A KIWI IN KERALA

A KIWI IN KERALA

NOEL GINN

STEELE ROBERTS
AOTEAROA NEW ZEALAND

GLOSSARY

banian	loose vest or gown worn by men
chappal	handcrafted leather sandal
crore	ten million; one hundred lakhs, especially of rupees
darshan	an opportunity or occasion of seeing a holy person or the image of a deity
dhoti	loincloth
jaggery	coarse dark brown sugar made from the sap of palm trees
lakh	one hundred thousand
lungi	length of cotton worn as a loincloth
paisa	(plural *paise*) one hundredth of a rupee
payasam	a drink of coconut, ground rice, and other ingredients
saip	(sahib) foreigner
teapoy	small, three-legged table for a tea service

Cover design by Matthew Bartlett. Photo on page 1: Annette Facer.
Thanks to all who supplied photographs.

National Library of New Zealand Cataloguing-in-Publication Data
Ginn, Noel.
A Kiwi in Kerala / Noel Ginn.
ISBN 978-1-877448-37-9
1. Ginn, Noel. 2. India. I. Title.
920.710993—dc 22

STEELE ROBERTS PUBLISHERS
Box 9321 Wellington, Aotearoa New Zealand
info@steeleroberts.co.nz • www.steeleroberts.co.nz

I'll walk, but not in old heroic traces,
And not in paths of high morality,
And not among the high distinguished faces.
The clouded forms of long-past history.

I'll walk where my own nature would be leading;
It vexes me to choose another guide:
Where the grey flocks in ferny glades are feeding;
Where the wild wind blows on the mountain side.

Emily Brontë

CONTENTS

FOREWORD

I first met Noel when he was about to return to India where he was living in a leafy suburb of Trichur, Kerala. He had a room in the home of a Christian family; first in the house, then later, a separate studio room among the trees where he had his 80th birthday celebration.

He was happy there where he wrote read and walked — but suffered from time to time from a feeling of isolation, missing conversation on literary subjects. Though he was never short of visitors; young men to play chess with, poor people who knowing of his generous heart would come to seek his help and advice.

During the short few years I knew him, Noel and I were very involved with India. Noel was living there continuously with occasional visits to New Zealand. I was living here in New Zealand and making long visits to India. We were in New Zealand at the same time and in India at the same time — separated by those grand mountains; the Western Ghats, Noel in Trichur, and I in Nilakottai, Tamil Nadu.

We exchanged visits; twice I enjoyed the hospitality of Noel and his host family, once taking two friends with me. On the occasion of our 1998 Illam anniversary, Noel and his friend Sojan came to us in Nilakottai.

Noel & I had a conflict in common; the New Zealand/India 'tug of war' or more like it, 'tug of love'. Loving, and yet being irritated by both countries while we were in them, and longing for the other; a predicament shared by many, including New Zealand Indians themselves.

In a letter to me Noel says;

'You're now back in fresh cool air, lucky you! Here it gets more and more humid — last night a whopping electrical storm that cut us off for 2 days & then blew my tube light ...'

'Should I must I come back to India, what do I want? I know that once back in NZ I'll long for India again ... I know that there will be the pull of India till the end...'

Perhaps we'd both had lives in India. In common with most Indian people, Noel believed in rebirth: 'Do not fear your death, you have been through that gate so many times …' he says in a poem. I have pleasant memories of sitting on the front porch with Noel in the early mornings discussing poetry and philosophy. I often think of his villanelle. It is good that this book of his is to be published at last.

> *'I think of faces I'll not see again*
> *Whose breath and body have been born away,*
> *The thought of death goes against the grain…'*

Jean Watson

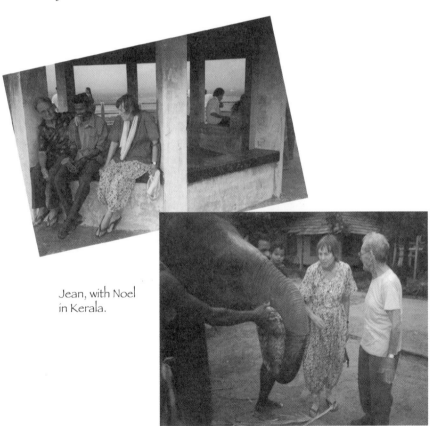

Jean, with Noel in Kerala.

INTRODUCTION

I first met Noel Ginn in 2000 when he returned from India to live with his nephew Howard Manins and his wife Liz on their beautiful Kapiti Coast farmlet.

I was 13 and for the next four years I shared many special times with 'Uncle Noel'. He was a mentor to me and became my proxy grandfather (by coincidence, Noel and my grandfather, who had died the year before Noel and I met, knew each other well in their youth).

Noel taught me chess and the basics of French and German, but most importantly he taught me about his view of the world and the history behind that view.

I was lucky to have shared with Noel his many passions and I cherish the memory of our times together.

He was born on 16 December 1915 in Wanganui, and in his youth became an energetic Methodist Bible Class member.

As a Christian conscientious objector Noel spent the war in a variety of penal institutions, from 1940 to 1945. Most of his first poems and letters while imprisoned were written on toilet paper, as blank paper was banned to restrict communication with the outside world.

Noel began corresponding with the young James K Baxter, sharing poems and comments from 1942 to 1946. He was introduced through Baxter's brother, Terence, who was in Hautu Detention Camp with Noel. Victoria University academic Paul Millar discovered a treasure trove of those letters, saved by Baxter, and published them in *Spark to a Waiting Fuse* in 2003.

After the war Noel became a horticulturist and largely ceased writing. He moved to Australia and in retirement lived in India.

At 80 Noel began writing again. His collection *Dweller on the Threshold* was published in 1998 — poems which, as book's jacket says, 'reveal the child on the edge of the adult world, the pacifist at odds with a world at war, the New Zealander encountering Indian culture, and the octogenarian reflecting on life and death.'

Noel Ginn had many characteristics that made him special, but the four that to me best summarise him and what he stood for were his vast general knowledge, his quiet wisdom, his wicked humour and his love for others.

Noel died in 2003 at the age of 87. He wrote *A Kiwi in Kerala* during his 1990s sojourn in India as a journal of his encounters and experiences of another world and another culture. It reveals many aspects of his spirituality and the discoveries he made along the way.

It is an honour and a pleasure to have been a part of publishing this journal.

Lachlan Mackay
Kapiti Coast
September 2008

Lachlan with Noel in Te Horo.

WHY, & A POINT OF VIEW

Friends suggested I write; one insisted, I said I couldn't. I thought about it and found myself time-warped to a drawing-room where a family party was in progress. It was in the days before radio when everybody got up and did something: danced, sang, recited or played an instrument. Even the little ones burbled nursery rhymes or sang in tiny voices, while the old told us what they did when they were kids. One aunt — a valiant soul who had fought adversity sang 'Shall we gather at the river', and we all joined in the chorus. Her voice, pure and true, swept to such heights I wondered how she could do it.

The flashbacks brought a message, no doubt. In the end I sensed I should get up and say my piece without demur although it was a bit late for the party.

While most of my schoolmates fell into jobs straight after school, and did well, I had no career. It is not profitable to look back, but I do envy of creative people who arrive on the scene clear about their calling as they soar above us on enchanted wings, their passage luminous. But envy is a shallow emotion with poor credentials and conceals the truth that these advanced beings, like anyone else, have had to work for their attainments, either in this existence or where other suns have had their setting. How else can we explain children like Mozart who appear as fully-fledged adepts? I doubt their brilliance and ability are gifts, arbitrary handouts, and not the fruit of hard work. If such gifts are to be had, what sort of a giver is it that withholds them from the bulk of humanity? It is altogether too simplistic an idea.

This assumption of earned abilities that carry over seems both feasible and far-fetched. Something similar is inferred in Eliot ('nobody's funeral, for there is no one to bury'), and in Wordsworth.

I do recognise, however, that for western people the notion of a succession of lives is way out. For most the too solid flesh makes only one appearance on the boards. Never mind, this belief, together with an unchecked wistfulness, has relevance for me and tells me that our endeavours have intrinsic value whatever the outcome. I am baffled, of course, and at times sense an implacable darkness. Then I switch to the positive things: the beauty of nature, the exuberance of the arts, the joyous reconciliation which flows from goodness, the sharpness and clarity of advanced minds, and not least, the closeness of love and friendship. It is an impressive list.

Laughter and a sense of absurdity have never been far away either. I look upon laughter as an unrecognised peep of paradise, an elusive yet contiguous state of being, and on absurdity as the monitor of what is really sound and practical. We can't allow despair a footing. We have covered certain ground and owe it to our unknown and strenuous past to continue to live strenuously. Buddha said something like this as he lay dying. For me the notion of a goal is inescapable, it's a fixture in my mind.

This journal has no thought-out structure; it is anecdotal and reflective, and made alongside the running stream of time. It invites random as well as sequential reading.

Since the decision to do this is recent, the setting is almost entirely in Kerala, the green south-western state of India where I now find myself. Because of this I have given the book its title.

Noel with members of his adopted family in Kerala.

THE HALL OF TERMINAL EXHAUSTION

A new month, a full moon. It is five weeks since I came down on Cochin, through the clouds glimpsing a network of canals, lakes, streams and inlets — a watery and wooded world with toy bridges linking invisible roads. I wondered if anyone would be there to meet me; was there indeed! I had a royal reception. It took five minutes to retrieve my bags and then I looked to the reception area and saw the fine head of Chandu above the crowd, bless his periscopic neck. Only he came into that area — it was restricted — and outside, to my joy was Sojan my host, then Nixon the merry one, Jose the brainy one and dear Mohan with no remarkable characteristic save that we all liked him. Finally there was Philip, who had driven the taxi from Trichur and was likeable too. It was a time for tongues and laughter, the pure pleasure of reunion. The ordeals of travel had tired my voice and it was fast giving out. The drive through rain to Trichur took two hours.

The journey had begun at Auckland and thirteen hours later I was in Kuala Lumpur, picked up and driven to my hotel, one of a chain. I was desperately tired so did not avail myself of the free sightseeing trip that the transit visa vouchsafed. The courier who organised this tour registered surprise and disappointment. Nobody could turn down an offer to see the capital of Malaysia! Well, I could; I told him I had been in Kuala Lumpur many times and my need was for rest, sorry. I forwent the tour of an energetic and aspiring city. It is not a mere town like Alice, but a city like Singapore. I had a cold admiration for its slickness and glitter, its efficiency, its technology and youthfulness, and warm enthusiasm for its tree planting and grooming. But it was all too much for my ungroomable mind and my aversion to surveillance and the drawing board. I wondered whether each tree, each blade of grass was dossiered. It was a night stop-over in any case, and my mind was on India. I was asked constantly what I thought of Kuala Lumpur and felt a heel that I was not agog with enthusiasm, but pumped what conviction I could into my responses.

It took three and a half hours to fly on to Madras and we landed at one in the morning. Why, oh why must arrivals be scheduled for the early demented hours? Nevertheless a surge of romantic joy arose to be once more in India, and I made my way into one of the immigration queues. India is not only the great mother, she is also the great teacher, albeit of the stern old school, and she lost no time in setting about her first lesson. The subject was endurance.

The time to clear immigration, recover baggage, pass through Customs and change money could not quite match the three and a half hours taken for the flight from Kuala Lumpur — it lacked but 30 minutes. Custom clearance itself was swift, however, and for the Customs I sing praise. The immigration queues, though, could have been photographed by reporters in search of copy of disasters in far away places, with stricken hordes queuing for relief. One hope and one invocation arose in the packed hall and added psychic pressure to physical pressure in the one-pointed surge to the barriers. Hour after hour we shuffled forward. The vision was of a bang of a rubber stamp on a passport. This operation required two hours. A young woman ahead of me, ill and exhausted, sat on the floor most of the time, except when we shuffled forward in blessed interludes. Nothing could be done, endurance was imposed upon us.

The luggage retrieval area was only half as tedious since it took but an hour. The carousel had broken down, some major hitch had occurred between cargo hold and baggage hall. Perhaps locks had jammed or the man who had the keys had gone off duty. The baggage appeared in dribbles, which suggested it was hand-carried from the plane.

Nevertheless at 5 a.m. I was at my hotel, enormously thankful and utterly spent. All the hoops and hurdles had been cleared and the race won. No Olympic medallist could have been as happy as I was with that graceless stamp on my passport. The Madras hotel is ancient and bears traces of former splendour. It is my base because it has become familiar. Though seedy and three-star I doubt, it provides what I want, a place for a night, two nights. The staff are beginning to know me. There is grave, courteous Boniface who works in the spacious dining-room, the most nostalgic area. I have befriended his little crippled son, for whom I bring a gift. He. I went there and looked on chaos. The furniture was piled to one side while workmen and carpenters were replacing the roof. The great fans were silent and no elderly waiters in cummerbunds hovered about. It was a deserted banquet hall in the stilly night. Boniface told me they were serving meals out-of-doors, did I mind? And that led to my second experience in Madras.

If there was an off-season for such hotels, it was now, during the south-western monsoon. The waiters kicked their heels. Boniface led me to the smaller of the two lawns. Before the entrance reared a splendid equestrian statue with Diana holding the reins. The sky was dark but not too dark, though colour had drained away. Small tables with full dining-room setting were on the grass. The lawn was edged by shrubs — hibiscus and *acalypha* — and trees. One flame-tree, its incendiary peak over, still bore a lone flambeau. Beside the lawn was a colonnaded walk, and an elegant stairway with a turn and landing halfway led up to its roof. I had seen mongooses on one of the lawns on an earlier visit.

By now night had removed shape and substance. She replaced the hot, moist day air with languid vapours wafted as if by silken fans. One banished day-serving concepts and images, they retired to their latencies and tall, round-shouldered shadows formed a back-cloth to this little plot of lawn.

I was seated with ceremony before damask cloth and serviette and a single candle was lighted. I took off my shoes and socks to feel the cool grass. The journey with all its demands and pressures withdrew, not blocks away, but light years. I was alone in a dark exotic bubble like a living black opal, with flecks of light and wisps of music from a hidden source. This was the ultimate glamour — it was India.

I ordered fish and chips! I had to. I knew the menu and couldn't do battle with their flaming dishes. To the locals, Indian dishes appeared mundane, whereas fish and chips was exotic. I chuckled at this incongruity on this incomparable eastern night where the troubled sky threatened rain and the moon floundered. I ate fish and chips in paradise. I told the waiter not to hurry with my order and he offered a beer. Wine would have been more to my liking but this is not wine country. Yeah, yeah, beer is okay, please, a beer. The remembrance of Ruby Wine made in India had to be suppressed. On the other hand, some Indian ales are great — I'm no connoisseur. The lager pricked the tongue and refreshed the throat. Kingfisher, it was called. My order arrived. It did not compare with the fish and chips of home. I should have known that gustatory experiences are not transferable. Still it was good and served my need. Dreams skirted the shrubby shadows. Other diners arrived — wraiths on the periphery. I remained undisturbed, enclosed in reverie. The coffee, black and bitter, was fine.

NIGHT~PIECE

A tropical night seen from a verandah never palls. Already it has removed the impedimenta of day, co-lessee of our planet. Colour and form, weight and magnitude, height and breadth; all are received into its capacious maw. A puttering worms through the dark; it is Chandu on his two-wheeler. For a moment a blinding beam leaps forward. He strides up to me, unbuckling his helmet.

'Uncle, Uncle, how are you?' Grinning and happy he greets me, a quick peck as he bends down. He is a beanstalk. I grin back.

'What's that for?'

'Reverence for age, Uncle.'

'Seems more like malice, reminding me.'

'Uncle, I must honour you.' He grabs a chair, sits on it back-to-front and shakes his thighs. This mannerism is widespread in India. If it suggests any purpose at all it could be a preparation for the next move. He springs up and switches on the fan and light.

'Do you notice anything, Uncle? Look at me.'

'I notice you didn't ask whether I wanted the fan or light on. You burst in and without by-your-leave or kiss-my-foot, took away the lovely night and put me in a draught.' I fend it theatrically.

'But Uncle, it is dark and I like the fan. Do you want me to kiss your foot?'

'No I don't, I'd be horrified, but nobody comes into another's house and takes over.' This idea is strange to him.

'But look at me, Uncle — is anything different?'

He looks directly at me. His hair is short, but that is not new. Formerly it was long and wavy with a smart mane; now it is short and boyish. 'Come on Uncle, look!'

I obey. 'Your face is like the moon, all pits and craters — hey, you've shaved your moustache! It makes you younger.'

He was pleased. 'That is what they all say.'

Moustaches are the norm, but his had been wispy.

'Good riddance, it was always pathetic.'

His shield of goodwill deflects the barb with a chuckle. He has an enduring concern about his appearance. He has one of those faces that is hard to assess. At even a little distance it sets off his carriage and elegance. He is, dammit, handsome. He knows, I know. He picks up a notebook from my teapoy and reads aloud, and I say 'More presumption.'

'But why, Uncle?' Again he is puzzled, 'I want to see what's in it. Why have you written in pencil? I can't read it.'

'It's an old notebook that's just surfaced, nearly 40 years old. I can't read it either, it is so faded, we need a stronger light than this.'

'Why didn't you use a pen?'

'No ballpoints then, only pencils. There were fountain pens but mine always leaked.'

He reads from a part which is a little clearer. It is about a dance and is altogether strange. I become interested. Some experience I had once undergone eluded me, some event. I had set it down. It is mine, was. He reads on and I become more and more puzzled.

'I'll look at it in the morning.' He riffles through. It is a forgotten notebook and has been in my pack throughout my wanderings. Tomorrow I shall get busy and transcribe it. I'll need full sun.

He has to go as he is just back from out-station and on his way home.

'Well, I make a move.'

'That's what the hero in the comic said when he saw the bullet coming, remember?' It's one his stories.

'So you're off. Good you called. I'm glad.'

He puts on his helmet and, with his black shirt and height, is transformed into a bandit. A couple of kickstarts and off he rides into the black bag of night.

I leave the light on and try to read from the notebook. It is rough and its entries have been made on the run. Over 40 years. There is this dance piece he read from; a story about a ten-year-old girl who joined a cactus society; fragments of a trip to Mangatepopo Hut; chatty notes about a hospital visit — nothing finished or worked up. Ah! a sentence from old Johnny Jaboor, 'To write a book musta be a good speller.' What made him say that? I find it poignant. This old illiterate Lebanese peasant whose world and wisdom could not translate into New Zealand ways. A dear friend gone. He wept when I left.

Morning had me peering in the notebook again but with more success. A passage about the Foxton Straight came on strongly. It was slight, about an ecstatic mood, still in its case intact. I went over the diary and read the account of the dance and thought I should bring it out of the woodwork into the light. There was a soliloquy on death; and life after death. Its urgency has faded, its relevance. Can I bear to go into all that again, relive anguish when I am now so different? Later knowledge barely tolerates earlier ignorance. I cannot relive that crisis. Yet the tracks of old suffering are still discernible, and no later experience can disturb the glow of past joys as if in jewel-cases. It had taken this disorderly notebook to reveal like a satellite old causeways and earthworks. I note a trace, I suppose genuine, of fortitude, a resolution to sit out the dark night and still enjoy life. At the end I had written:

Knowing that all
Who come must go,
Why are we stunned
When this is so?

Must we endure
Life's overthrow?
I am afraid
this is so.

Heavy stuff.

WALYAR

A runny nose and unreliable innards have made a bid for my attention, I resist on principle, servants should stick below stairs. Fortified by such strong-mindedness, I climbed the high step of the bus and made my way to a hard seat. Sojan and Victor were with me, We were heading for Walyar and would take two buses; the first to Palghat would take two hours, and the second on to Walyar half an hour.

The first was express. It made few stops so could speed; it hurtled over pot-holes through crowded suburbia and then, with greater abandon, devoured the less populous countryside. How it parted and penetrated the traffic is special knowledge of the East. If called upon such a bus could part the Red Sea without needing divine assistance.

Having established that the driver was master of his craft I relaxed and gave myself to the green landscape, for no prayer of mine or exercise of the will could aid or hinder our progress. The Trichur exit was narrow and leafy, as most of the lanes, but I became aware that this lane was more luxuriant. This quarter was the poshery of the town, its west-end, though we were heading east. One after another I descried through the foliage porticoed and colonnaded mansions, some elegant, several pompous, others fortress-like. Driver, driver, go slow! Our architects would never be so bold as to design the likes. Here there was no lack of rupees and no curb on whim and folly. When it comes to design, adornment or the single distinctive touch India is never at a loss. But alas, the will to create beautiful structures and inviting precincts is rarely exercised in the business area which is uniformly ugly and inconvenient. The spirit of beauty has long ago fled before the scourge of commerce and taken refuge where it has always been at home, among the temples and in the humble-tumble houses of the poor.

Everything is done by hand, concrete-mixers, power-tools and cranes are not to be seen. The west looks upon this as backwardness; the women mixing the cement on the ground, the human chain that hands bricks up floor by floor, and bamboo scaffolding. The west builds with machines, and there is no chance for the hand-crafter's touch to come through. We must decide whether technology diminishes while hand enhances the beauty of the end product.

A house, almost in the same league — with style and distinction, but not size — is being built next door where I live, so I have seen the patient toil. The other drizzly day, for instance, I saw three men pushing a handcart laden with bags of cement. They had come from afar. It was hard work on the dirt lane and harder still on the quaggy grass of the site. They were gasping *Uh! Uh!* in turn, as they strained. They unloaded and left only to call an hour later with another load. They were small and wiry with lungis furled. Such skinny legs and arms. Unlike the fleshy west, they were made of steel. I watched them prop the shaft and unload. One man put a plastic sheet on a bag then backed and bent to take the weight. He staggered into the half-completed house. This pathos got to me — it was not a matter of the picturesque but of survival for these workers whose fate is to push a hand-cart through traffic, through life. They were exhausted and looked starved. One felt their bondage and their patience. Such scenes are common.

The mansions gave way to lesser dwellings still deep in the underworld of trees, and they too ended as we mounted an embankment. For a while I looked through the bars of the bus down into pools of shade, and caught my breath as I looked on a winding stream with banks colonised by ferns, *caladiums* and other plants seen too fleetingly to identify. It was too sylvan, too idyllic for my idea of India.

The wind tore at the hair, fingers became numb as they gripped the rail of the seat in front, for the windows are not glazed. Much later, when we got down Victor said he had been riding horses. It was exactly how I felt after all the bouncing. The road cut through vast plains of padi which reached the horizon on one side — green padi under the open sky. The padi to the other side ran up to where the western ghats took their craggy stand, dark and wooded. Then we plunged into forest once more through a long shade-tunnel. It was natural beauty in perfection — trunk and vine, thicket and bush, overhead branches, and the emerald sails of banana palms. I tried to take in all this beauty. I began to muse. Leaves have a role, not for embellishment, but for the actual underpinning of life in the planet. Does it all come down to leaves, then? A leaf. An invention of such moment that in comparison the invention of the wheel is a triviality — without leaves a dead planet except for a few moulds and lowly organisms. The thought came blindingly as if no man had known this before. In the leaf is sewn the key of creation.

I spotted a traveller's palm, unique in its predilection for two dimensions. We expect palm leaves to wave in all directions, caressing the air that cools them. Not so the traveller's palm. It stands firm, rigidly holding up a fan that never fans, like a piece of art deco. Is it true that in its axils the thirsty traveller can always find a noggin a pure water? I tried to recall its botanical name but it eluded me. I thought it ended in -*ella*, so went through the alphabet, but with no success, mainly because I could not picture the shape of the word. The thought of a bird persisted and I came back time and again to my censor with *crowella*, which he curtly dismissed every time. I handed the search over to my subconscious and thought of other things. Half an hour later the answer was there quietly waiting. It was *ravenella*! No one on the bus was aware of the triumph which I had to myself. I rejoiced, marvelling at the resources of the mind.

Another familiar plant appeared on the way. It was *mussaenda*, with blooms of vieux-rose, pink and white. I had no difficulty with that name. I adore this plant even through its blooms have no claim to elegance such as the iris or the lily. They look like handfuls of scrap material hastily stitched together, or the daubs of an impressionist who has no interest in botanical detail, but it has its own style and moves in a high society, it leads and does not follow. Its haphazard flowers reminded me of a favourite aunt when I brought her bunches of asters every year, for I grew lots of these peppery-scented annuals. She would fill an old vase with water and shove them in all at once then fluff and ruffle them into some sort of arrangement. Her success fascinated me, for it was an age of floral art classes with its mystiques, focal points and critical appraisal.

We reached Palghat. The bus station is a hideous necessity. Long ago I decided that without help I cannot travel. There have been many times when I have asked directions and the person I asked would rock his head from side to side. I am never sure what it meant. The signs on the buses are in Malayalam script, never English. The shouting conductors can be helpful. As each bus arrives there is a rush as to a gold strike. I have Sojan as my guide and leave it to him whether to join in the rush or ignore it and wait for another. Once I saw a flight of six or seven dhoti-clad youths chasing a bus. They looked like affrighted apparitions in long white nighties. They came and went in a flash.

Catching a bus is not simple and straightforward operation, there are refinements and subtleties. One buys a ticket, having found the right vendor, then finds a queue of inordinate length standing before a closed bus. When the door opens it is like a share issue that opens and closes in a minute. So what does one do? On one such occasion Sojan was calm and unflustered as usual. He began to chat to two small boys while I was consumed by urgency. I find these sharp-witted urchins attractive, but first things first. I was pleased though to see him give them a coin each; he is gentle and kind. We went off for a coffee; stalls abound. I am too inured to confusion to ask questions, (how would we be able to get on this bus along with a million other determined travellers?) We came back. The bus was full and packed. Sojan forced his way through and I followed. Halfway along there were the two small boys sitting with plastic bags. They had nipped through the queue and bagged our seats. There is another method, more direct. It is to put one's luggage through the bars of the window onto an empty seat before the door opens. The luggage serves the same purpose as the small boys.

The second bus, however, called for no such strategies, as Walyar is not populous. This village sits on the Tamil Nadu state border and Kerala buses must stop there. The run was through pretty areas, trees everywhere, with half-hidden houses and hovels thatched with palm leaves, the more primitive no better than humpies. The traveller's glance falls upon a picturesque scene, it cannot assess the quality of life, whether the currents that flow beneath are sweet and pure.

With dismay I looked on the street-and-a-half which makes up the township of Walyar. 'You will like it, Uncle, we want you to stay a week, ten days.' It was supremely ugly. Victor took us to his hotel, what we call a restaurant. It was simple and spacious, a place for the locals. A stainless steel beaker of coffee, with a plate of biscuits, was set before me. As it was late in the day he wanted to show us what he meant when he sang the praises of Walyar.

We turned off the main road and walked through the Monday market spread out on the ground, then entered a long road. First impression was the absence of traffic noise. Old trees met intermittently overhead — *abbizzia*, *peltophorum* and flame trees. They fretted the sky and blocked the heat. We wandered on and I began to feel more peaceful, no longer stressed and shaken by the rampaging buses. Peace lay upon the place like a green mantle. The trees thinned. People walked and cycled by. Cottages were scattered either side the road, they stood back among low vegetation, placing a seal of simplicity and underscoring the peace. As the road climbed, the dam came into view. An immense horizon met the paling landscape. To the left were the heavily forested ranges, rough and irregular. The forest descended and occupied the catchment area. The trees would be preserved.

One of the enduring images I have of India is of people walking; bare or sandalled feet have trodden these roads for millennia and still do. It is a strong image, and of feet, not footwear. One sees an individual or a small group walking, it is no great matter, but when one sees hundreds of people walking, only the dullest can be incurious as to the destination. Many holy and revered feet have walked here, and infinitely more which were not at all holy, moved by routine, necessity or upheaval. One senses a compulsion to move. Some pattern is being served, it is not mindless.

The dam was manned by guards who offered no check as we went through the barbed wire onto the causeway. The light was fast weakening and a loaded cloud advanced from the north-west. It carried night in its folds, and rain. Sojan pointed to a boat pulling from the farther shore of the lake; his eyes are sharp. I could just make out the movement of oars. The silence and vast skies compelled us to stand and watch, and await its approach. It was as if in that vast panorama this was the only event. It could be Palestine and the lake of Galilee. The fishermen in their dhotis as Biblical figures, the robes are not unlike. If Palestine is a holy land then India has equal claim to that designation. She is still steeped in wisdom and strong in intuition, and for those who would seek wisdom, the skies are conducive and the mountains commodious. As the lakeside air brushed my face I wondered what India has to do with this tumultuous age. Much more than I can tell.

We moved down the embankment and along to the shore where a score of locals had gathered to watch the fishermen unload the catch and free the fish from the nets and sort them, weigh and sell them. The boat was heavy and clumsy and the oars crude. The fish were flat and broad, about eight inches long.

'Would you like me to cook some for you, Uncle?' Negotiations took some time and there were others before us. Night had conclusively ousted the day and threads of rain began to connect heaven and earth. We had one umbrella and I was in the middle. For me the walk back was euphoric, glory having descended with the dark and the rain. There was peace, the dying light and the thick tropical night.

Men, women and children were still moving homeward, carrying bags and bundles. In its endeavour to absorb all detail night was not entirely successful for defiant lights from the cottages made their stand. What was spared absorption was modified and subdued.

The restaurant, Victor's, as all its kind, had a cement floor, plastered walls and metal furniture. There was no evidence of any aesthetic consideration. It functioned well. The working area was a dark catacomb rather than a series of doorless rooms. In one, onions were heaped upon the floor, another held bundles of firewood and I saw a woman add yet another to the heap and receive payment. In yet another I saw a young man scaling the fish we had bought at the dam; what the cooks were doing over their wood fires I was too bashful to find out. I was shown a small room where I could take a nap should I desire. I returned to the public area and sat down with another beaker of coffee, but first water was set before me.

Outside was a continuous roar of traffic with the surge of stopping and starting vehicles as each was examined. All lorries entering Kerala had to be searched by the border police. Fumes seeped inside. The police, all young and agile, strode about in khaki uniforms with tight trousers and large-buckled belts. Each carried a probe about four feet long. From time to time they came in for coffee, helping themselves to biscuits — what the arrangements were I do not know. Their work was arduous and boring. They clambered over loads and opened the tops of tankers. This went on day and night. Customers came and went, a bearded man of about 30 came over to me and asked did I mind if he were to talk with me. I indicated a seat. His name was Stanley and his first question was my good name. His second was my country, and when I said New Zealand he repeated what he thought I had said — Switzerland. This so often happens. He was warm-hearted and outgoing. He told me he was a graduate in English literature and was a schoolteacher, and took every opportunity to speak English with an abroader. Two major interests he had and they were English and the Gospels. His father was a headmaster and his mother a teacher. His church was the Church of South India which I believe is in fellowship with the Anglican Church.

My friends joined me and their conversation took over. Stanley pulled out a Malayalam New Testament and told me he was reading the Apostles. This puzzled me until I realised he was referring to the Acts of the Apostles. Victor slipped away to cook our meal.

I was hungry, I was ravenous, and at last the fish arrived, graced with a sauce, and on a separate plate sliced tomatoes and onions formed a geometrical pattern. I cannot recall when I have ever been regaled with such appetising and distinctive flavours. The sauce contained fresh coriander as basic flavour, then there was ginger and a number of herbs. I found myself appraising it as if it were a wine, and longed, one yearning moment, for a light white wine — a chablis, I thought, as if I knew all about it. The fish, though freshwater had character, but I had difficulty with the small bones. Such fish should be eaten in silence and without haste, I did neither as I was plied with questions and the others, fast eaters in any case, finished as I talked. Then instead of sensing this slight misalignment they continued to engage me, compounding my discomfort. They would be thinking that oldies, slow in most things, were even slower in eating. So under the gaze of five pairs of eyes I doggedly ate my meal.

The visit then ended as we had to go onto Coimbatore that night, but pressure to return was strong — 'Stay a week, ten days, Uncle, I'll rent a cottage for you.' I could not fix a date at this stage, nor did I entirely go along with the idea, in spite of my romantic moments on the road to the dam. Such moments cannot be replicated and it is not wise to try, since the variables and subtleties are never under control.

Stanley was also going to Coimbatore. He sat behind us and was rather left out of our talk, though ever attentive and smiling when I turned to him. We alighted together and he went his way. I would like to meet up with him again. Many such I have met and it is more and more borne in on me that I cannot take up the many friendships offering. If any desire further contact I leave it to their initiative. For them I have novelty value, and a friendship is not based upon novelty. It is useful when getting around but it holds illusory elements. Meanwhile I capitalise on it.

LOVE WITH A DIFFERENCE

I lie on my couch with a booklet that has just arrived. It is from my foster son in North Borneo and is called *The Spiritual Sword*. It consists of a series of articles which are mainly expositions and sermons upon passages of the Bible, written with earnestness and missionary zeal, and they reveal a wide knowledge of this unique compendium of early Jewish and Christian writings.

I read some and try to capture their spirit of enthusiasm, but know all along that it will evade me. These writings are for their faithful, not me. I cannot subscribe to their premise which is that the Bible is the basic unquestionable authority in all matters. Years earlier I considered another premise, that of the Catholic Church, which lays claims to being that absolute authority. The case is impressive, but again I could not agree.

So I disappoint him. I disappoint him also because I will not discuss his beliefs or enter into argument on the basis of Biblical authority. He has a sturdy homespun faith and has formed his views after painstaking study. He is sincere and courageous, he is practical and direct. Our friendship is longstanding and is reinforced by a shared sense of humour. In his case it is forever bubbling and has special charm as the Chinese way of thinking surfaces through English speech. I am enriched by him.

Nevertheless I am disappointed by my inability to look upon his fundamentalist church with other than a cold eye. We will have to put up with this unbridged gap of understanding. There is always a danger when a difference in understanding arises. It is that when the mental processes lie exhausted and the disagreement unresolved, the conflict will transfer itself onto the emotional plane which is far more energetic. First there is perplexity, then a little disappointment, followed by exasperation and resentment, the two that always go hand in hand. They give place to criticism of a progressively more acrid nature, until the final degradation of antagonism, condemnation and hatred.

It is a familiar and deplorable descent that blights personal as well as group and international relationships. The hope is that those involved recognise what is happening; to do this they need the ability to distance themselves from emotions and stand as true observers. Who can do this?

A few days later I was reading an article on religions of the world. I have always regarded religions as divisive but inevitable expressions of growth. I read a statement that surprised me. Professor Ursula King, who is head of the department of theology and religious studies at the University of Bristol, spoke at a conference this year in London. She said that 'few people, whether Hindu, Buddhist, Christian, Muslim or whatever have any idea how complex and diverse religions are.' She quoted statistics compiled by David Barrett who since 1982 has annually published statistics on the membership of institutional religions. He states that in 1982 there were 20,870 distinct independent Christian denominations in the world. So, she asks, who speaks for Christianity?

One thing has always repelled me in the Bible, it is a pervading sense of man's misery and inadequacy. It is degrading for man to believe that in sin his mother conceived him. There is no gainsaying man's errancy, terrible and bloody in its expression throughout history, but he is a learner who works through mistakes on his evolutionary path. I lean to the definition that sin (a word I distrust), is missing the mark as in archery, and that through trial and error, cause and effect, man must find his way. The same good book, careless of consistency, proclaims man's quasi-divinity; he is set a little lower than the angels. This is more encouraging and cheerful. I like that line of thinking which looks upon sin as a choice of the lower rather than the higher option. But like sickness its contemplation is a morbid exercise.

There are phrases and passages in the old Bible which I cherish and I have felt cheated by the wilfully prosaic nature of modern translations. Phrase after phrase comes to mind with mysterious thrilling resonance:

'When I consider the heavens, the work of thy fingers.'

'If I take the wings of the morning and dwell in the uttermost parts of the sea...'

'Ye shall know the truth and the truth will make you free...'

I cannot bear the loss of these passages. Poetic and intuitive writers have filled the Bible with treasures, and Jewish thought has its own glory. The poets and seers did not know their words would fall under the scalpels of theologians and dogmatists, they were illuminated by another source and were free in spirit. But their words have fallen into the hands of dissectors and polemicists; their space which formerly transmuted the music of the spheres now has the sounds of the library and the turning of pages by myopic fingers. I might be taken to task by scholars if they read this, I might have to modify my statement. My fault will lie with my love of freedom of spirit rather than the bondage of the law.

I digress, for my theme is the pain of differing. Each takes his stand on preferred ground, but all must move on, we must recognise this. It is wholesome that we differ. On our journey we depart at different times and from different places; we use different transport and there are many stops. Only at times can we travel together, absolutely together.

Mother Mary, New Zealand writer Jean Watson, Noel Ginn, Mini, Alexa, and Sojan George outside the home where Noel lived with Sojan's family. Trichur, India, 1995.

AND IT RAINS

It is evening. A long time in my cane chair. Sojan is visiting Roy nearby, while his mother and wife Mini are watching a video next door. I turn off the porch light. It attracts insects and then they come over to me. It is muggy, I would take my shirt off but for the mosquitoes — as it is I am slapping my ankles. I do not try to think, and the ever-fossicking mind which never explains itself brings out a memory of an old *New Yorker* cartoon in which a plump overdressed society woman in a bookshop says to the hovering salesman, 'Just grazing.' The humour is evergreen.

The fireflies hold my attention. In an old pastoral poem they are called 'country comets' and I ask myself if the image is apt. Are they really? Electric blue, otherworldly and eerie. I concentrate on these vanishing jewels pinned for a moment on the velvet night. Bright desire so softly extinguished. The light is better inside; I am not ready for reading and return to the sit-out, drawn by the enchanting night.

Mini arrives. After the video she met some girls from the village and they wander back to the house together. She brings them to see me. They are so pretty and it is charming how they huddle and push forward propelled by curiosity and pulled back by bashfulness. They want to see me, they have heard so much from Mini who has endowed my prosaic facts with glamour. I am a foreigner, a symbol. She holds out an object in her palm. I recoil, it is repulsive.

'What is it, what is it? Is it a spider?' I cannot see in dark.

'Not spider.' The body is three inches long.

With a tangle of feelers or legs, it is ugly and tough as a cane toad. I am only a moderately squeamish person, but I am revolted.

'Won't it bite you?' I am sure it is a spider.

'No bite.'

'But what is it? Are you going to eat it?'

'Ess, eat it.'

'Oh, no, it is horrible, horrible.' She and the girls laugh.

'But what is it?'

'Njandu.' She shows where a leg was removed, which gives me a clue.
'Is it from the sea, a crab?'
'Ess from sea. Not from sea.'

When Sojan returns I learn that it is not a sea crab but a fresh-water crab from the padis. Small boys collect them for food and they are pronounced delicacies.

*

Françoise Sagan's book, *The Still Fire*, is my companion for half the night. It has descriptions of the gentle countryside of Aquitaine, with a slow introspective beginning and with hints that the pace will quicken.

*

Another day, with steady persistence rain is falling. I install myself on the sit-out but there is too much spray. The air is cooler so I put on a cardigan. Sojan is bare-chested but I am a softie, sensitive to changes in temperature. Besides, my cardigan needs an airing, unworn too long it can gather mildew. I drag the chair into my room and go on with my book. Françoise Sagan is a great writer. As suggested in the early pages the story crescendos to a big climax.

Now the rain ceases, but there is no sun, no sun on my shoulder. Even so the muddy path is firm, but not the ruts. Chandu arrives on his new Hero Honda to take me into Trichur for shopping. I have to cash travellers' cheques, buy stationery and some chappals. I try them on, and the assistant remarks on my white feet. I chose a pair studded with small cones both sides of the sole which are supposed to massage the feet. I suggested a pair for Chandu as he lost the pair we bought last year in Colombo, but they do not stock his size, whereupon I said, 'Serves you right.'

INTERVAL

There is a floating moment on awakening when consciousness returns. It is brief and hard to seize. One moment oblivion, the next a resumption of the body and the environment. It is an important moment, and if one is attentive and attuned one can glimpse one's self returning to the body, as if on a call, as if to its *pied-à-terre*.

Usually the first component of one's consciousness catching the dawn light is the emotional nature, the mood. Whether this is pleasant or unpleasant mostly depends upon one's contentment or discontentment with life and the current situation. Then gradually the other elements that populate consciousness take their places.

It is that first evanescent moment of return which interests me. We know that during slumber the brain never ceases its activity, and that one of the functions of sleep is to tie up loose ends of the preceding day, undo the knots and generally clean up the office; similarly the bodily form has fatigue drained off and cells replenished.

In that moment reports come in on unsolved problems, hard-to-assess situations, and matters that are purely intellectual. They come from a higher part of the mind. On the other hand the known things that have been mishandled or shelved send messages from the subconscious, for it is loath to burden the daytime awareness with old unresolved matters. There comes a time when temporary storage must cease. A messenger arrives. It could be a busy time if we care to pay attention. The deputation is momentary but it does not come in frivolity. It is a good idea to sensitise ourselves to this oracular moment and also to watch when significant interstices and intervals occur during the day, for if ever we are to receive flashes of insight or the clear light of the intuition these are the portals of entry. We do well to watch them.

All this because I awake exuberant. It matters not that the body creaks somewhat and occasionally says 'Careful', but if there is moral support from the upper storey of one's being, then one is chuffed, charmed and goes one's way rejoicing.

MY FRIENDS ARE YOUR FRIENDS

Nixon called yesterday. He told me the night before he would come today at 9 a.m., then elasticised it to between 9 a.m. and 10 a.m., a good Indian precaution. In fact he did not come until 4 p.m., and my greeting was 'Nine already, I didn't know it was so late.' I was not put out, I had been busy. Besides I knew his heart and it is bell-true. The bus strike which was to have released him from work did not take place, and he had to go to work after all.

He came on his brother-in-law's scooter. He is a sunny character, a modified Groucho Marx, with wide slightly bulging eyes and open features. He is immaculately groomed as he is a salesman for a Japanese firm which is fanatical on grooming. Above all, he is merry, and, supreme bonus, devoted to me.

We met two years ago at an evening of celebration. If I had then to describe him in one word I would have said madcap. He did not pursue our friendship on a subsequent visit and I was puzzled. The reason became clear, however. He was self-conscious about his lack of English. On the first occasion he had been drinking and the effect overrode this factor. I recall the others around the table and the plates of cashews and dishes of diced-beef — it was an evening of hilarity. The inferiority apparently went deep for he had pride. He told me English was a status symbol he coveted. He had become teetotaller and had also given up drinking tea and coffee, and confessed he was forced to do this as he was fast becoming a drunkard like his father. I saw his father one evening as he returned from the toddy shop. 'See,' said Nixon, 'he can just walk.' Poor bloated and defeated man.

So his ban on alcohol had the effect of energising his complex about English, that was why I did not see him on my second visit to India. But after I left he began sending me short notes in English and told me he was taking classes. On my third visit I saw him briefly as my stay was short, but I realised the ice was broken. Letter-writing continued, so that when I arrived this time the friendship was established.

His motive in approaching me in the first place had linguistic purpose but now it was a case of devotion. He is naturally kind and befriends people in need, as I begin to find out. For instance, a man, Bharat Singh, was obviously lonely. He is a middle-aged man, exceedingly small, who is superintendent in one the central government services. He is highly intelligent and has a sweet retiring nature. Transferred from Bhopal in the Hindi-speaking belt, he was isolated as few in Kerala speak Hindi. English is a slightly better medium, but it is not the basic language, Malayalam. Malayalam is a formidable tongue, for him as for me. Bharat Singh wanted to improve his English, so Nixon asked could he bring him along for conversation. He had to leave wife and family behind in Bhopal. His wife has been unsuccessful in her efforts to obtain a transfer from her job to this region.

We were on the sit-out chatting, Sojan, Nixon and I. Eventually Nixon said, 'Then?' on a rising inflection. It meant, 'Shall we make a move?'

I like pillion-riding; it provides an intimacy with the surroundings denied four-wheelers. The intimacy threatens to become too much, for a tumble is always on the cards, as we wobbled through tortuous tracks and lanes worsened by the monsoon. Their disrepair militates against danger from speeding traffic — one cannot keep to the left but must choose the best track. Once on the larger sealed roads one's enjoyment diminishes as black chugs of diesel pour from trucks and buses, attacking eye and lung, with added outrage from the silvery discharge of auto-rickshaws. I do not mind the traffic jams and the confusion, the weaving and stopping which becomes a game, an entertainment, observing how the problems of congestion and jamming sort themselves out. But the fumes… Nixon hoicks and spits. I begin to think a little more will be curtains.

'We are going to the hospital.'

'To see Martin's mother?' Martin is the brother-in-law.

'Yes, any problems?'

'I would love to see her.' Poor lady, she is an asthmatic who has had a heart-attack but doesn't know about it. She is out of danger after some days of monitoring. The corridors are narrow and thronged, blocked whenever a trolley passes or a patient is walking on crutches. Martin's mother has a room to herself. I cannot say I recalled her, but I knew immediately who she was, so much like Martin with long face and aristocratic nose and intelligent eyes.

She sat on her bed looking at me steadily, and beaming her smile. It was not a surface smile but came from some interior light. I was always conscious of her radiance. She put out her hand and held mine a long time. I kissed it and she bent forward slowly and kissed mine.

We did not stay. Others were in the room and Nixon wanted to take me for a coffee. We made for the canteen, but found it uninviting and went outside to where the scooter was parked. He had told me of a nurse who had looked at him, and he wanted to see her again. She wore a yellow sari, he said. So he had been there earlier.

'Is it a romance?' I asked, but no, he did not want a romance. She did not appear. We left. He had been arranging a plastering contract for his unemployed friends, Shelton and Nelson, brothers. Their family was poor and he had been taking them vegetables. We went to another home where I knew he had been helpful. We met Shelton and Nelson on the road. They were well-built young men with strong faces, both shy in my presence. Nixon told me their grandfather was an Anglo-Indian.

Back to the hospital. Again the handshake and slow smile of the old lady. She began to speak but Nixon couldn't translate for me and I gathered she was a little senile. I warmed to her, and some understanding leapt through circumstance. Whatever her mental state, she was full of love. We also had to check on the nurse of the yellow sari. 'She must have gone home.' We waited by the scooter ten minutes. 'Give me ten minutes,' he said.

We decided on a movie. It promised action and violence. Had I demurred he would have given way, so I agreed to see *Shanghai Express*. But there were further calls to make — how gregarious people are — and we weaved along many roads and lanes on visits until it became too late for the movie, so it was deferred to the following day. The business and charitable calls were over but there were still social visits to various homes. On the roads too, for they too are meeting places. We met Vinod, a tall, handsome auto-driver with eager face and infectious laugh. He was standing with an older man by a stone post. In this country I see people everywhere standing motionless for long periods. We ran into Simon, the national hockey rep turned coach. He is a neat, keen little man with supple physique. He wants me to see his gym some time. There was another chance meeting with a man I had met once before — it was after a wedding reception where about ten young men had gathered in a nearby house and were sitting on the floor in dim lamplight. While others drummed he sang a long song of what I was told was unrequited passion. He lowered his voice to enhance the drama. Nixon by my side whispered a translation. This gentle artistic man was a policeman.

We visited four houses in succession and each provided a lively welcome. The details of the stranger had to be explained, and there were predictable questions. There were cups of coffee, a banana, a cake and some sweetmeat. The older men asked the questions while the women and children crowded the doorways. Arun appeared, a likeable soldier on two months leave from Delhi. He was 22, an army clerk in his third year of service. His English could sustain a tolerable conversation. His house was the last we were to visit, the first half of that evening.

We returned to Nixon's house and I drank coffee again, and then, since he had returned the borrowed scooter, we walked from place to place again. It was dark among the crowding thickets and hedges, and under the palms, mangoes and jackfruit trees. I could not see a thing but my companions who knew the warrens had night vision. I tended to trip, not being accustomed to my new chappals, so they guided me as a blind man. Nixon said he wanted to protect me from the stones, which bulged. 'Is that right, Uncle?' he asked and I suggested we would talk about the stones that stuck up and were in the way. 'But all the stones are in the way.' He and Arun repeated the expressions as they steered me past puddles and ruts.

Arun's life was regimented with but a half day off on Sunday. He lived in barracks and, more favoured than most, had a room to himself at the far end. There was drill from 5 a.m. and breakfast at 8, followed by long hours in the office. It was a dull life only partly compensated by the issue of three bottles of rum a month, a private's quota. He said he did not drink and I assumed that he traded this rum. His salary was from two sources within the army system and yielded 1800 rupees a month. I remarked it was good pay and he answered that they were soldiers and gave their blood for their country. Fair enough, fair enough. After 15 years service he could, if he so chose, take his pension.

We reached his home — he murmured some needless deprecation of the place but the large room we entered was spacious and clean. The ceiling was thatched. Theirs was a military family and his uncle, a strong old man with snow-white hair and close-cropped moustache led the conversation. I was grilled once again. Then his father, who had been sleeping, opened his door. He looked older than his brother, and frail as he swayed towards a chair. He had a smoker's cough. Arun told me his father was a drunkard and that his health was bad. Drunkard is a judgemental word outside India; we would prefer to call him a heavy drinker.

Again we returned to Nixon's home, this time for supper. I was so stuffed with coffee, cakes and bananas that my appetite had vanished and I had to work on my praise of the food. There was a plate of pappadums and a beef stew with delectable flavours. It was then that Arun took leave of us. He was a good companion.

Nixon told me he was a good man but with some qualifications. For instance, he did drink, though he said otherwise. He held things close in his mind and could not be a deep friend. His father took something derived from opium and Arun did also. I gathered it was milder than opium. He had done some wrong thing and it was told to me but I must never say a word to anyone what I had heard. He was forgiven and his transgression put down to the hot blood of youth. But his brother now, there was a good man, and a great friend. I must meet him some time. Soon he would be back on leave.

When the time came for him to take me back to my place no auto-rickshaws were available, so we walked through the twisty lanes and then crossed the path through the padi fields. Here was open sky and a little light from a crust of moon entangled in filaments and shreds of cloud. We came upon the main road, and still we walked. We chatted about the military family we had visited. I said I liked Arun, and Nixon agreed with my opinion. 'He will get better,' he said. We sat upon a high wall in the dark. I could have got there alone but Nixon legged me up. Autos went by one after another, but they were occupied. Eventually an empty one came and I was pleased, for I was tired. The evening had been kaleidoscopic. I had looked into many houses and on many faces.

I made a composite image of the face of Kerala. It was male, for women are ever in the background, it was about 25, hair strong and wavy, thick moustache, bright black eyes and dazzling teeth. It was handsome, sensitive and smiling, above all it projected friendliness. Keralites are group-conscious and that is a mark well above average for humankind.

THE ACRONYMIC PLAGUE

The teapoy is in place once more on the sit-out, on it a plate of porridge, a cup of coffee and the *Indian Express* English edition. The morning is sober-suited in quiet grey, Milton chose those words. I find the papers baffling, and if I allow it, exasperating. In one respect only: for the life of me I do not know what all the initial letters stand for. Today, for instance, there is a cartoon drawing of a gallows made up of the letters JPC — what do they stand for? There is no one about to tell me. I take the front page and read on. First report is that Mother Teresa turns 83 today and well-wishers send bouquets and good wishes for a speedy recovery; she has malarial fever. Comment on her condition is made by the superintendent of AIIMS to PTI. An attentive reading of the text is rewarding for I find that AIIMS refers to All India Institute of Medical Science and I guess that PTI refers to some press association — well and good. The main article deals with a row at the CLP(I) meeting in Bangalore where chairs, microphones and teacups filled the air with their dangerous trajectories. That too clarifies. The CLP(I) is Congress (India) Legislature Party. I can now say Tally Ho.

The next headline: 'RTC Staff Stir Called Off' is enigmatic. The strike was of the KSRTC employees. I can't decipher this one although I turn to Page 9, col 1 as directed. The strike was called off by the Samyukta Samara Samithi, comprising representatives of six pro-LDF trade unions which are listed as CITU, AITUC, UTUC, INLC, the Labour Union, and CISF Federation — a cheer for the Labour Union. A conscientious reading does not help me here, but I know it is about buses and unions. Next, there is an uproar in RS over camera surveillance. I ought to know by now that RS refers to the supreme legislative body of the land, the Rajya Sabha — I have seen it but forgotten, I am deservedly benighted since I know nothing about the political parties — yes, I must do a course on politics, would six weeks suffice? The parties referred to in this article are the SJP, BJP, JD, AIADMK, CPM & KPCCI — surely there are others.

Contractions serve and are here to stay. We might eventually revert to hieroglyphics or ideograms, each with its cargo of meanings. They are fast gaining currency in the EC and USA, they have given us NATO and the UN, and a thousand postulants queue for recognition. In a small country like New Zealand one can read the headlines and then focus on the articles that arouse interest, but here in plural India it is not that simple. The coverage is not so much of the activities of a billion people but that of almost a fifth of the human race. It is too large to be a microcosm of the world. How can I then voice criticism when what I register most is awe?

These reflections must not end in petty complaint. In the *Indian Express* I read the daily tragedies that are enacted in a thousand places in schools, hospitals and institutions, in public places, private places and among the tribals and primitives. Misfortunes and wrongs are brought into print — the plight of individuals, the plight of groups, injustices, muddle, ineptitude and fumbling in high places, the paralysis of the will-to-good and will-to-honesty all because rampant greed rules in this land; and finally the destruction of the very land itself.

All these calamities flow into one's pent emotions until they threaten to overflow and bring devastation. The reader cries enough and turns to the sports page. In sentimental vein he can think of it as the still sad music of humanity, in petulant vein he can state that this civilisation is 'an old bitch gone in the teeth.' Ruth Prawer Jhalvala describes it crisply as the manifest byways of human affliction. It is all these, all here in India, in perpetuity, whether one looks upon degradation or misery or upon a poetic moon above silhouetted palms.

In earlier days newspapers did not exist, there were lamentations but they were largely unheard, they could not be poured into microphones or amplifiers, nor disseminated to the news-stands of the world. Today it is different. Technology has worked to give us all, and we cannot handle it — we put our fingers in our ears and do the crossword puzzle. But the journalists work on. They are the hunter-gatherers of this age and bring in great sheaves of disaster. The appetite of the world's presses is insatiable and unwholesome, that is if we allow it.

There is a law which goes something like this: for every action there must be a reaction. There is recognition that this law not only applies to the Newtonian universe but also to living human beings. He who thinks he can stop an apple falling or a thought spreading is an ostrich, and in line for a great surprise. What then can we do with all this mass of news, when one piece alone can fill a horizon? Today I read a long article about not-too-far-away hill tribes riddled with tuberculosis, without medication and sanitation, and all unemployed. The state authority makes noises and calls for a bowl of water in order to rinse its hands. In this single case one can rally to the sides of those who demonstrate and agitate, but what of all the other woes and evils?

Crises are happening around us and it is the best informed and most aware who suffer most and bear the brunt of world agony. To many this may appear to be a curious assertion, but let us consider what is happening. Many are bearing physical pain to the utmost limit of nerve capacity, many are overcome and driven out of their minds by emotional agony induced by the events of this age. To these must be added the relatively few who suffer mental agony as they wrestle with the problems of humanity. They front up to the three places of suffering. They stand on the physical plane and keep their nerve, they control emotion on the emotional plane, and on the mental plane they work steadily on world problems. Their capacity to identify with life in all its aspects is greater and brings immense suffering. There is one more source of suffering. It is due to the trained ability of the imagination to see future suffering, hidden in the womb of the present. This rarer type of suffering is gethsemanic, and few there are who possess the kind of capacity or strength that can endure it, but their number is growing, hopefully in geometric progression.

Our thoughts have been ranging from the concrete to the abstract and back again, and that is their function. We have glanced superficially at this ephemeral number of the *Indian Express*, remembering that ephemeral refers to a day. What would we have then, what would we have it say? Tell us then, and keep on telling us, Oh, *Indian Express*, of the shame and disgrace of our race as well as the glory. Keep on, keep on, all you journalists and commentators. Tell us wherever there is a shortfall of compassion, reckless devilry, political shenanigans, or failure of integrity, we need your vigilant and tireless columns. We need them badly, and perhaps some, but not too many, of all those initials.

A MEMENTO MORI

As the years amass incontrovertible proof of mortality, the fact of one's own demise etches itself deeper into the consciousness. In the early and mid-years, when the pulse runs wild and energies are unbounded, one knows one is immortal save for the unlikely falling brick. Doubts, hideous ones, that creep in and scare us come in the night, but daylight is a watchdog that chases them away and we go back to our games. That stage passes sooner or later, and the realisation of mortality dawns, and it is impossible then to avoid emotional and mental reaction.

It is unworthy of the unique body and soul one possesses to run away from this relevant fact, yet most do; decent and honourable people who make the world go round banish the matter to a future session of thought, like politicians who pass thorny issues on to a sub-committee, and further, until they run into the sand. Most ordinary people, who would never think of cheating others, cheat themselves in this matter and go to extraordinary lengths to circumvent the contemplation of death, saying it is morbid to think of such things. It is not, though, it is unhealthy not to, as unhealthy as the neglect of a rotten molar which could poison the system.

Those who dare to look squarely on death and allow a place for it in the planning of their lives come away with a different expression. They catch a glimpse of something which, whether a peep or vision, enheartens them. They take courage because they have taken fresh stock of all those things which have furnished heart and mind over the years, and they reorganise themselves. Those who have lived entirely on the emotional and physical planes come away with acceptance, and some hope; those who have striven mainly on the mental plane come away with a new slant on reality, with the knowledge that there is work ahead of them still, perhaps in a new medium; while those who have found their souls and live in its universal quarters come away with excitement and anticipation much like school children at the beginning of a new term.

So it cannot be as bad as one thinks. In fact anyone who has given death its honour and place, knows one is over the worst, and finds something to go on with, and no longer finds naught for one's comfort or:

That the sky grows darker yet,
And the seas rise higher;
Night shall be thrice over you,
And heaven an iron cope.

No, it is not like that. Having extended their viewpoint they get on with life's business which is to go on and not stop. I think it is a sane idea to give a thought to one's passing, but not like Thomas à Kempis in abjection and mortification, but with a businesslike appraisal about measures to be taken.

JAYAPRAKASH

It is the hottest day for some time and I say 'Huh' and flop my head on my chest. I do not complain, but Sojan notices and soon a draught of cool air plays on my back through the grilled window. It is gratefully received but my papers blow everywhere.

I've been wondering when I first met Jayaprakash. First I thought it was at Ranjith's house where I met four students who boarded there, together with his mother and a delightful lady teacher who was fluent in English. No, it was another occasion, for Jayaprakash lived nearby, he was not a boarder. Yes later, Ranjith brought him and three other students to visit me on the sit-out. I remember now. There was Sajeevan the short, nuggety one I made much of; Titus, tall and handsome; and Santhosh who wore round Gandhi glasses. I would say that Jayaprakash was the youngest — he was still growing and had yet to fill out, though many Indians never do. He looked so young. I recall an impression about his voice which was in a high register and slightly strangled in the back of his throat and had to go too far to project properly. His teeth had braces. Otherwise he presented a bright, fresh appearance. That was a year back and I more or less forgot about him, until one day recently I had been wandering in the cool air. As a foreigner I am a little self-conscious when I move into narrow and intimate lanes, for I have no business there. They are the leafiest and the walls are entirely mantled with moss and fern. This is a true charm of the Kerala village.

I heard someone running behind me but did not look around, until I realised the runner was making for me, coming directly toward me, calling 'Excuse me, excuse me, sir,' and there he stood slightly breathless in front of me. I smiled and greeted his fresh bashful face.

'Do you remember me, sir? Do you remember me?' I stood still and gazed upon him so anxious and thoughtful.

'We came to see you, with Sajeevan, Ranjith and Titus, we came to see you.'

It was then I recalled the lean sweet face, the braces and the high voice. He was delighted that I remembered. We fell in together and walked a hundreds yards or so, when he said 'This is my house.' It was almost pure Tenniel among the trees, with knee-high hedges flanking a path to the low-roofed tiled cottage. He could not ask me in as he was on his way to a class — they have them at all hours — but he promised to come and see me. His great aim was to gain confidence in speaking English. I could see what a tussle he had with shyness and only his determination had forced him to approach me. After the first flood of greeting he became tongue-tied.

Ranjith brought him along several times after that and I enjoyed his enthusiasm and naivety. His father was in hospital. For years he could not work because of asthma and now he had an ulcerated leg. His mother was the breadwinner and she worked for the press. I learned also that his braces had cost 3500 rupees, a horrendous sum. Later Ranjith told me Jayaprakash was considered to be the cleverest of their group.

I ran into him again, this time on a major lane. He told me his father was out of hospital. Would I like to meet him? Now? His father, 52, was a small man and I took to him straight away. His face had an air of suffering, almost sanctity. Our conversation was minimal but that did not matter.

One day when they came Ranjith told me that the next day it was not only his birthday but also that of Jayaprakash. Would I come along to his, Ranjith's, house as they had a cake to cut. I went and took along for each an envelope containing a birthday-card and some money. It was a shy occasion and I had to make the going, but in the end they were all chatting — three others were there. It is an embarrassment that I have to be the centre of interest but I realise they probably have never moved more than 50 kilometres from here and that to them I am a symbol of a bigger and perhaps unattainable world.

Tomorrow I go once more to Jayaprakash's house, for it is the season of Onam and they want me to share the ceremonial meal. He had a parcel which he opened and he showed me the textbook he had bought with the birthday money. It was a colossal volume on computer science. He asked me to autograph it.

ALLEPPEY

Sojan announced a trip to Alleppey to see a boat race. This would take place at 2 p.m. and then we would leave for Cochin and go onto Malayattur, his wife's village, where she was staying, as custom prescribed at a certain stage of pregnancy. We would then continue our journey back to Trichur.

Previously I had passed through Alleppey on my way north from Trivandrum but my memory is all a-blur with coconut trees and banana palms ... I recall seeing many streams, canals and waterways. We caught a bus to Ernakulam and another to Alleppey. On arrival we called on Sojan's friend Shyam at his shirt factory — a new venture in a new building. Shyam's father is an ayurvedic doctor whose profession had yielded enough wealth to provide all his son's needs as well as capital for this venture undertaken to occupy his time.

Shyam Kumar is a pleasant man of 30 who will become plumper as time goes by. We went upstairs to the factory door where we took off our shoes. Our welcome was like sunshine — smiles on all faces, plus curiosity about me the foreigner. We examined the various machines, button-holing, buttoning, locking, collar-fusing and many heavy-duty sewing machines. There were some 30 workers in a relaxed and harmonious atmosphere. Shyam introduced us to his cousin Ramesh. Neither of the cousins knew much English and I was surprised, as usually in these parts affluence and knowledge of English go hand in hand.

The four of us then left by car for the beach where Sojan and I intended to obtain lodgings. After the clutter of Alleppey the beach was restful. The west coast of India and the Arabian Sea filled my mind and stirred my imagination. The sea was calm as it went about its daily praxis, laving the shore. This was the legendary Malabar Coast. Immediately before us was the Lakshadweep Sea in which are set the Laccadive Islands with their Nine Degree Channel.

I reflected on the innumerable vessels of antiquity that had plied these waters century after century back into the recesses of time, all traces obliterated by the unrecording waters. The sand was ivory, and a substantial jetty ran a hundred yards into the sea; it continued a railhead, built by the British but is now abandoned. We watched some youths bathing near it. One ran back to a pile of clothing to get a smoke, took a few puffs then ran back into the waves to give his companions a puff. What they were smoking I do not know.

We pulled into an inn yard but no accommodation was available, nor would there be in the entire city because of the boat race. What to do? This was a matter for my friends to decide, and as they showed no concern whatsoever I did not worry. We drove into the grounds of a high-class hotel and entered the dining room. It was filled with Western tourists — uninteresting faces in my uncharitable eyes, but for my Kerala friends quite otherwise. It took half an hour for our order to be taken and a further hour before we were served. Clearly the staff were unable to cope with the influx. When at last the food arrived it was disappointing. The soup, harbinger of things to come, was stone cold, and that is unpardonable in any restaurant — unless, perchance, it is gazpacho. The steak, I must allow, was passable, but the vegetables were not properly cooked and tasted of oil fumes. My friends later complained about their dishes. The cost was high.

We slept in the shirt factory — it was airy and had fans — Sojan on the cutting table and I on a camp stretcher. Mosquitoes were on patrol but I had a repellent, Odomos (what we call Dimp). The toilet was large and tiled and gleaming, the hand-basin light blue and spotless. There was a floor toilet and ample water supply with which to fill an outsize bucket. There was a bailer.

Though the race did not start until 2 p.m., Shyam sent us off with his driver at 10:30 a.m. We were privileged, for crowds were moving on foot towards the ferries. Even the tourists were on foot while we swanned through. We stopped at a ticket booth and paid 100 rupees apiece before boarding a ferry. The roads that brought us there were narrow and had canals either side, large enough to take sizeable craft and both road and canals were overshadowed by spreading trees. They led to a great lake, at least a kilometre wide and so long I could not guess its length. The left bank as we entered was entirely furnished with stands as far as eye could see. Behind them was the everlasting backdrop of coconut palms.

We headed for an island, obviously man-made, for it was precisely rectangular and had wooden shoring. It created a channel of about 80 yards to the shore and in this channel were markers for the finishing line. So

46

we were destined prime view. The island, at a guess, was a hundred yards long by 40 wide. It was tented over in makeshift fashion. The foreground was provided with fifteen rows of folding chairs, while behind them was a grandstand of rough timber, nails sticking up in places, and tied with innumerable bits of rope. Sojan, clever with crowds, got me a seat right on the water's edge and by 11 a.m. we were in place with thousands of others. A youth beside me said the crowd was two lakhs (200,000). The long wait was in no way tedious as there was plenty to see. The attraction was the snake-boats, some 120 feet long, sixteen of them, manned each by over a hundred men. There were also smaller boats paddled by women, and they held 30 apiece. The crowd thickened, until the island could hold no more. The stands on the shore also filled. I felt privileged being in such a place, but then a shower arrived and being on the outside, I was soon wet. Eventually it stopped and the sun came back to dry me. The thoughtful organisers were handing out eye-shades and these were a boon.

By 1 p.m. I was agonising for want of a toilet. I had noticed a scrimmed corner as the ferry pulled in, but there was no way through the tightly set chairs, so Sojan escorted me around the water's edge hanging onto the canvas eaves and grabbing poles, and in one case a spectator. Even so, it was a walk to the paradise gardens in terms of blissful relief. Back, purring with comfort, I could dare to drink a carton of chocolate. In the intervals when little happened I returned to my Agatha Christie at a stage where the plot was beginning to grip.

The main races were those of the snake-boats in four heats of four craft each. It was wildly exciting — the roar of the crowd and the precision striking of the water by the paddles, and the crescendo towards the breath-taking finish — it was awesome as the paddles struck the water sounding like bullet shots. At the stern of these mighty canoes four men stood with long-bladed oars which they wielded like the rotors of a windmill, so there was the contrast of the frenzied paddles and the slowly revolving oars. They generated incredible power. The spectacle of such unison was overpowering. The winners raised their paddles and held them horizontally over their heads.

At one stage the sixteen boats were together for official viewing. They performed a kind of paddle ballet augmented by cries and chants. In the centre of each boat stood a pace-maker and he held a stomper with which he pounded the floor of the hull. I couldn't see this but learned that there was a socket with a spring set in the bottom, so the stomping was as pestle and mortar. It produced a hollow sound which with the paddle blows harmonised to produce the bullet shots.

In the lull after the race one crew drew near and I was able to look down at the paddlers individually. They were bare-chested save for two crews who wore black and white banians respectively. Bodies and hoisted dhotis were drenched with sweat and spray. They glowed, for high currents of energy had been surging though them and they were still charged. I noticed a couple of older men among them and learned that the crews were from separate districts and it was no small achievement to assemble a crew of a hundred fit men. As a stranger, I had no favourite to barrack but for those involved and their supporters it was a matter of intense suspense and pride. They moved along, receiving plaudits and banter from the spectators. I marvelled at the slimness and sheer length of the craft which they were able to propel — as I calculated — at eighteen kilometres an hour over the fifteen hundred metre course.

There was an island nearby set aside for officials and the media. The chief announcer evidently had a winning humour for he had the Malayalam-speaking crowd rolling about in merriment.

Towards 6 p.m. the thoughts of two hundred thousand minds turned to departure, and the pressing and crunching began. As each ferry broached the island, those nearest the landing stage heaved forward. The young and agile leapt from the grandstand onto the roof of the ferry. Among them was a group of Germans in shorts and hefty foot gear. They appeared enormous in comparison with the locals, huge shapeless beings of another race. There are many Indians six feet tall and more, but these blond men were giants. They were not arrogant or assertive, but kept to themselves. I leapt to grab the roof and swung in, a bold feat for such as me.

Our plans for continuing on to Cochin and beyond received a check when we saw the situation at the bus-station. It was submerged by thousands of would-be travellers, in chaos and urgency. We went back to the shirt factory. Shyam was still there and it was apparent that we would be spending another night among the sewing machines — enjoying another seamless night — my brother-in-law would approve the pun and would add that it was fitting, I could do with his comments.

Shyam and Ramesh, ever considerate, drove us about three kilometres into the country to a different style of restaurant from that of the previous evening. There was a curving drive-in among trees, and an attendant escorted us past the main building to a summer-house much further back.

It was circular and in the centre was a round table to correspond. It was stone. A stream ran alongside. The beauty of the night was the décor, and the croaking of frogs the music. We were delighted. Sojan and I were served with cold lager immediately while our abstemious hosts drank water pure and undefiled. We retailed the events of the day and they shared our pleasure, for they had listened to the broadcast of the main race. Food arrived with little delay and was infinitely palatable, and our appetites were sharpened by the seven-hour fast on the island.

I was content when they began conversing in Malayalam as I had much to think about, the immediate past and the immediate present. The moonless night exerted its power to dissolve that which is tangible, allowing entry to its own mysteries.

ONAM

Today is the second day of Onam. It is the culminating festival of the year just as Christmas is in the west. The two festivals correspond in their mythology and in their joy and goodwill. The simplified story of Onam goes like this. In the early days Kerala was a garden of Eden, inhabited not by Adam and Eve, but by a whole race of people, the Malayalees, who were ruled and governed by a Christ-like king. His name was Mahabili. There was prosperity, there was equality, generosity and justice. Truthfulness was the most exalted virtue and no thieves flourished.

So harmonious was this kingdom and exceedingly beautiful in this lush and fertile part of the world, that the very gods and devas became jealous of King Mahabali. They feared his power and envied his popularity. One day, they argued, he would rule over the entire world and this thought was abhorrent. They decided to cut him down to size. They approached Lord Vishnu and asked him to do something about it. He himself then appeared before the king in the form of Varuna, a dwarf, and humbly explained that he desired to do penance, and for this purpose he needed a plot of land to be measured by three footsteps. The king readily acceded to this request. Thereupon Varuna assumed gigantic stature. With one step he encompassed the earth, with his second, the heavens. For the third step Mahabili offered his head and Varuna placed his foot upon the king's head and pushed him deep down into the nether kingdom of Pathalam. The dispossessed king made one request and asked the Lord, still in the form of Varuna, that he may be allowed to return once a year to be with his subjects in the beloved kingdom. Permission granted, he visits his people on the day of Onam.

The celebration coincides with the end of the south-west monsoon when the land is at its most lush and fruitful, and when the first harvests have been gathered. Everywhere I see floral carpets, posies are set in the stems of plantains, crackers are fired and special foods prepared. Like Christmas dinner, the special Onam meal — set on a plantain leaf — is central to the celebrations. Kerala-style curries and payasams are prepared.

The latter is a kind of porridge made with rice and coconut and is thick and sweet. I detected but could not identify an aromatic flavour somewhat like the bay but there are no bay trees in this tropical land. Maybe it was cardamom.

This morning there was a sound of treble voices singing as a file of small boys, aged 8 to 11, appeared. Two were completely covered in grass, some carried staves, and most wore masks. They danced before us, singing, clapping hands and waving staves. They were re-enacting the story of King Mahabali, and in the end one fell upon the ground and a grass-covered boy placed his foot upon him and the other pulled him up again. The merriment and enjoyment of these boys was delightful. Sojan gave them money and off they went like carol singers. Happy, happy boys. I think of Keats and his 'Ode on the Grecian Urn' and wish he were here to share this revelry. In the distance I hear chanting and the beating of drums.

I visited many places, the first being the home of Jayaprakash, where I ate a special meal prepared for me. At the table were Jayaprakash, his brother Rajeevan and myself. On the floor beside us a brass lamp burned and before it on a banana leaf was a helping of rice for King Mahabali, whose visit brought so much joy. The existence of brother Rajeevan was a surprise. He was a year older than Jayaprakash and had the soft gentle eyes of his father. His brother resembled him but I read a slight difference in their expressions, the older boy I thought was happy and dreamy whereas the younger, who was also dreamy, gave an impression that his dreams were under the control of a questing intelligence. The mother, the ministering servant, beamed happiness. Her sister, her family and neighbours crowded the room to gaze upon the foreign attendant.

Later we went to their sit-out and looked out on the scene. My first impression was correct — it was Tenniel storyland from this angle as well. The path was gravelled with small red stones and branched around an urn-shaped pedestal planted with what I supposed a curry bush, it was Tulasi. I chewed and tasted a leaf — it was not the curry bush, though it possessed a marked flavour. Verdure and leafage billowed to make a tall background of shade trees. Attracting my gaze was an ashok tree. This beautiful specimen gave the final touch to a romantic picture. There was little deliberate landscaping as such, not much more than the hedged path and the urned feature, but the touches were right and the effect so agreeable that the most skilled gardener would approve.

The ashok tree is to India what the slender cypress is to Italy. It is the readiest and most elegant symbol. It is not a sombre pine but a bright evergreen, most like a mast. The central trunk is hidden by drooping springy branches drawn in closely together and densely furnished with lance-shaped wavy leaves. Its self-grooming is faultless.

Well into the evening I found myself in the area where Arun and his military family live. Unlike western gardens where boundaries are asserted, the properties flow harmoniously together leaving many open undefined areas. I entered Arun's house and enjoyed the customary payasam before joining the throng outside. A group of women circled a lighted brass lamp set on the ground. They were singing, dancing and clapping hands. A leader gave the refrain which was taken up by the others. The steps and arm movements were simple and measured and the circle rhythmically contracted and expanded about the lamp. Little children joined in, as did some men for one of the dances. This went on as others watched. A little boy brought me a chair, for which I was grateful. The single light bulb on the verandah was switched off. That was better as there was a full moon high overhead which added mystery to the night shapes and other-worldliness to the singing group. It was easy to envisage this scene as one of a series going back through the generations far beyond memory. It was not a performance but a spontaneous expression of their rich legacy of happiness, given shape and feature by a genial mythology.

*

Another day has arrived, and again there is a visitation, this time heralded by drumbeats. Four small boys in little shorts appear. Faces, trunks, legs and arms are painted in stripes — yellow, black, dull red. The near-black is their own pigmentation. They look comical and I come to life.

'Tigers, they are tigers,' Sojan says.

They come right up to the steps, two bigger boys beat the large drum, one each end. There is one other big boy, who is the collector. The rhythm is established and it is syncopated. The boys begin a lively dance. Part of the routine is to freeze action at intervals. They build up enough tension for us to envisage the hostile jungle. They stop suddenly. No words are spoken; Sojan gives the collector two rupees and off they go to the houses behind us. On their return they smile and wave vigorously. Their painted smiles are grotesque.

SOME ADDITIONS
& A LITTLE SUBTRACTION

I checked my wallet the day after. I reckoned I had 1150 rupees. There were only 750.

'Sojan, what were our expenses yesterday? I can't tally with what I have here.'

There was the:

mattress	770
rubber cushion	75
auto	20
iron	415
	1280

Correct. Plus the 10,000 for the house addition. So total paid out equals 11,280. The travellers' cheques gave us 12,400, so that leaves 1120 rupees. Plus the 30 roops I already had in my wallet. Makes 1150. It must be 1150. I know I had 1150. No other purchases? None. Then 400 is missing, perfectly clear. Missing.

It was a happy evening, one of the celebratory days of the Onam festival. I mention only Nixon's name for we enter finger-pointing territory. If I named the others implications could be drawn. We mustn't tell Nixon.

There were six of us in the small rented house. Two were busy making chapattis there on the floor in our midst. We others sat round, sang, danced and yarned. Nixon was incredibly funny dancing, as was his friend, former pupil, a professional now, they said. It was the first time I had seen live break-dancing — fearsomely energetic. There was a little brandy. I had a glass to please and threw the ghastly concoction down in one draught. Let it compensate by making me merry. How can brandy be made from cane sugar, I ask you?

A stew was simmering in the first room. It got later and later and I became sleepy. The friend nearest fussed over me, spread out a mat and rolled some cloths into a pillow. I settled down on the hard floor. 'Sleep, Uncle. What's that Uncle?' he said. It was my wallet sticking up as I stretched out. I always carry it in my front pocket. He took it out. I remember he took it out to examine. I was virtually asleep. I remember that, and I remember I was thinking he could look at it if he wished. A deep ten-minute sleep followed. It cleared the fatigue. 'Here, Uncle, your wallet.' He handed it back and I stuffed it in my pocket and thought no more about it.

I recounted this to Sojan who hadn't been to the party. He pondered, and I'm glad he said we shouldn't tell Nixon. 'You should be careful, you should always be careful,' he murmured. The loss is not big when its worth in reckoned in foreign currency. But it is a disappointment. Had the friend come out and asked I would have given (a phrase I've heard before).

More days passed and the cutting edge of the hurt dulled. Robbed by a friend. Yet really he is a great guy. Are his values so different from mine and those of my friends at home? Most I know here are scrupulous about money. What to do and how to act when we next meet is my question. A scene of righteous confrontation? I have no stomach for that.

I recall a phrase used by a worthy but rather domineering woman once. It was a committee meeting and each member was to speak out at a public meeting on the issue that exercised us. Our treasurer, a quiet, somewhat inarticulate man, demurred. Then the scornful words, 'Call yourself a man!' I often recall that blackmailing phrase. He called himself nothing. The assumption was that men by definition are strong, bold and assertive and that women are weak and timid. What a cock-eyed point of view.

No, there would be no confrontation, I would avoid confrontation. I would avoid him then? Show coldness? or withdraw friendship? The point is that I did not know how I felt, except that I still liked him.

Today I awoke wondering who and where I was in time. I looked at everything from an incredibly long angle. The immediate scene was not in focus. I have similar sharp alignments when standing on a mountain, the grandeur eliminates that which is small and petty and brings on a godlike emotion in its universality. Here I was in a new environment with new friends. What would four hundred rupees mean in 50 years time?

Sur la place, chacun passe. We leave it at that.

MALAYATTUR & ST THOMAS

Mini has been counting the days till the new arrival, 36 days to go. It is time for her to go home. Her packing has been proceeding carefully and thoroughly, and first she cleaned and polished her suitcase. She, Sojan and I took the bus to Malayattur and this entailed a change to another bus at Chalakudi, as ours had broken down. The second bus took us on to Angamaly. The third bus was to Kalady, and from Kalady we hired a three-wheeler to deliver us an hour before midday to her home among the trees. The last section over granite stones was particularly bumpy.

Our welcome was spontaneous and joyous. Mini's brother Johnny was disappointed that I was to stay only one night, as he wanted to show me around and discuss plans for his new house. At present, he, his wife and little boy live in the family home. Francis, the man I had previously met who had lived in Italy, was not about — out of station, they said.

Looming in my mind was a visit to the famous chapel on a hill nearby where St Thomas rested in prayer and meditation for fourteen days, and where he had planted a cross and, according to some, erected a small shrine. This was the site of his momentous visit to Malayattur and it holds pre-eminence for pilgrims over the seven churches he founded along the Malabar coast. Sojan had bought for me a small monograph entitled 'The Historicity of Apostle Thomas', in which are cited the sources of knowledge on the subject, and these I must study and assimilate if I am to take advantage of my chance to visit some of these places.

Mini, Sojan and I set out early in the afternoon, presumably for the purpose of making this pilgrimage, but I am learning not to presume, even though my turn of mind calls for clear destinations and stated times. This is not the Asian way, not the Indian way. I am disconcerted therefore when expectation is not met by performance. If India is a state of mind, can I complain because I do not possess it? How hard it is to let the days unfold and bloom naturally and not rush in to direct them with itineraries and timetables, thinking that today I'll have this experience, I'll do this one thing. Yet a traveller must plan to some degree unless he is under no constraints of time or means, in which case he can afford to drift and follow the vibrations as they register. The traveller in India must protect himself from delay, frustration, annoyance and pettiness — all corrosive destroyers of peace of mind. Otherwise he will never see the beauty of squirrels at play, otherwise he will never take time to watch small boys bowling their hoops, or watch a woman collecting a wild herb for use as a mosquito repellent. He will not discover that before occupying a new dwelling one must first boil milk in the place, and one must not move in on a Thursday, the most inauspicious day of the week. Finally he will never allow himself to stand still and motionless for hours at a stretch, as do so many here, undergoing who knows what spiritual or mental refurbishing, or receiving ineffable insight.

To walk along the shady lanes of Kerala villages is surely nourishment, as is the contemplation of moving or still water. The tall, airy shade, the crannied walls, the harmonious shapes and colours of habitations, as well as the twists and turns, though all on the way to some destination, are themselves destination, the place where the mind lingers — when away from Kerala it is to the image of these lanes that the mind returns.

The shade notwithstanding, it was hot, especially when we came to the road which was but sparsely shaded. Hot, but not like the tongues of flame that play upon less favoured regions of India. Along the lanes were strewn stretch after stretch of hay, heavy coarse hay. It mattered not if vehicles or cows or goats passed over as it lay drying, but if a shower threatened it was quickly gathered up. The hay then gave place to hundreds of mats woven from bamboo supplied by a rural development agency. This cottage industry is of immense benefit to the community. The mats too, had to be dried. On the main road men were rolling up and tying them, and as we waited for a three-wheeler, the pile grew higher. The roads and lanes served not only for communication but also as working area, since other level spaces are virtually non-existent.

The spin in the auto for the next part of our trip drove cool air into our faces. We got out at a dead end, and were fronted by a tall and massive Portuguese church, belting out a hideous din of pop music high up from a balcony. But why, oh why? Across the street was a flight of steps leading down to the broad strong Periyar River, a surprise after the clutter and diversity of the village scene.

I recalled a similar moment of surprise when for the first time the mighty Mekong River came into view behind the market place and I saw its immense progression. There were many steps down and we sat on them and waited for the ferry to draw near. It was paddle and pole and very little of either; a man was vigorously soaping himself as he stood waist-deep in the water. The far bank had a landing place and a track leading up into the undergrowth. If the view from the bank was satisfying that which we saw as we were borne along in the rough-hewn boat was even more so. Far in the wooded eastern distance we saw the ghats, while downstream a horizon of palm tops rose above the water, infinitely remote. One of the two old ferrymen placed a conical coolie hat as large as an umbrella upon my head, and the trite phrase that ends a flawed poem of Wordsworth came to mind — 'And oh, the difference to me' — but I gave no thought to the woman who 'dwelt among the untrodden ways,' for the hat kept toppling sideways so that I had to hold it firm.

It was a stiff scramble up the bank but soon we were through the boulders and scrub into another of the endless shady lanes. We walked a couple of kilometres before coming to a sign which indicated the way to gardens and an elephant kraal. Enquiry yielded the information that the elephants had been transferred elsewhere, all save one baby elephant. It was in a solidly built elephant house which had great beams instead of rails and rafters. There was the baby elephant with one foot chained moving

ceaselessly back and forth. Its keeper led it out of the building to a water-trough and then to another area, training it to kneel, to raise one foot after another, and to reverse. It was two years old, a sobering thought that such growth, strength and intelligence could come into existence in so short a period.

Three young men were also watching the training lesson, they stood much closer. Suddenly one began shaking his lungi and a cloud of dust, or what I thought was dust, was shaken out. It was not dust but smoke for he had set his lungi smouldering with cigarette ash, and the fire had to be beaten out. It was in tatters below his knees but he

57

furled it to the folded position and no one need know how near he had been to immolation or nakedness.

The garden had neat tight hedges alongside narrow paths and these led to summer-houses. There was a grotesque effigy made from naturally contorted wood. The fanciful mind of its creator had also produced a large cone out of some kind of clay and snakes moulded from clay wound around it and reared their cobra heads. The feature of this small garden was its aspect. The land fell away before an immense panorama of rolling forest and hills with the broad Periyar winding its way in the foreground.

By this time my legs were delivering messages. I did not feel sleepy-tired but leg-tired and I faced the long return to the ferry with a dwindling stoicism. If a young woman nearly eight months pregnant could move along effortlessly and joyously, so should I. But I heard a voice saying, 'You are old, Father Time, you are old.'

I sometimes marvel how significant communication can pass between strangers on the way in this country. With no word spoken a deal can be made, a situation clarified. Perhaps this phenomenon is born of necessity in a polyglot land where action and intuition is quicker than words. A car pulled up on the empty road and in a trice we were seated inside. I neither saw Sojan nod to the driver nor, on getting out by the riverside, pay him. Again the words surfaced... 'and, oh, the difference to me.' Wordsworth was having a day of it.

The phrase hung around like a horse-fly; I blessed my good fortune to have a ride. Again the simplicity and timelessness of the ferry ride. This time the ferryman was wearing the coolie hat. We hired a car to take us to the place of pilgrimage, the great sanctuary of St Thomas.

Sojan said he had planned for our walk to take place later in the day to avoid the heat. I envisaged a short climb up some steps of a hill to the sanctuary, but was taken aback when he told me the walk was five kilometres. I looked at the track before me — it was uphill, through outcrop rock. Does it get any steeper than this? Yes, a little. All the way? Yes. I felt indignant and deceived but said nothing, but how was I, a crock, to make it? Why wasn't it explained before I had squandered my energy on the elephant walk? And my legs were mutinous. 'It will take four hours there and back. Allowing for rests.' My god! I felt for my puffer.

In the idiom and spirit of my country I decided to give it a go. Imagination came quietly to distract me. Along this way, nearly two thousand years ago, Thomas the Apostle walked. He would be in his 50s at least. He had sailed, perhaps, from Socotra on the main trade route. How did he go the length and breadth of the Malabar coast converting the heathen in Aramaic, a difficult unknown tongue? Enlightened beings no doubt have ways and means. And I thought of this man so little mentioned in the scriptures — once in each of the synoptic Gospels and the Acts. In St John's gospel he fares better. He is mentioned as Di-dymus the twin, the one who doubted what was told him and said he would believe only if he could touch the wounds and as a result was rebuked by his Master. Because of this very human story Thomas has become the archetype doubter, the sceptic, the scientist, the one with two minds, the one who hangs on to what he knows. How many sermons have bored millions over the centuries because of this incident? Perhaps he did have faith but insisted on bringing his faculties along as well, could this be so? And is it a good thing in the story, that the Master of Masters condemned this investigative approach to reality. Martha was also chidden over her priorities — spiritual matters to take precedence over practical issues of the day. So was Thomas in a similar case? There is a difference to ponder on.

Whatever the answers, I did not have to doubt the authenticity of the tradition that a man of tremendous personality and spiritual power had toiled up this stony slope of Kerala. I did not aspire to merit or blessing, but I did find it a fascinating exercise to try and put myself in his place.

High places of the earth have long been regarded as power points through which incoming extra-planetary energies are channelled. The word antenna had no currency in the first century, but Thomas must have noted his teacher's predilection for high places where he could withdraw into silence and receptivity. And he must have observed how refreshed and energised he was on rejoining his followers. It would not be beyond the inductive power of a careful mind to conclude that energies from unknown sources had entered into the being of this extraordinary man. Thus Thomas had learned to head for higher ground; and here he was in unknown territory, himself transformed and possessed of the same pulsing currents of energy as his Master and instinctively heading for the heights as he bent his shoulders to the task of revealing to these Malabar people the ways and techniques whereby he had acquired these transforming powers. Maybe he observed as he headed for the highest peak of the ranges that the way was not untrodden. Other feet had walked here in another tradition. Had he that breadth of outlook and inclusiveness of mind to recognise that these Hindoos also were aspiring people and that the attainment of their greatest exemplars was of the same order as that of his Galilean Master? We can but surmise.

The knee is a hinge and the leg a lever. The fact that climbing is an act of leverage is forcibly affirmed by the actual climber, and for a tired climber the whole employ of consciousness focuses on this activity.

A lichened boulder to negotiate. Observe the colours of the rock, the lichen and ground blackened by humus, the infinitely small *adiantum* fern. Large ants moving quickly about their affairs, but why such pace, such hurry? Pain behind the knee, the length of the leg. Stand to take in the view, the land falling away. Do not look up. Are you tired, Uncle? The sweet voice of Mini. Of course I am tired. I hope my testiness did not register but I was angry. For Sojan the problem was a simple equation, an old person needs twice as long to allow for rests, therefore he needs four hours. What else was there to it? He should have known my capabilities. I did not fear for the legs — they would fold or otherwise, but to allow tightening of the chest was lunacy. Again I felt for my puffer.

It was no use. After less than a kilometre I had to stop. You go on, I'll wait for you here. This they would not consider. We stay together They did not voice disappointment. They had done this walk before. The descent was also a matter for concentration. Feet moved clumsily, skidded, tottered, staggered. The driver went down ahead to try and get the car closer. The edge of exhaustion had been passed. How stupid to think I could make this ascent. Mistake, mistake, mistake, and still I was bitter at what I had missed.

Did I really think St Thomas had been in this place? I must leave historicity to the experts. Dr John Ochanthuruthu, a historian of the University of Calicut has this to say: 'The authenticity of the St Thomas tradition in South India cannot go back further than the 13th century. So far as explicit support in favour of St Thomas tradition in South India is concerned I have no doubt the answer must be none. Neither the Church Fathers nor the Apocryphal Acts say anything explicitly about Malabar.'

It is odd that I who possess a good share of scepticism in my make-up regard this question as academic. The old saying that energy follows thought is exceedingly pertinent here, when caught up in the living energy of the tradition. Thought and energy have created this story and it will endure. From tradition and mythology one teases out some truth of an enduring nature. That it is enclosed in a suspect matrix does not contaminate the jewel in the lotus.

*

Many of the homes I enter have a similar design. They present a broad front to the road but there is little depth. First entry brings one to a long narrow room little wider than a corridor, usually furnished with a sofa, invariably uncomfortable, and with two or three hard chairs. As there are grilled unglazed windows the entire length one has a verandah feeling, one is not quite inside. If the owners are Catholic or Orthodox there are pictures of the Holy Family; if Hindu, of their prolific deities; and both are excruciatingly bad. In addition are photographs of the dear departed. Either end of this first room may lead to a bedroom. A central door leads to a similar but broader room furnished in better style, but still austere. There is sometimes a television. The central room will lead to a bedroom one side, which in turn will provide access to a second bedroom, but I have had no chance to verify this. From the central room with its borrowed light one passes — often down a step — to the third narrow strip, much like the first. This rear area serves as a kitchen one end and for storage the other with a dining table adjacent to the kitchen. Throughout, the floors are mirror-finish concrete, either black or venetian red, with skirting of black paint on the cream plastered walls. The back door has steep steps; the builders of these houses display no knowledge of the relationship of tread to riser, they always get it wrong. To the far end, with outside entrance, will be the toilet area, unless there is a freestanding place in the yard. Most often a handy tap serves at the back door for washing hands and mouth after a meal. The water splashes into a rough channel — not a drain as we know it. The water then runs on to the base of a palm tree.

The feature that strikes a visitor from grassy New Zealand is that the ground is bare — even in green and pleasant Kerala grass does not invade at the slightest opportunity. The soil is reddish and always swept, and the effect is agreeable. From the yard one steps into the green shade of coconut palms, bananas, mangoes, neem, sometimes the scented champak, and a host of broadleafed trees, which provide that restful brooding atmosphere so often lacking from urban properties. The poorest villager is provided with the surpassing riches of the plant kingdom.

In Mini's house I am given the grandfather's bed. It has a slight give in the webbing and for this I am grateful. I eat alone on the verandah — I must call it that even though it is not open — and am closely observed by all. The women never sit down with the men. Kindness surrounds me. 'How is it, Uncle?' I am used to this questioning and vary my answers from

'Quite nice' to 'Very interesting flavours' and 'scrumptious', but usually stick to 'Quite nice', so that the question now incorporates the answer: 'How is it, Uncle? Quite nice?' This time it was an accurate appraisal. There was plain rice which I had specified, preferring plainness to fiery additives, and chicken pieces boiled or steamed with a stunning savoury sauce. Mini's touch was in all this, she knew my ways and limitations.

Towards ten in the evening the household retires. The night had been observed, as shawl after shawl of darker hue had been thrown around her magnificent shoulders. I did not have to talk much as conversation reverts to Malayalam as easily as water runs to lower ground. Its animation and force provide interest along with the other sounds of nature.

The bedroom was of moderate size and bare save for the wooden bed and a table loaded with luggage bags and baskets. The door to the verandah was carefully bolted. The other exit was a drawn curtain. It led to internal recesses where the members of the family retired — except for the grandfather who, I discovered later, slept on a kind of long table in the sit-out.

Johnny was to share the room with me. He is half-brother to Mini and ten years older. He is slight of build and frail from some explored but unidentified cause. I did not realise this frailty, as the slight build of many Indians belies their strength and endurance. He has a part-time job on the buses, conductor or second conductor, and has taken a liking to me and complains vehemently that my stay is for only one night. Though married happily enough (what can the term mean?) there is some hunger or restlessness about him, common among people with mental ability who live in a cramped or isolated community. They have unexercised faculties calling for stimulation. His semi-distrait expression swiftly changes to eagerness upon meeting strangers. I must have passed his assessment favourably for he proved mindful of my needs and was avid for conversation. Though to my knowledge most people of India sleep on the floor, or the ground, seeing them do so elicits a pang. Yet it is clean, for shod feet never enter their houses, and mats are first unrolled — besides it is a practical and sensible usage of space. To the hard beds of India tribute must be paid for the superb posture and grace of the people. He slept at my feet.

He unrolled his mat and for half an hour played with his baby son until he slept. He then took him away and handed him over to his mother. He had a light blanket. I told him I would have to get up in the night and was concerned lest I disturb the household as I floundered about. He insisted that I must awaken him and he would guide me. He proved to be one who on wakening was instantly in command. He lit a candle and guided me down the labyrinthine way.

The next day our Trichur friends would arrive by car to join us, or rather would pick up Sojan and me for an overnight stay in the hill station of Munnar. They were to arrive early but not so early that Johnny could not take me for a misty walk about the houses and padi fields and not before the high-spirited sun replaced the soft luminescence of dawn with hard, vivid colours, the reds and yellows of *canna* and *ixora*, the gold of marigold, orange-red of *lantana*.

People, mainly women and children, were thronging a temple called Madumal, bringing garlands. The terrain had swelled to a small eminence so that we looked across miles of padi and plantation. The open space of the temple was not defined by wall or hedge but by natural contour and in the centre under its own roof was a crude and garlanded nandi bull. It had been many years since it had been ridden by Shiva, but it was still on duty awaiting a summons. Johnny told me the Malayalam word for temple was Ambalam, hence the term Ambalamkkala, temple bull. As neither Johnny nor I was Hindu we could not enter the temple but I saw through the entrance a galaxy of lit candles and a priest ministering to the faithful gathered about him.

We inspected the site where Johnny's house was to be built. It would fit in among the trees. We left the lane to re-enter the family property through the trees from the rear. On the edge where they ceased just before the house was a bed of plants resembling ginger. He told me the name in Malayalam. It was like, but not, ginger. He bandicooted a root and cleaned it for me. Smaller than ginger pieces, it was also aromatic; the flesh was yellowish-red. As I chewed a piece I could twig the distinctive flavour but not put a name to it. Later Sojan told me it was turmeric. When a baby is born it is rubbed all over with the pulp. The canna, the banana, turmeric and ginger belong to a family very much in the service of humankind.

MUNNAR

Friends from Trichur spilled from the white Commodore: Nixon, Bharat Singh, and Jose, bright-eyed with excitement. I greeted each as they came through the gate. Then I made a mistake. I thought I was greeting Philip the driver, I had only seen him that once on the occasion of my arrival in Kerala at the airport. Besides, I didn't see too clearly. It was not Philip whom I greeted but a colleague of Bharat Singh on transfer from Nagaland. The name caused merriment, so strange it was, sounding like October but in fact Athuba. He had Tibetan features. He was slightly built with quick lively movements. The real Philip then appeared. How had I mistaken his face, so different? Though they had some refreshment on the journey from Trichur, they welcomed the meal provided by Mini's household. Sojan and I made our farewells and joined them on our trip to Munnar.

As we crossed the broad Periyar, Sojan pointed to distant ranges. They were seen to advantage from the bridge looking straight up the river.

'Runmudi,' he said.

'The St Thomas sanctuary, you mean?' Runmudi was the highest visible peak, conical from this angle, but actually table-topped.

'So this was the small hill you told me about!'

At Easter a great throng ascends the mountain chanting an ancient Syriac text. A Portuguese word, I'm told, has ousted one of the time-honoured Syriac words, suggesting the processions began in the Portuguese period.

From Malayattur our route took us direct to Kothamangalam along the gentle foothills before turning east into higher hill country. My map names this territory the Cardamom Hills, though Sojan tells me he has never heard that name — to him it is just part of the Western Ghats. Broader vistas appeared as we rose, and we came on the surprise and delight of waterfalls. One, by the roadside, astonished me with its pounding energy and volume. It came from directly above, tumbling to our feet in the wildest, whitest exuberance.

We were merry and in high spirits from the outset, we passed a toddy shop all on its own, slowed down, then reversed. They tasted a sample before buying bottles. I had remained by the car with Philip. They brought me a glass, then another, for I quickly downed the cool sharp refreshment — Philip, as driver, would not drink. For all the love of alcohol these young men had, they drank very little. I could take no more than the glass pressed on me. It had no effect except to lie heavily on the stomach.

Much of the landscape was taken up with tea plantations, lightly shaded in a few areas by the large *grevillea* of Australia, the silky-oak. For miles we saw naught but the low-plucked tea bushes, but the grandeur of scale saved the prospect from monotony. Then suddenly we would plunge into forests. Occasionally, looking down from the car, we could see splashes of red on the green treetops below. I was asked what these flowers were — I the tourist — but my knowledge was meagre. When we came across specimens closer to the road I identified the red parrot-beak tree or *Erythrina indica*, which has so successfully colonised Australia that many presume it to be an original part of their flora. It is murderously thorny. Another red-flowering tree took longer to get to for scrutiny. It was the tulip tree or *spathodea* which came to South India as an ornamental shade-tree from Africa and liked it so much that it made its way into the native forests. I might not be quite right here as there are various species of *spathodea*. I thought the flower unmistakable. By the roadside at frequent intervals poinsettias were thriving with flaming bracts as red as holly berries at Christmas time.

There were two discoveries exciting for me, since they were known in New Zealand. They were the wild *calceolaria* and the *erigeron* ground cover. At first I thought the drifts of yellow where the tea bushes met the road were the cursed goat-foot oxalis, *pes capri*, and so was delighted when going up to them I saw the unmistakable pouches or slippers, bright full-moon yellow. I believe they are migrants from South America — India is too old not to have migrants. The *erigeron* with its rose-tipped little daisies tumbles down the roadside banks.

As I looked for plants Nixon and Athuba were dancing on the road — they needed no toddy to stimulate them — both were incredibly supple, but expressed themselves in different ways. Nixon was a self-taught break-dancer who through hours of video study had mastered the routines, developing them into routines of his own, apache or hood. He was an actor born. Athuba on the other hand derived from an infinitely graceful tradition. Unlike Nixon, who stamped the earth with joyous energy, Athuba barely alighted, but floated with wraith sinuosity, singing a quasi-falsetto song which later, to my astonishment, I discovered derived from Baptist hymns. His note was clear and flutelike, he was self-absorbed in some secret joy, then changed suddenly to camp sensuality, only to drift once again into his dream-world. In the mountain setting on the highway it was bizarre. We posed for photographs, more toddy was drunk and everyone sang, with a zest for enjoyment that was entrancing.

As the road twisted and turned upwards through the heavy forest I began to notice what I thought were young coconut palms growing closer together then usual. But that could not be; I could see no beginnings of a trunk. From the car they reminded me of seedling nikau palms about four feet high. I wanted to know what they were. We were not on a botanising trip so I couldn't devote my whole time to this pursuit. In any case I was in alien territory without books, plant census or guide. Whatever they were I was intrigued, for they enhanced the forest floor and adorned the banks. I wondered aloud.

Jose answered, 'Cardamoms, Uncle.' What! knowledge in our midst! and what exciting knowledge — cardamom, queen of the spices. We stopped and went among them. Each clump threw up a score of stems like aspidistras. They were thriving, vigorous plants. 'See, Uncle, the fruits, I know it because we grew a plant at home,' said Jose. At the base, lying on the ground, were bunches of green berries like grapes but smaller. I picked a berry and chewed it. Hardly any flavour. 'They have six processes to go through, Uncle. They fetch high prices on the market.'

Jose picked a bunch. 'You mustn't, you have no right. Hide it in your pocket.' Yes, we had no right, however large the planting. Nixon's rebuke was necessary.

I was back in Sydney, my last days there — formative days after Wanganui, beloved home town I loved and left. New experiences crowded in. It was 1969, boom time in Australia. Among many experiences was the inestimable one of meeting Neil and Barbara, themselves Kiwi expatriates.

Tony, a Kiwi friend, had told me about Barbara and Neil, how they made their own muesli and also how they made curries with individual spices, scorning powder from a tin. One evening he took me to dine with them at their home in Vaucluse. My interest in curries, already roused, was heightened that evening. The meal was memorable for the chicken tandoori and the Barossa Pearl wine that accompanied it. We talked spices and we talked shares. At the end of the meal when we sat back with black coffee and Hennessey's I had a surprise, for Neil had put a cardamom seed in my coffee. Good coffee stands on its own, yet now it was enhanced. The bitterness remained and along with it arose a hint of fragrance, a suggestion of exotic airs, and Hennessey's sealed the experience.

The currents that washed us together have parted us with the same gentle motion. Neil had suffered during the war and old age was not for him, while Barbara, as far as I know, lives on in Noosa.

The valley town of Ademali provided what we had not expected, a high-class restaurant, where we lunched. The two bearers (waiters), Kabeer and Suresh, joined in our merriment and served us enthusiastically. Photos were taken and they included the cleaner of the landscape window who was grinning through the glass. I had vegetables, chilli-free, with rice, but they were not fully cooked, a fashion I find tiresome.

From Adimali we began to climb through changing vistas. It is a world for contemplatives as well as tea planters and spice growers. As we climbed even higher the panorama stretched like an immense animal, strong and laid-back. The soul of Kerala was taking the light.

At 4.30 Munnar came up, the place in mind. In contrast to Adimali it was on a ridge. A little further on and a little higher we came upon a lodge and booked in. There was a curving drive halfway around the building and we parked under a grove of eucalypts. The land dropped away from the trees to reveal another valley. The first impression of the lodge was its generous space and spanking cleanliness — it gleamed. The room we hired held three single beds which we put together — six would sleep there, the other on the floor. I went for a siesta while the others consulted the cook and then went off in the car to buy chicken and vegetables. They also bought beer and brandy.

My sleep lasted two hours before I rejoined them in the lounge/dining room. Athuba was making a salad. Jose and Nixon were singing and dancing. Philip wanted a walk after driving all day and asked me to join him. Further up the hill was a chapel, before which he made a sign. It was closed and I wanted to sit inside for the silence, but here outside was nature's greater silence.

An evening such as this with its depth, which trees and plants scented, and light movements of air oxygenated, is one thing when alone, but quite another when shared. Philip was receptive also to the mysteries and imponderables of night, and our chatting was minimal. A contentment descended, for it was a moment when a passing acquaintance could change into a friendship. Could it last? I wondered how far his existence and mine could touch. Our differences were many, but under the stars they were nothing. Athuba joined us and announced that the meal was ready. We lingered a little then made our way back.

Four students from Eranakulam joined us and brought with them four bottles of beer. Nixon did not drink much that evening, maybe he had less than a quarter glass of brandy. Jose said afterwards he had drunk a huge quantity of toddy earlier. He suddenly fell ill after two hours of dancing and singing, left to vomit, then fell asleep on the bed. Thinking back on that evening I realised how modest the intake of alcohol had been. Jose and Bharat Singh did not drink while Philip confined himself to a single glass of beer. The fact emerged that it was Athuba who had accounted for three parts of the brandy bottle. Yet he too drank rarely, according to Bharat Singh. Nixon slept for well over an hour then reappeared blank and wide-eyed. He made for the bottle and I tried to dissuade him but he said he must have it. In no time he was the life of the party again. His recovery was short-lived and he collapsed again. He lay on the bed unstirring till morning. There was speculation that the medication he had been taking for bladder stone, together with the drink, was the cause of his condition, but the simple fact was that he was allergic to alcohol and had often told us so. At various stages one or the other went to bed.

The students were interesting, they were recognised by Sojan as belonging to the old princely family of Cochin. One was in his last year of training as a homoeopathic doctor. They called him doctor and thrust me forward for him to look at my eye which had suddenly become bloodshot. He said he was not a doctor yet and that I should see a qualified man.

Jose and I were the last to sleep. I was on the outside of the vast bed and he on the floor. As I went to lie down I found one of Nixon's sample batteries on the mattress — he goes nowhere without his trade samples, and I said to Jose,

'Poor Nixon's lost his battery, no wonder he can't sparkle.'

The remark struck us as funny — perhaps it was the late hour and the sight of the five sleepers each in his blanket and dead to the world. Perhaps it was the thought of our merry, irrepressible friend whose vitality had twice switched off suddenly. We could not control our laughter, especially when, arranging my blanket, I found a second battery. It was hilarious complicity. We subsided with a few more lingering outbursts and sniggers at greater intervals. Finally silence and darkness.

I awoke first and had the bathroom before the rush. Our plan for the day was to head south to Thekkadi and Periyar Lake wildlife sanctuary and then return to Trichur, not by the same route, but by turning directly west before going north. We had a drawn-out leave-taking of our Cochin friends and, after photos of the group in front of the cars, we parted. This was about 10 a.m. An hour along the way we came upon a tea factory and sought permission to pay a visit. This took half an hour to arrange but eventually we entered the compound, admired the flower beds, and passed into the ramshackle ad hoc jumble of tall tin buildings.

The scent of tea pervaded. That in itself was a reward, for the sweet airs that hovered over the tea plantations gave no hint that out of this sea of shining green would arise the tangy aroma of the cup that cheers. It was true then, that these long aerated benches of leaf-tips would, step by step, transmogrify into crunchy packets of tea upon supermarket shelves. We were to see how this came about, and followed an extremely small Malayalam-speaking guide. We went through noise from sieve to sieve and looked at the leaves as they moved along the conveyor belts and shakers and through huge maturation cylinders. I could not benefit from the guide's spiel and was thrown a single word in English. As I knew the technicalities were set out in encyclopedias I could look up later, I did not mind. What mattered was that I saw the leaves arriving green and splendid and turn into black tea, shuffling down the conveyor belts and gently trickling into bags, in five grades. It was a muddly visit nevertheless.

Sojan had bought fresh wheat-flour buns, baked nearby in the western style. My homesick palate rejoiced and I did not miss the butter and raspberry jam.

Nixon wasn't well, he was listless and faint. We had to get him to a hospital, else he would never make the trip back. At Kumily, after enquiries, we found a small hospital. He was admitted at once. Later the friendly little junior doctor told me he was suffering from acute alcoholic comatosis, or that is what I thought he said, he spoke so rapidly. He was given an injection and put on an intravenous drip to counter poisoning of the system, and later put on another drip of glucose to restore the depleted energies.

We debated what best to do. Here we were, 250 kilometres of bad mountain roads from Trichur, and due to return that evening. It was already mid-afternoon and Nixon would be on drips for many hours. It was decided that we should go on to Thekkadi to the wild game sanctuary, return to Kumily, take our meal, and then according to Nixon's condition, reassess our plan, hopefully taking him back with us overnight.

We arrived at Thekkadi resort as the sun was declining. The grounds had preserved the natural forest, and its roads and parking areas were well maintained. A large tourist hotel dominated the scene, aspected down to the long arm of Periyar Lake. Large noticeboards gave information about boat trips which took tourists to the viewing areas where tigers and elephants could be seen. These trips took two hours and the last trip for the day was returning, so that was that. We gazed down the long empty lake. We wandered about. There were information boards to read, there was a display building stocked with photographs and illustrative diagrams about the various animals and information about flora and fauna protection. There was information as to where one could buy postcards but it disappointed as there were no other buildings around. There was no one to ask. Unexpected and startling was a series of large photographs of elephants mating, explicit and detailed. Was it unseemly that nature should impose on these ponderous, awesome creatures the same urgencies that had preoccupied man down the ages? And what had happened to Indian prudery?

Back in Kumily we found Nixon on a bed with a drip into his left arm. We did not all go in. The room was a concrete box and it held two beds; on the other was a lively middle-aged man undergoing treatment for back problems. This included traction. A harness about his waist had reins on each side which led to the foot of the bed to engage a network of ropes which ended in a single rope, which ran over a pulley and dangled a bag of sand. Though no graffiti announced the fact, I knew that ahead of Kilroy, Heath Robinson had been here.

'How are you, Nixon?'

'Yes, I am okay.' He had a mannerism of spacing and emphasising each word. 'I am okay, I've been sleeping.' There was still a lot of sleep left in him. I held his hand, he smiled, then let expression drain as he relaxed deeper. I knew he had taken in my comfort. He rallied, 'The nurses, I like the nurses, I like the nurses.'

One nurse he liked was tying the traction rope anew as the bag of sand kept slipping second by second to the floor. Sojan took over, and after a struggle succeeded with such a tight knot that the heavy instrument of traction was prevented for all time from evading its duty.

They came in briefly to see him. Jose and Philip were more eager to chat up the nurses in the corridor. I stayed on longer sitting there — it was an old occupation… so many times. Sojan called me. The doctor wanted to tell me his difficulties, his struggles to rise from a background of poverty, his low salary which was not even a third of my pension. Meanwhile he examined and pronounced as temporary the haemorrhage in my eye. He prescribed drops.

Knowing that it would be as late as eleven at night before Nixon was through with the treatment and thoroughly rested, we went for our supper, then wandered about the main streets of Kumily. The others went back to the hospital. The scent of spices gathered and dispersed in the night air. Sojan and I spent some time in a spice shop, talking to the assistant. We bought a tourist package of eighteen linked plastic bags which held samples of all the spices grown locally.

Nixon was ready. He was not one to dramatise his condition and knew what could or could not be done. We were in for an all-night ordeal over rough roads that demanded total vigilance on the part of the driver. For over eight hours Philip concentrated on the road ahead. Is there some merit in this routine achievement? Meditators — in spiritual, artistic or scientific fields have this ability to focus and concentrate. Is there some link or inference that powers of concentration acquired in physical work will be applicable to more significant enterprises in the drama of life? Is it all that big a jump from taxi-driving on mountains at night to traversing the mountains of the mind? Behind both is the will to keep going. It was Philip's strength and endurance that returned us to Trichur at eight the following morning. Each of the passengers was in his own private bubble of exhaustion. Discomfort and fatigue are woven into the transport systems of this country; this is a factor which contributes to the resilience and stoicism of its people. We in the West who readily complain about minor shortcomings of our transport systems have no conceivable idea of the Indian scene.

Athuba, Bharat Singh and Nixon above all, after a quick fresh-up at their homes, went on to work, while we more favoured ones who had no such urgency, did what most in the whole world we desired to do. We slept.

Nocturne

Towards 6:30 Praveen took leave and asked would I care to walk back with him to his house. Already visibility was lessening I was overdue for my evening walk. He comes frequently for conversation and I am mindful that I must keep on talking on any subject and accustom his ear to English sounds. He pays the courtesy of full attention. First I had to put on shoes since snakes are about after dark, and chappals offer no protection. From his house I went on further, a kilometre or so, to the main road, then turned back. As ever, the night was velvet. The road back takes a sharp turn right then runs for a short, heavily shaded length before turning left to the temple. It was on this darker stretch that a shape came towards me. It veered sharply from left and to right, a cyclist I thought, avoiding puddles. It was a drunk and I made room for his wobbling. Even so he came straight for me and fell heavily against my shoulder. I held him in support. He hugged me and began to sob while I at a nonplus began to comfort him. He was kissing my face then went on his hands and knees to kiss my feet, I fending and raising him. This scene continued awhile, then he took two small bananas from a plastic bag, peeled each gravely and presented me one, indicating I should join him in ritual eating. Then he resumed his hugging and let escape a sob or two. At this point a man came out of the dark and assessed my predicament. He scolded the poor befuddled man and steered him towards his home, but not before a final abasement and kissing of my feet. My rescuer knew me, as I used to watch him at play hockey with his friends in front of the temple. He took my shoulder and walked me back; it was his responsibility, he said. He asked did I play chess and I said at an elementary level. Then he would come to me one morning next week for a game.

MALAYATTUR REVISITED

It rained steadily all night and as I wandered the next morning I had to choose the firmest mud to walk on. Later some drying would take place. The muddy sections were few so I could concentrate on the delights of the morning. They were three; the green shade; the light draught of air that only a spinnaker could register; and the stealing perfumes which played hide-and-seek and defied identification. Had I knowledge of the flora I would have tracked down the scent. Instead I had to bypass curiosity and enjoy the scent in its own right. The writer Ernest Raymond came to mind. He was generations back. In my early teens his reflective and sentimental books excited me. I recalled two titles — *Tell England* and *Adventures in Contentment*. Others eluded me but the essence of adventure they invoked was heady, as was his skill in alerting the senses. He taught me to seek out and enjoy the marginal things of nature. There was a poem I wrote under his influence which began;

Oh, I have loved the velvet rose
And sought her mystery to seize
As on her bowing stalk she blows
And spills her scent on every breeze.

What surprised me about these lines was that they brought tears to the eyes of a young poet, a friend, who though younger had greater judgment and poetic experience. He gave no quarter to the rest of the poem, but these lines stirred him, he said, and recalled Blake's lines:

When the stars threw down their spears,
And watered heaven with their tears.

Poetry was a passion but I could not write. Phrases and images came, but with no power to mould them into a living artefact, they remained fragments.

Raymond had driven me to it; the beauty of nature was an obsession, almost a torment. I recall other lines I liked at the time but now dismiss and relegate to the great discard.

Who can assuage the pangs of incoherence
Or mitigate the dull underground moan of soul
Bearing the barometric thrust of beauty?

Questions beyond my ability to answer. My mind switched to the two preceding days I had spent in Malayattur, Mini's family home is among the poorest and simplest but, scaled down as it is on all material levels, it has its own authenticity and completeness, as life in the Middle Ages had its own authenticity and completeness. This is what I thought, but I cannot assess their longings for a bigger world, nor indeed the extent to which these people live in the modern world. The simple annals of the poor prove not so simple.

It is the walks, either through the forest or along the lanes to the vast panoramas of padi, that beguile me. The sheer abundance of forest with its walls of green and roof of green, latticed with skylights of blue, overwhelm me. In what cleverly landscaped garden could anything surpass this? How long has it taken man, and then not completely, to realise that nature is not interested in considerations of geometry and architecture? Prissy balance and precision, spacing and grooming, is the kiss of death to nature. Here there is no tyranny of straight line or the nonsense of a right angle. The tracks and lanes follow the dictates of feet and terrain.

Yet by using straight lines and right angles man has found a way through nature to greater knowledge and powers, as well as to greater follies. I do know that a crooked natural path nourishes the spirit and that we need all the tangles and untidiness of nature. The memory surfaces of a friend who deplored nature because of her untidiness — He was a solicitor. I have no thought to denigrate the profession but precision was important to him and the prime attribute of reality. After all his love of precision led him to the stars. He was also an astronomer.

The family owns 20 cents of land, about 1/5 acre. I work it out. Three harvests a year are reaped from this padi field. It is enough to keep them in rice most of the year. Now a question arises. The son has to build a house and is forced to sell this field to help defray costs. This must not happen. Surely there is some other way.

When we arrived the sit-out was a threshing floor. The women had cut and carried the sheaves on their heads all the way to the house. They were busy threshing and winnowing. I had seen earlier the way sheaves were tied a wisp or two of rice straw, a twist and a turn and the sheaf was firm. I saw how skilful feet can be in this threshing stage. Heel and ball of foot alternately rolled and ground the sheaf, then turned the ends into the centre and rolled at again. There was a sharp beating of the sheaf on the floor and it was stacked on a pile. There were no flails. This processed pile was gone through later — a practised eye noted if the sheaf needed further beating.

The floor was deep in stalk-ends, trash, and rice. Periodically a home-made broom, not unlike a besom, would miraculously skim away the dross, leaving the rice on the floor. This was later transferred to great bronze urns to await winnowing with sieves. The threshed sheaves were then sold to farmers as cattle feed. The yield in rupees from this transaction was meagre, but in this lowly economy every rupee counted. So the great stretches of padi were the untrodden pastures of the cattle. The stubble was worked back into the soil but there was no dung. Later the winnowed rice would be bagged, then protected from rats against which unremitting warfare was waged.

I wanted to enjoy the last lights as they faded on the padi but Johnny and I were surrounded by children laughing and joking, keen for fun. Rarely did they see a 'saip' (sahib) and the young eager faces were at first a little over-awed. In their varying expressions they took on the beauty and diversity of flowers. They knew a few expressions in English and quickly found out my name, age and country except that Switzerland and New Zealand was one and the same. The mothers and older women moved in and I wanted to go on but Johnny would not allow me. They do not often have such entertainment. I admired the children's dresses, asked them to give me their teeth and asked their ages and names. One little boy about ten put his arm about me — he was not cute or fetching but the epitome of a healthy young boy. His name was Martin, so I called him St Martin. His family was Catholic.

Two old women had great heavy loops of plated gold standing upright above their ears in defiance of nature. I guessed that in earlier life the earrings they wore were excessively heavy as the lobes were distended a couple of inches and no longer used, and there was a later piercing high on the ear. I asked for one as a souvenir and said I would wear it. No, we could not grow coconut or padi in my country, which puzzled them. Then what did we live on? Where do we get rice? I explained the dominant role played by wheat and potatoes. They knew about po-ta-toes but laughed at the way I said it. And what was my religion? Always a question of importance in India. Temple, mosque, church and school are the major institutions in their world.

The following evening we did have some quiet moments on the high ground overlooking the padis. The scene was reminiscent of, but much vaster than the cornfields of Van Gogh. It also was the playground of light. Thin earthen banks separated the various properties. Which was Johnny's field? Away beyond some pylons to one side. The vast plane of padi wore a headpiece of jungle, mostly palms — a darkening corona spread from east to the brighter west. Now the colours were subdued and we re-tinted them with our memory of former light, they became pastel and infinitely tender. Who could capture such light, such beauty and splendour in word or paint?

I had to meet Jessy's family. Jessy is Johnny's wife, a tall woman of grace and beauty. We met the first two brothers in their adjacent shops which at a guess sold similar goods, groceries, cakes and soft drinks. Anthony, the first, was grave like his sister. This gravity, which had no element of mistrust or scepticism, was characteristic. He wanted to give me something, a cake, a drink, something. Finally he cut a wedge from a kind of tart, still warm from the oven, containing coconut and fruit. It was delicious and the fact that I was enjoying it pleased him greatly and he thawed. I felt his integrity and sincerity. Our conversation was limited as we had to make use of Johnny's interpretive abilities.

Brother Raphael made a quicker impact. He also wanted to give me something and came up with a packet of Nice biscuits. He said he would come to the house later and take us to a toddy shop, and on my urging, since he had mentioned kurkas, he agreed to take me to see what sort of plant it was and how it grew.

The walk to their house was alongside a clear shallow stream — such clarity of water is rarely seen except in the mountains. A smiling family greeted us. Two toddlers were a focus of pleasure and joy. I met the wives of the brothers. There was a young man, also a brother, sitting on a low wall. He gazed at me with intense concentration, then smiled. The smile was virtually permanent — with mouth open. He was deaf, completely deaf. The family had sought treatment for him to no avail and his development was thus retarded. He was eighteen, a fine-looking youth. Anthony had given me a small packet of groundnuts and I broke it open to give him some. His grin broadened as he carefully picked off the skin.

On the verandah was a large heap of freshly dug kurka roots, more the size of ginger than sweet potatoes. The tubers had not been washed and were being sold on the spot as customers called. The nutty flavour reminded me of new potatoes. Raphael appeared and shortly after we found lunch set out for us. They spared me the chillied foods and gave me vegetables, a bowl of kurkas and an omelet. I ate all the greens but could not manage all the kurkas or the omelet.

Raphael then took us outside and we went along the path by the stream and crossed where it was bridged at the main road. Retracing our steps on the opposite side we eventually came to the kurka field, a couple of acres or so of low ground. The plants grew on long beds three feet wide and raised about four inches. The leaves were strangers. I crushed a leaf but it had no scent. The stems were weak and of soft tissue, they rooted readily where the nodes touched the soil. Raphael dug into the soft watery earth with his fingers and broke off a root, surprisingly hard for a bog plant. He washed it in the stream and gave it to me. I nibbled at it and realised that unlike a potato it could be eaten raw. The flavour, however, was neutral and I agreed it needed cooking to enhance the flavour. It is an palatable root vegetable and a fine supplement to the diet. I could see that because of its water-loving nature it could flourish in few other regions outside Kerala.

It was a long walk on the main road to the toddy shop, an undistinguished concrete cube. The entrance was narrow and it had ugly unpainted concrete walls. Small eating rooms led off a short passage. Inside the one we entered was a long wooden table with a form of equal length against the wall. It was bare and its bareness was repellent as if it were a cell. Perhaps outer trappings were superfluous and of no moment for soon the customers would be experiencing the comforts of intoxication. There were many dishes available but only Raphael wanted to eat. A dish of fried pieces of meat coated in sauce was ordered with a bowl of toddy and three glasses. I tasted the meat at Raphael's invitation. It was tasty but after a moment the fiery sauce hit me. Johnny did not eat and Raphael did not drink. He explained that Raphael was on medication, therefore toddy was out. It was sharp and bitter, in fact horrible, but I managed to empty my glass.

We had no expectations and no illusions, there was nothing wicked and nothing alluring. We left sober. There was strong agitation in the district for toddy shops to be abolished because of the high incidence of drunkenness. We came across a young man lying on the road. Two men nearby transferred him to the side. I noted he was lying with his head downhill. He would be there all day.

Johnny told me then that Raphael had a stint in a mental hospital caused by his brooding over the caesarean birth of his child. His wife was perfectly healthy, but he felt guilty about this operation and was convinced he had harmed his wife. Worry had gnawed his confidence, though he appeared strong and seemingly well-balanced. His wife was again pregnant. This is how I understood it, for Johnny could not explain clearly and also I was told in confidential asides.

A small man arrived. He had a withered foot. It was Paul, another brother-in-law. If it were fair to say so, he was more friendly than the others, more animated. Perhaps it was a bigger event for him as he could not work and had no preoccupations of business to occupy his attention. He wanted Johnny and me to stay the night. As it was, Sojan and Mini would be staying with him. I resisted his pleading. At such short notice I did not want to stay. Afternoon tea was an occasion. Four types of cookies and sweetmeats were provided. How thoughtful they were, how hospitable.

Our return was by ferry, bus and auto-rickshaw. The ferry ride was further down the river this time. The great Periyar never varied pace on its way to the sea. Johnny had forgotten to bring the kurkas. It had crossed my mind but I did not try to speak up, not wanting to be pushing household matters. Why didn't you speak up, he asked. I wondered too. The next day when Sojan and Mini returned, they brought the kurkas.

Back at Trichur we have counted the cost and are going to build a new room. The small room I occupy is perfectly adequate, through dark and, I suspect subject to damp, but I have no problems, I am satisfied as things are — a haven. The new room will lead off the front porch directly, so in a way will be cut off and shielded from sounds — they think of the crying of the new baby, still sleeping in the womb and soon to awaken.

It will possess a western toilet as a concession to stiffened joints that tend to go into seizure and labour when using the eastern counterpart. This is a measure of prime satisfaction.

Sand is the first requirement, then bricks and metal, Sojan's grandfather owns a granite quarry, and he deals in river sand which he can deliver in one of his trucks. So we pay a visit to by bus his mother's family. It is twelve kilometres from the city. We stop right at their office building and enter to the greetings of Sojan's affable aunt and after warm chatter she provides us cakes and scalding tea in a burning glass. After this kindness she takes us to the old house further back on the property where the old folk live. I meet grandfather and grandmother 82 and 79, and a maiden aunt who is 80. These worthy and fine-looking people have the same gentleness and old-world courtesy that my father's seven sisters possessed. They were composed and calm and had the gift of communing in silence. No one spoke English. I sat on a hard but high quality settee, and before me was a small table graced with a jam jar. It held a single spray of *syngonium* already beginning to put out white roots. A spent bloom of double red hibiscus choked its mouth. Only then I noticed seven or eight small fish in the jar. The house was spacious and genteel and cool draughts wandered throughout.

Grandfather took us to the river, along a metalled path, walled and shaded. Maidenhair fern greened the walls. It was a long arcade of shade and stillness. Suddenly at a turn it opened to a sizeable stream, wooded right down to its sandy banks. Grandfather led us downstream then we plunged back into the trees, still on his property. The dense planting was not strictly forest, for so many chosen trees had been planted. This was so completely another world that thoughts, values and preoccupations underwent a change, like a cabinet re-shuffle with a new forest deity presiding. I could have stayed there hours, years, that was my mood. We followed a path, I was avid for knowledge of the denizens. One small tree by our path was so perfectly shaped and furnished with bright foliage that it captivated me. It most resembled a camellia or lilly-pilly. I crushed a leaf and smelled it, tasted it. Nutmeg? Sojan and his grandfather conferred in Malayalam. It was a nutmeg tree.

I had a little nut tree
Nothing would it bear,
But a silver apple
And a golden pear.

Wide of the mark or not, I was in fable land. I looked for its fruit, no silver apple or golden pear, but a nut little larger than a medium plum, not perfectly round, spheroid. Beneath the outer coating was a black sheath with a bright crimson tunic splitting to expose the black nutmeg. Nutmeg and grated nutmeg! Familiar from childhood. The discovery stopped me short. It had been a long journey from childhood through the world to this little nut-tree.

Another small tree twelve foot high, standing clear as though planted, also caught my attention. It had the same symmetry and height as the nutmeg but was woefully unleaved as though ravished, as though lacking trace elements, or needing more light. Yet it functioned well enough. Perhaps that was its normal penitential vestment, I did not have to ask its name, the scent of leaves was pure clove. I knew the clove was a *eugenia*, therefore akin to the lilly-pilly — its name came so pat, *eugenia aromatica*.

Taking our leave and in search of Uncle who managed the business, we engaged an auto. They own many properties. We found him and his son Benny in a granite quarry. I recalled his stocky figure and strong genial face. About ten workers were with him. A rocky defile led to the arena of the quarry with threatened vegetation crowding the cliff edges. Thin-armed but strong men were wielding sledgehammers in the heat. They bounced off the granite slabs until a crack appeared, then a crowbar was used to widen the fissure. As the boulders and slabs were reduced to one-man rocks they were carried to one side while petite women in saris hammered the smaller rocks into metal or chips and then filled their baskets and carried them on their heads to the main heap. As I could see it, three grades were produced — the heavy one-man rocks for house foundations, and two grades of metal.

The drainage was erratic, for even the ground surface changed under the attacks of sledgehammer and crowbar. A cliff-fed streamlet connected the pools and puddles. They were everywhere and small fish swam in them as well as their predators, the frogs. A truck lurched and manoeuvred its way in. The men loaded it by hand with one-man rocks. I was invited to sit on a selected rock, which wobbled until Benny wedged it with a stone. A worker brought sweet tea in a steel beaker. It was hot trudging into the quarry, and I was glad to sit and watch these labourers at their slow, rhythmic toil. Twice a week a contractor drives in with an air-compressor drill to work on the cliff faces. Apart from that all the work was manual.

One of their empty trucks arrived and we went with it to get the sand along narrow roads brushing the scrub as we went by. It was a considerable distance from the quarry to the riverside where the sand was piled. A truck was there ahead of us and we had to wait while the men loaded it. They used curious tools, half shovel and half hoe with the handle almost parallel with the blade. Ferry boats were anchored nose-in to the bank. They spelled peace and idleness more than any other symbol. Such boats are featured in thousands of paintings and photographs the world over. One was in use and the 45 minutes we were there it was kept busy. One of the other boats was used by the sand men as they worked the river bed. They dived into the shallow river and scooped up sand from the bed into strong colanders or chatties and tipped the golden contents into the boat. The quality was excellent and unvarying. When the boat was laden they poled it to the landing and painstakingly discharged its cargo. It was sold on the spot.

An old man came down the slope with his two bullocks and led them into the water. He scrubbed them painstakingly before allowing them to wallow. He then performed his own ablutions with the same thoroughness. This done and his clothes rearranged, he touched the beasts lightly with a switch and drove them across to the opposite bank. I watched them feeding as soon as they reached green leaves, then saw that our truck was backing into position and five men stood by to load. I had only glanced at the truck, but when I turned my head back the man and his beasts were gone.

It was a long and lumbering journey back through the dusk to the little house in Evanoor. The truck was hard to manoeuvre to the entrance where the labourers, jumping down from the sand, began unloading. Having unloaded one side, the truck turned about so that the other side could be discharged onto the same heap. Everyone works long hours and no one has ever heard of overtime. I doubt if it has an equivalent in Malayalam or any other of the myriad tongues of India. It is an unknown term.

PAUL

Do you remember me? Jose had brought along a friend late in the afternoon. Again I deplored my inability to remember names and people; I would not make a successful diplomat or public figure, for in such circles it is imperative to honour one and all with one's memory. This man had such a pleasant face, but my shelves of recall were bare. Paul, of course, of course, I had met him twice, but briefly, while pillioning with Chandu.

I had been told of his arch-conservative family and his inability to break the mould — there had been something — a failure? A jealousy? I was unable to take in what I had heard. All I recall was the impact of his fresh, smiling face. He was 26, an electrician employed at the nearby sub-station. I wondered why he should come and see me. His English was serviceable and he had no study incentive. I suppose that Jose just brought him along.

Just then Laj arrived. He comes daily to inspect the house which is a building next door and which should be ready for him and his parents within two months. The talk centred around typing and computers, he is a student, and we discussed their capabilities. I told them that as far as computers go, my knowledge was zero in that field, a complete ning-nong. Ning-nong, Uncle, what is it? The conversation began in English, was infiltrated by a few phrases of Malayalam and then completed overrun and occupied by that rippling tongue. Paul, who had not spoken, beckoned me to come inside and talk — we were on the sit-out and I was slightly surprised that he should provide this initiative. But Kerala people observe open house and have different ways. To my shame I cannot recall our conversation. I am not one for detail but for general impression, for instance I identify plants by their general appearance. Maybe if I were a psychologist I would be a gestaltist. My father could recall a conversation word for word and years afterwards. My admiration has an element of envy. Maybe our conversation amounted to trivialities. We were in my room sitting on the bed and he plied me with personal questions. What had I done in the past? What was my object in living in Kerala? My shirts were on a rack and he was interested in the origin tags on my clothes. Some of the talk now comes back.

He asked would I care to take a walk with him. Jose had to be on his way to see a friend who had landed in hospital with a broken leg, and Laj was but passing by. I preferred an hour later when it would be cooler. Then I realised this had been his idea in coming to see me. It was sultry. I wondered what route he would take. We wandered first to his home to leave the bicycle. He lived in the main street and the house frontage was right on the road — a nondescript aspect. Inside was entirely different, disclosing amplitude and substance. Spacious tiled rooms opened one into another. The impressions were of taste, restraint and a touch of opulence. We stayed a moment, with but time to meet his married sister, Roshni, and grab an umbrella, for dun clouds were marshalling.

The roads we trudged were busy, therefore smelly, and we had constantly to step from the tar seal to the berm. Yet it was enjoyable. He told me he loved God and asked about me. I am not at ease when conversations take such a turn but his pure shy joy in this confession spoke an interior happiness. I did my best to come in with my own affirmations and joy in life. I had to get away from church language but he displayed no proselytising zeal. The road was long, but wide enough to allow for horizons that are denied the lanes, and to partake of their airy, unappreciated sustenance.

At the junction with another main road we came to the entrance of the sub-station and I knew his purpose. I was in for a visit, and met, in different sections, three officials at their desks. It was not a grand tour and I did not have to bear the impact of technical information. In one place I saw long banks of controls, like petrol pumps, and I thought of inspection parades, anything but their intricate purposes. The bird-brain said that was what sub-stations should look like.

We did not entirely retrace our steps, but cut through the vast grounds of the Engineering College, pleasant after the roads. I saw four young men in front of the main building chipping weeds at a furious pace. They were students. Surely there was some project afoot, for no self-respecting gardener would work so fast. The grounds were untidy and maintenance half-hearted, save for one locked and chained area which contained low hedges designed to simulate walls, parapets and balustrades. The topiary was meticulous and there was a maze of geometric design — from outside I was unable to discern the patterns. The devotion expended on the hedges did not extend to the paths and flower-beds that accompanied them. Is it fair to say that nothing is completed in India?

Do you know Simon? I do indeed, my memory scored at last. The hockey coach. Paul told me he was a famous coach and had represented his country. Yes, he was a famous coach who had once represented India. We had passed the ponderous main building and wandered across to shade trees; beyond were the hockey grounds. Simon had spotted us and came over. It was fast becoming dark and the teams were still practising. We sat on the concrete surround of a tree and watched.

A sports field in an urban setting lies open to more sky than any other feature. Even parks which honour space have shade trees dividing the sky. So it was refreshing to sit there, just to sit. Sports fields unwittingly bring down the maximum light from the sky.

The ground was almost totally bare of turf and consisted of cemented red gritty soil; levelled, it is ideal for hockey. I watched, but unless the play came our way, could not see the ball. We talked of the changes in the rules since my day and how the game had speeded up. I reminisced how, when an Indian hockey team had visited New Zealand before the war, a test-match was played in my home town. A member of our hockey team was selected for the national team. His name was Thrush, and he was a forward, so that whenever he gained control of the ball and commenced a run the crowd sang 'Bye Bye Blackbird'. I was a ball boy.

The players came by, thundering and scrapping, and as quickly moved on. Black rain clouds with heavy bales showed unmistakable purpose as the cease-play whistle blew. We were surrounded by the players; young men and women had been playing together and a vortex of energy enclosed us. Some chatted, others listened, not sure of English. A saip, or foreigner, is a major curiosity. The first spots fell, foretelling another night of rain, and we had some little way to go. Our heads and shoulders were kept dry by our umbrella but feet and legs were soaked. It was not unpleasant.

We have been waiting for Mini's baby. A message comes from Malayattur that it would arrive on the 14th. Today is the 19th. Sojan has been shuttling between us. First it was to be in a few days. Two days pass and labour pains have not begun. The latest news is there will be a caesarean today. Sojan's mother made a day-trip. Mini is in the hospital. Her half-brother Johnny came to see us one day. He was intending to take me back with him and was puzzled that I should demur. I did not feel it was right for me to intrude at such a time. I said I would leave the timing of visits for Sojan to decide. Later when he turned up he agreed it was not appropriate just now. I shall go later.

A telegram — I think it was — came while Kunjumon and I were playing chess. I pricked up my ears, as I thought I heard the word 'death' floating on the stream of Malayalam. It was a chilling thought. It took some time before Kunjumon translated the news that Biju's father had died. I knew who it was — Sojan's uncle. He and some of the family had made a quick visit less than a fortnight ago. He was driving. It was sudden. Heart, I thought, or a stroke. Sojan's mother prepared my meal and then left to visit the bereft family. She could not tell me on her return what had happened, and my interpreter had gone home. My surmise as to the identity of the dead man proved wrong — it was a relative of that man. The words denoting relationship are not the same as ours.

THE HOCKEY TOURNAMENT

The sky was moderately furnished with clouds, they did not presage rain, but I was mistrustful as a low rumble kept up all afternoon. Mainly it came from the east and the south but I thought prowled around the entire horizon. Mid-afternoon the rumble turned to a growl. Kunjumon had no need to remind me of his promise to take me to the hockey tournament at four this afternoon as I, of memory poor, had remembered. By now the clouds had thickened and darkened and I said we were in for heavy rain. He did not think so, or that is how I took it. When English is rudimentary I am often far out in my conclusions and have to cross-check. When I took my umbrella he looked tolerant.

The grounds are nearby, and as we walked along he asked did I remember Balankutty. I did not. When he grabbed my shoulders and acted drunkenly and said 'By the temple,' I knew that Balankutty was the drunken man whom I helped and that Kunjumon was the one who came to my aid. That connection made, I understood that this man lived nearby, in fact on the bend of the lane. He said that he had been drunk again and had bitten a man. There was an uproar and the bitten man's brothers came to his house and tore off some of the roof-thatching. As we drew near we saw a young man working on the roof. It was not Balankutty though. I looked around and there was my alcoholic friend on the path. We looked at each other. I remembered his face and the missing tooth. I smiled and spoke but his face remained blank. Kunjumon spoke to him and there was a spark of recognition, but only a spark. He was a troubled man who only gave the rudiments of recognition.

The game had begun by the time we arrived. It was women's hockey, one team in black and white and the other in red and white. Some of the girls were barefoot, others had the lightest of footwear — only the goalies wore protection. In a skirmish near the sideline where we were standing I saw a girl take a fast ball fair on the shin. She stooped to rub it, limped a couple of steps, and was off and away again.

I found it hard to see the ball in that light, except when a new ball replaced the old — this happened twice while I was there, I found the play intensely interesting, especially when close by. I saw no goals scored but there were many crowd-stirring runs and attacks. Rain had started, not heavily but steadily, so we hoisted the umbrella. One could have made a special study of the supporters, all of whom were students of the Engineering College and the girls from the rival colleges. They busied themselves chanting and jumping, arms upthrust high, as their team made a spurt. Their antics orchestrated the action. After a whistle for obstruction a voice called out LBW.

The rain stopped play, or so I thought. Everyone, players and spectators, walked down the ground to the far 25 yard line. I could not make out what it was all about. A goalie crouched in her den, arms spread-eagled, as an opponent took a shot at goal. There was tension as we watched and a din arose at the outcome, shrieks of delight from the supporters of the winning side and lamentations from the losers. I assumed that because the second half was cancelled the event was to be decided by a goal-shooting contest. There were several of these contests. One girl came off crying into the arms of her schoolmates. The goalies alternated and each result was recorded. The final trial was won by a girl in red and white and that success evidently was the clincher. A frenzy of rejoicing and hugging followed. Groups swept from one to another. There was some tussling and fighting. I am ever a poor witness and had to ask Kunjumon what was happening. He said 'excitedment' and I guess he was right. As we walked back we were surrounded by the players. A few had umbrellas, most became thoroughly wet. It did not appear to bother them as most were in tears and the soaking was nature's empathy.

WALKABOUT & THE BABY

The early morning inviting, I went walking. It becomes a habit. I was not so much wrapt in my thoughts that I could not suspend time to watch a goat ripping off posters from a concrete wall and eating them. I thought, this is as it should be and if all the goats that are currently tipping the balance of frail eco-systems towards desertification could be assembled before all the hoardings of the world what a great world this would be.

I met Valsan, who was shifting cattle to the temple area for grazing. He took me along a path by the lake which I had not explored before, thinking it private. Valsan is excessively shy and cannot speak English. The path had been churned and chopped by the cattle and led to the padi fields, where I thought there was a lake but was wrong. There was no defined shore-line since it was temporary inundation. Today water was widespread and clear enough to see submerged pasture.

He directed me to a small hall on the side of the path. The door was open and I could see bands of psychedelic colours from a TV. It was too early for viewing. Near the doorway Kunjumon faced a friend across a carom board. They were busily flicking a black dice or taw against the counters, endeavouring to sink them into the four pockets. They were intent and silent in concentration. This is the village den, and I was surprised to see how well-built and serviceable it was. I did not stay long. About midday Kunjumon arrived wanting a game of chess. We are not evenly matched but soon will be as he thinks more than me. It will not be long before he has the better of me. I tell him when that stage is reached I play no more. He was to call again at four in the afternoon to take me to the hockey tournament, but was late. Meanwhile the thought of a chess pattern that I had once mastered came to mind and I set out the board with the idea of reconstructing it. I failed and was disappointed for I wanted to use it against Kunjumon. Also, I regretted having no grounding in chess. To embark upon a study would take time I wanted for reading, so I firmly banished the idea I had first toyed with, as I had earlier abandoned the idea of learning the Malayalam language.

At four Nixon arrived and seeing the chess-set he wanted a game. He is a quick thinker and scuttled me three games in a row. Midway through our game Chandu appeared. He had come from a course run by the radio broadcasting authority as he is to be a casual announcer. He kept telling me what to move until I told him sharply to stop. Nixon was unperturbed. I always get rattled when a third person does this. By now it was 4:30 with the sky darkening. Kunjumon arrived and seeing I was engrossed in chess he released me from my promise to go with him. I offered him an umbrella as it was certain to rain. Chandu left and we played on.

Nixon's purpose in calling was to take me into the city to meet Athuba who wanted me to write a letter for him. But Sojan was the one I had been really waiting for; on my mind was the thought of Mini and the delivery. We left an hour later, walking down the main street to the rickshaw stand. We ran into Kunjumon who told me that the girls' team, which Simon coached, had lost their game. Taking an auto, we had hardly gone half a kilometre before Nixon discerned Jose and Christopher in the gloom. They packed in beside us. Athuba was not on time and we expected this, but a friend, Narayan, was there and he took us to the lodge where Timothy, a fellow Naga man, was living. Both were colleagues of Athuba. He arrived, then Timothy left as he was busy with a group of tourists from Nagaland who had to be taken to the station for their five-day train journey back to their home state. I quailed at the thought of such a daunting ordeal.

Athuba is a delight, with quick-silver mind and fast flow of speech no matter that his English is at a tender age, his faculty of improvisation never fails. The Naga people are Indians, of course, but their mind and style are Tibetan. Words are delivered staccato in the rush to communicate. Coupled with this urgency is a constant flow of wit and gesture. He and Nixon are constantly mimicking the manners of others.

Yet he did not indicate why I had been summoned. 'Wait, wait' said Nixon to me in an aside. Narayan had to go then and I learned why Athuba had not come to the point — there was no oriental manoeuvring, he simply did not want Narayan to be privy to the matter in hand. It was for an application for a transfer back to Nagaland that he wanted my help. Gradually I learned what he wanted. He had married a year ago and wanted to be back with his wife. She works for the Treasury of Naga State so there could be no possibility of a transfer outside her state. Athuba on the other hand was employed by the Federal Government as a superintendent of the Khadi Commission, consequently, in theory at least, he had access to any part of India. He gave me a draft of the facts and I wrote a letter on the spot, sitting on Timothy's bed. I felt my draft was a bit smart and too congested with detail to finalise, so, since there was no hurry, decided to take it home and work on it there. I thought I did tolerably well as all were talking at once and involving me with questions. I told Athuba that too much detail about his career and circumstance took the punch from his request which must above all be succinct. I promised to try and do just that as though it were an art form. I felt I could come up with what was needed.

Timothy, who had more of the Tibetan look than Athuba, spoke excellent English and gave a history of the Naga people, a vigorous mountain race which valued independence and resisted the British efforts to subdue them. He spoke of his hatred of the British with passion. He told how when at last they were conquered the British traders began to develop the opium trade as they had done in China. As a consequence there was a decline in strength and virility as the opium took over. He was particularly bitter that the British made no effort to teach the people English during their occupancy. The sparse tuition they did obtain was due to the efforts of the American Baptist missionaries. Now it is the turn of the Indian government to dominate them against their will, for they still want independence.

It was time to move on. Nixon, Athuba and I left the large modern lodge to step into pitch darkness and rain. There was a blackout. The three of us crowded under an umbrella and sought transport. Nixon wanted change so first we went into a state coffee house for a snack, coffee, and the change. The coffee was excellent. Two fried eggs sufficed for me, an indulgence, and the others had parottas. The place was thronged. A man came over to chat to Nixon. He was introduced as Luke and had plenty to say. He had a business in computer equipment located in the same building. He was persistently curious about me and asked if my profession was preacher or teacher. I was horrified and eschewed any suggestion that I had a profession. He began to tell me how high his qualifications were in English and that he held a Bachelor of Arts in English literature. This coffee house, he told me was similar to the old English coffee houses frequented by Steele and Addison and other writers. I added Johnson to show my approval, for he was earnest. But what do you do? What was my profession? By now I decided to be difficult, I said I was retired. But what do you really do? To appease I said I was a horticulturist. He was nonplussed and did not want to admit his ignorance of the term. But what is your mother tongue? I decided he was a bore. There was a cross conversation between the others and I gathered silence about me, not in rebuff but in self-protection. I had not come there for gruelling. I had been friendly and mimed that there was too much noise to talk at any length. When he left Nixon told us that he had twice mentioned to him the BA in English literature. Then we left.

At ground level the streets were thronged with wet feet, and just above head level was a stratum of umbrellas, in between were purposeful faces and bodies. An auto was hard to get, for my suburb away on the outskirts has the worst roads of all and they were further deteriorating in the monsoon. They ignored us as we clapped, some refused outright. At last though, Nixon and I were on our way back. My first thought was about Mini. Had the baby arrived? Through Nixon, Sojan's mother told me that Sojan had rung to report no change but that a caesarean operation was definitely set down for the morrow. The power had been off all evening and I floundered in the darkness, first with my plate of rice and then to bed, where tiredness required no light. The forecast of the baby's arrival was October 14th, it was now the 18th. The news of a possible caesarean alarmed and silenced us. It was quite tolerable that other mothers have caesareans, but the thought of our Mini under the scalpel and the little treasure undergoing dramatic rescue from the quarters that had now fulfilled their purpose, disturbed us. She was at the renowned Hospital of the Little Flower in Angamaly. Sojan was there, as well as Mini's mother and father. They slept there according to custom, exactly where I do not know except that Sojan slept on the verandah. All Tuesday we were in suspense. I kept saying to myself no news is good news, and wondered if it were the other way, no news is bad news. There had to be some news, some word, it had to come, and it did, expected and unexpected, as it chose its own moment. On the 20th, Wednesday, a boy was delivered. Sojan's mother took the bus for Angamaly and I followed the day after. Sojan had quickly returned to Trichur and took me there the same day.

I found Angamaly the typical confusing, rather dirty city, throbbing to its own dynamo.

The hospital is vast for a provincial town; it is modern with broad corridors presenting a clean spartan aspect. The pebbled garden of the maternity wing was immaculate. A saried worker was twitching pieces of small paper and other rubbish through the pebbles, flicking them into a pan and then tipping the contents into a bin. Mini's room held two beds. A smile from radiant Mini greeted us. She was lying on her back and there was a small bundle by her side. The first sight of a newborn babe stills the mind and opens the heart. There it was in minutest perfection, surprisingly light in colour, and one could imagine some resemblance to Sojan. Light was still alien to the little one and on being lifted he opened his eyes the merest slit to reveal his own light. It was bright crystal. The room was full, not only with Mini's family, but also that of the other young mother. I saw her baby too, quite different from Mini's. It was smaller and had a trace of an old man look. I was surprised to see it smile, such a quirkish grimace conveying an amused tolerance and acceptance of earthly existence. If this was the delightfullest Puck then Mini's baby was an infant Buddha wrapt in contemplation.

We went on to the house in Malayattur and the following day Mini, her baby and her retinue arrived. In three months she would return to her permanent home in Trichur. The caesarean had not been necessary, there were many stitches and Mini has to recover.

WYNAD

For penance addicts, India is the place to be. I formed this opinion on the long journey to the district of Wynad. Had I thought to recite the penitential psalms while on that seven-hour rack I would have emerged cleansed and shining. Instead I emerged dishevelled and with wind-whipped face and a tailbone calling for intensive care. The buses were excessively crowded as workers were to go on strike at midnight. Hence all and sundry were minded to be in another place by that deadline. At one bus junction I had my first experience of being crushed to death as everyone outside the bus pushed to get aboard while those leaving tried to get off. I held my shoulder bag with all my strength and was carried helplessly in various directions. It is terrifying to be held in such a mindless embrace.

But again Sojan had worked it for my advantage, and had bagged a seat. Even so I had to endure a thigh forced against my shoulder, such was the crush. Our destination was Wynad which is not a town but an area of the Western Ghats, vast and extensive enough to have fastnesses. In one such I heard about a dying tribe under decimation from tuberculosis and poverty. The government has pledged to do something about these tribals. The district touches the three states of Kerala, Tamil Nadu and Karnataka. The main town is Kalpatta and there we intended to stay four nights. It was dark when we arrived and we put up at a lodge. It was clean and roomy. The only fault I found was that the western toilet (an advertised feature) did not function. I asked the room-boy, Manoharan, how it worked, i.e. flushed. He said proudly, I thought, 'It is under repair.' For him this was a triumphant phrase.

The following day we were able to contact a friend of Sojan, a partner in a motorbike firm. He was up here relieving the partner who was the permanent manager. He came from Trichur. He took us to his apartment hidden in the forest. There were three apartments adjoining and his was the furthermost. It had three sizeable rooms, one behind the other, then a toilet area and a back door onto the hillside. It had the homeliness of a bach. The view was of tall forest, the ground level dense with coffee bushes.

A stack of firewood was by the door. The only negative feature was the lack of privacy, and that was a matter of adjustment. I was at ease. The slow life invites one to enter its rhythm where the temperature is that of a summer day at its best and the cicadas sing in the mountain air. We walked back to town — it is largely downhill. We found a hairdresser where I had a close haircut under the gaze of curious eyes; it cost ten rupees.

On our return we went in search of meat, stopping by the fish vendors on the pavement outside the market. Sojan went off and after 20 minutes returned with a kilogram of good beef steak. For this he paid 20 rupees. Meanwhile I waited in the auto. A young fish vendor's face lit up and he held out a fish and grinned at me. With his fellow salesmen he quizzed me. He knows now that my total Malayalam vocabulary consists of two words — *pal* which is milk and *meen* fish. In turn I learn that his name is Ali and that therefore he is a son of the Prophet. I gazed at his strong handsome face and wished I were a painter. I thought of the kick he gets out of life; he radiated joy there on the pavement and among the smells.

Sojan returned, Ali reached over to shake hands and we drove back through the trees to the apartment. I took a rest. Not long, for midday found me on the stoop with my book. I was reading a biography of Alexander Blok, a Russian poet who died in 1921. Years back, a friend Rodney had given me a copy of one of his prose works, *The Spirit of Music*. It made little impression on me, as I read it hastily and inattentively and only as a duty, for I was caught up in other interests. I regretted my lost opportunity to become acquainted.

A large broadleaf tree at the doorway served for shade, a place to tie the clothesline and a support for the pepper vine. I heard kitchen noises; Sojan was busy cooking. A clatter as a curled parchment leaf feet landed at my feet startled me. Immediately a similar scene came to mind when I sat one day in a park in my home town. It was autumn and still and the clatter of a large leaf had startled me. It was intensely red. Then I saw a single leaf of silver birch, small, quietly glide down and alight, just like a woman who is late, slipping into church.

Theoretically it is autumn here since the coldest days are coming and the monsoon is almost over, but the parallel is not exact, it will not hold for the rhythms are different. The cold is welcomed as the year is at its best. I then realise that the tall trees in this plantation make it shadier still because of their green muffs of pepper leaves all the way up the trunks. Green-muffed trees, that's something new! There is a dreaminess in the air, a languor, an autumnal pause. I am sure it is autumn as it throws long shadows across my mind, evoking other lives, other places and times, not melancholy though touching, telling that life is long and will go on and on. The nearest to melancholy that I feel is the simple thought that all is unseverable and connected, therefore we should cherish each other and all that is. And we do nothing of the kind. If all is empathy, held together by empathy, emotional and mental, should we not stop acting as fragments and learn about what the Russians call *sobernost*, togetherness? Everyone at some time has had such a thought. Does it make for melancholy? I shall think about it — the tears in things.

Sojan's meal was served in a stainless-steel dish with straight rim and consisted of the boiled raw rice I enjoy, the beef, diced and fried with herbs, and a side-salad of cucumber, onion, tomato, topped with finely shredded cabbage on which lemon juice had been poured. The 'others' will be here soon and as there are only two plates we ate ahead of them so they can use the dishes. The others are the partner of the firm and the mechanic, as both live here. They have the same name, Suresh. The older Suresh, the partner, is big and plump. He is 28, while the younger man is the typical slim Indian youth of 25. Suresh the mechanic comes from Calicut and frequently goes home. The place suits admirably as it is within walking distance from the shop in the main street.

That evening as the four of us have supper, another man arrived. He is Jose, a tall, bearded man, fit physically and mentally. Sojan was able to prepare food for him from the midday meal. Jose is married to the sister of one of the partners and his house nearby in Trichur is known to me. Through this connection he learned of our presence in Kalpatta. He is a field supervisor on one of the many tea estates belonging to the tea empire of Harrisons. His tea estate, Mariamman, is beyond the town of Mundakai, 35 kilometres further on into the hills. He invited us for a visit the following day and to stay overnight when he could show us over the plantation and the tea factory. He went back this same evening on his motorbike, but not before he had some brandy with Sojan and the older Suresh. The younger Suresh was teetotal. That night I slept well despite the hard wooden bed. There were no mosquitoes in this high country.

Because of the strike we were denied the use of sight-seeing buses. In any case I was not eager for any more long trips as I was tired and aching. The nearest tourist spot was Lake Pookat and Sojan negotiated with an auto-rickshaw driver to take us there. Three-wheelers make the going laborious on such trips. Pookat is a nature reserve and its entrance consists of many aggressive noticeboards mostly in Malayalam script, a large guarded gate, and a guardhouse-cum-ticket-office. We had to buy our tickets at a window facing the road, then present them to the ticket collector three steps away who let us in.

It was pleasant, obviously a small lake among dense forest. A sealed path girdled it and a walk was indicated; the alternative was to hire a boat propelled by pedal. I was too tired to do the place justice and privately asked myself had I crossed sea and ocean to visit this unremarkable lake; infinitely prettier lakes abounded in my own country. But, tut! that is no way to think. The driver came with us and talked interminably in his lingo. I would have preferred his silence.

Though said to be 75 metres at its deepest, the edges of the lake were shallow and reedy. One small bay was entirely covered by water lilies holding up blue chalices. I did not know enough to determine whether this form was identical with the blue north-Australian species.

I could not shake off fatigue-induced melancholy, and hid it. One vantage point, however, held me. From this angle I could see into tier upon tier of lofty forested hills, each paler as distance intervened. I knew that the smaller of the wild animals dwelt there. At least I had found a touch of grandeur.

A light meal in a rotunda restaurant concluded our visit. I chose tea and cucumber sandwiches and stressed there were to be no chillies. They disappointed for they were thick and dry and excessively peppered and I was gasping. In my mind were the thin cucumber sandwiches served at the croquet green. When will I learn not to have expectations while travelling? Still glum, I decided it was a beautiful place, but nothing to write home about. I leave it slumbering with a *Do not disturb* sign on the superlatives.

I had to discard my pyjamas as the seat of the pants had split and the cloth is too thin to patch. I had found them always hot, so decided to buy a lungi. This is a six foot length of cotton cloth not quite four feet wide, used as a wraparound. I would use it only indoors as I consider it unsuitable for westerners, and I would never use it furled to the knees, as the intricacies of folding and tucking can only be mastered by such as me early in life. I have yet to master its use and am alert to its perils, I am wary of coughing or sneezing lest the whole strip fall around my ankles. It pleases me now as night-attire, so cool and light.

A jeep took us to Mundakai and on to Jose's plantation the following day. The last short stretch, signed *Temble Road*, was steep and ended at a wooden gate which a woman opened for us. Each time she opened the gate a young bullock tried to enter the garden. It was journey's end. The villa was large and solid, its stone walls plastered and pointed white, and it had no beauty. The smiling servant closed the gate and took us inside, carrying one of our bags. Jose, she told Sojan in Malayalam, was at a managers' conference and would meet us in the afternoon. The inside of the villa was superior to the outside. It was conceived on generous lines with cool corridor, high ceilings and spacious rooms which collected coolness and invited repose. It was built by the first English planters over two centuries ago, and only the wooden ceilings had to be replaced. Later Jose told me that though it is pleasant it can become claustrophobic during the continual monsoonal rains. I envisaged a pile of long Russian novels with which to meet the siege. There was a smell characteristic of old farmhouses which burned wood, half smoky, half musty, ever so slightly nostalgic and romantic.

Jose's wife was away; I thought she was visiting her little son aged five who lives with Jose's parents in Coonoor, just before Ooty. While Sojan and the servant prepared lunch I wandered about the rough garden. The range of plant varieties indicated someone with a gardener's passion. Except where volunteer plants of the uncultivated areas bordered the front terrace it was uncluttered, almost bare, and the gritty red soil was exposed. There were many bought plants in containers awaiting a chosen spot. First love obviously was roses, but not the voluptuous tea-roses I have been accustomed to. Rather the selection was of small-flowered species and single roses of earlier days. Each one registered in its attenuated foliage the ordeals of survival, I longed to feed, mulch and water them. One single white rose exuded a perfume sweet enough to dismiss all the dullness and tedium life could ever hold. I returned to it again and again.

Besides the roses other plants were spaced, temporarily, without thought of effect. There was a tired hydrangea pining for a cool glade. There were plants of the fragrant herb tulasi, acalyphas and many crotons. But I do not like crotons any more, I have seen too many. They lack conviction and exuberance as garden subjects and I wonder what I once saw in them, the same way years later one wonders what it was in an earlier infatuation that was so beguiling. Coleus were there, another plant I have grown out of. Why is it? Familiarity? Are they really decadent in the eyes of one who loves alpine plants and the starkness of the mountainside?

In the hedgerow a *duranta* was disporting blue flowers. At first I thought it was heliotrope, though at the back of my mind I knew I was wrong, the scent was similar though weaker, and the flowers approximately right. The foliage said no, no way, as did the strong stems. Later Jose, who has a degree in botany cleared up the doubt. Duranta of course. I was abashed for I had handled so many durantas in Queensland. The base of the hedge was laced with maidenhair fern, its delicacy and elegance belying its hardy nature.

The villa was sited halfway up a hill. It stood within an amphitheatre of ranges many leagues across, not at the centre but towards one of the circling ranges. In the late afternoon they rose dark and forested, presenting a close horizon. Between the villa and the range was a low rounded hill covered with clipped tea bushes.

Jose apologised for his late appearance; the conference was obligatory. We sat talking and drinking tea. He told us that on the crest of our hill was a small temple we must see. There was a steep track. Could I manage or should I go up on the motorbike? I thought I could walk. We had heard of this temple on Temble Road, some tale of destruction by wild elephants. There were plants of interest on the way which provided excuses for a pause. In any case a climb which does not allow halts to examine the wayside weeds and shrubs is mechanical; none could agree more readily than I. I saw a solanum, many healthy solanums with characteristic potato flowers, and large, blankety leaves. Jose identified the species, *nigra*. He showed me a legume perennial in flower, exquisite in detail; he could not identify it. A major tenant of the wayside flora was the orange-red form of lantana, carana, a ubiquitous traveller. None of the lavender species *montevideoensis* has settled here, they have all gone to Australia. I came upon a full-grown mushroom, the whitest I have ever seen, legendary white. What had been the sequences which placed this delicate story-book character among the rough hardy plants? It was poisonous.

As we climbed higher the extensive view unfolded. Immediately before us were rolling hillsides of tea bushes, which extended to steeper slopes. In the valleys and lower places were, symbolically, the lines, the living quarters of the workers, while nestled into vantage points higher up were the villas of the administration. One landmark was the tea factory. The 360° view was unobstructed. To the south east were the Nilgiri hills, the blue mountains. The true name of its most famous hill-station was Uthagamandalam but the English had shortened it to Ooty. To the north some 150 kilometres lies Mysore, to the west the hills gradually subsided into the plains of the Malabar coast. This point was the meeting place of three states. Kerala, Karnataka and Tamil Nadu. To the eye these distinctions signified nothing, for the consciousness was filled with an immense play of light on the monsoon sky and the mountain-girt landscape. It was changing subtly before our eyes. Its sustained silence was magnificent and the walls of the ears tensed, straining for a sound. Nothing but waves of silence. I wonder what the scholarly codgers who prepared King James Bible thought when they passed the phrase 'I shall lift mine eyes unto the hills whence cometh my strength.' Had they experience of solitudes and high places? Decidedly they knew the high places of the language.

We were taking the view from holy Indian ground, for this was an ancient world. Simple stone walls formed the compound of the temple. Candle lights could be seen within. There were two old priests officiating, one pouring a libation onto a stone in the compound. They did not mind visitors. I looked for signs of devastation wreaked by the elephants. Jose spoke to the other priest, not the one performing the libation, who retold the story with animation, then Jose translated for me. In the rainy season the elephants withdraw into the depths of the forest and cavernous places as the thunderstorms of the late monsoon frighten them, but in the dry season they roam about. A herd came to this hill and made its way to the summit. The large iron gates were locked but a single gate at the rear was open and a baby elephant pushed its way through. It soon realised it was alone, for the adult elephants could not pass through. It panicked and began to rush around and cry out. The scene is easy to imagine — cries from within and anxious trumpetings from without. The adults stood about helplessly. The walls are solid rock and can withstand attack. At one side of the compound a lesser temple building incorporates part of the outer wall in its structure and in it was set a wooden shutter of a window about eight feet above the ground. It was this window the elephants smashed. Eventually the distraught prisoner stumbled on the exit and was restored to its kin to be comforted and consoled.

The unifying green of the landscape with the baize top of tea bushes belies the immense labour of maintenance. The bushes are kept down to about four feet, the optimum height for the pluckers, most of whom are small women; men also do this work but they have not the same patience.

In plucking, the growing-tip plus the next two leaves are snapped off. But the pluckers, for whom bulk is of more importance then quality, more often than not include the fourth, fifth and sixth leaves and even twigs. Gradually the height of the tops increases so that every fourth year there is a drastic trimming, more than a foot will be removed. There is fertilising to be done four times a year and such is the response in growth that plucking takes place every ten days. This plantation, one of five in this part of the Harrison enterprise, spreads over 2500 hectares.

I asked about new plantings. These are of modern, cloned varieties and any gaps that occur in the 200-year-old plantations are filled with these. All the original bushes are from seedlings, it remains to be seen if the clones have the same durability.

I sat on the terrace gazing at the strong, gloomy range not so far away. Even this rampart is utilised, for it is underplanted with cardamom plants. I watch the labourers weeding in the distance, making out sickle movements and some grubbing. Weeding is a continuous part of the maintenance. Over 200 years of weeding have served to provide the work that has nourished generations. A slight wind stirs. It is warm and the stirring refreshes.

I gaze again at the nearest horizon. Against the sky, its crest does not trace a worn and rounded line as ancient mountains should, but is more like a graph. I suppose therefore the ranges are young. No geologist is here to answer my schoolboy questions. I wonder then if Mt Kinabalu of Borneo is younger still, for its outline is freakishly jagged. It is too late, I decide, for me to take up geology. Suddenly in life I find my time must be husbanded. Though too late, I want more knowledge. I have studied plants to my limits (and forgotten much), but have neglected the rocks and stones of our planet. I owe them apologies, or at least some contemplation. It is not realistic wanting to be a polymath when one has the capacity and patience to grasp only rudiments; the wish and this fact have to be reconciled. The way to knowledge is slow and laborious. Is there no other supplanting way whereby one can gain command of vast tracts of learning? The practical and conventional answer is no, no other way, only by sweat and labour. Agreed, agreed, but even in agreeing to the necessity for mental toil, I suspect there is another way. Certain experiments and experiences ... books beneath the pillow at night ... in Russian experiments, hints that advanced beings let slip of intuitive ways to knowledge. We are often told about the dramatic and final breakthrough in some scientific discovery. The scientist has gone to his limits along the way of experiment and ratiocination and then lets go for a spell, his concentration leaves the field. It is then that a flash of intuition brings answers bearing with them their own unassailable authority. What to do then? The answer must come from within. And what of all those who have died with no knowledge of life in all its subtleties and complexities, who have never travelled outwardly or inwardly? Has the sip they have taken from the chalice other purposes than an understanding of the planet?

Maybe to those who have worked strenuously in any one field giving their all to that chosen territory, answers will come from within concerning other fields. If there is such a thing as truth it is too strong and enormous to grasp. How does one grasp light? The nature of light too has proved evasive; as soon as we have demonstrated that it travels in straight lines we find that it bends. So truth is a long way ahead of our perception. It dawns upon our wondering minds that the ultimate foolishness is for us to consider what we know as the final and unassailable truth.

The rounded, rather conical hill breaks into a ravine at the right and the forest takes over. Here and there are the palms with fronds with 'arms outward stretch' as in school drill, and right in the midst of the sombre greens is a *spathodea* in a carmine-orange blaze. It is all so much like the forest in New Zealand. One could be way up the Whanganui River, at Pipiriki say, or Tangahoe. All we have to do is substitute tree-ferns for the coconut palms, cabbage trees for the *areca* palms, and Christmas-flowering rata for the *spathodea*. For the imaginative this presents no difficulty.

I did not notice that the workers had gone behind the hill out of sight; their voices, however, reached me. For a while I heard a buzz as though a pump had started up. It grew as loud as a helicopter, then five men came round the hill with spray engines strapped to their backs like Martians. They wielded long wands from which emerged broad clouds of spray. In no time they sprayed the entire hillside. I must ask what is the ravager they are repulsing. I fear the spray is poisonous and nobody wears a mask.

Sojan appears from nowhere. Jose too shares this gift of materialising. Maybe my habit of sinking into reverie makes it easy for them to perform the trick. He brings food. I ask what the main dish is, the other was a small fried fish. He replies 'Rubber.' It looks like porridge, I have visions of regaining youthful suppleness through ingesting a form of rubber. No, not rubber but *rava*. Again we hear differently. To my question what the main dish is Sojan was thinking of 'dishes', to his answer 'rava' I was thinking of rubber. Rava is made from wheat. It has more texture than porridge and it contained nutty additions that enhanced enjoyment. I turned to the fish, which separated cleanly from the bone and was tasty. I found it possible to think lovingly of the animal kingdom even while consuming one of its members.

Now Jose appears and I ask what the spray is for. It is to combat blister-blight caused by a fungus whose host dwells in the forest. And the spray, is it poisonous? Somewhat. Through the plantations silky-oak trees are spaced on a fairly open pattern. I know they are grown to provide a measure of shade but why such wide spacing and why the defoliation up the trunk? The answer comes that the amount of shade the plants can take without encouraging fungus in the rainy season has been worked out precisely.

He had arranged for me to visit the tea factory, but I did not expect that I would be given a conducted tour by the assistant manager, the actual tea maker and king-pin. He was a Mr David, a man in his mid-50s. His English was excellent, his explanations lucid and his manner natural and friendly. I was honoured. He was born in Colombo but had spent over a quarter of a century tea making in this factory.

We met in the delivery yard where trucks brought in the bales of newly-plucked leaves. We climbed a broad iron stairway, much like those on a ship, to the first floor and I wondered why these steps should be so substantial. I did not ask when this factory was built but assumed that it was as old as the plantation itself. It certainly gave the impression of being excessively sturdy and durable, unlike its counterpart I had visited in Munnar. It was as if the builders were thinking in terms of centuries, not decades. In the event it has proved more durable than the British Empire under whose dominion it was conceived.

Already the scent of tea had filled my nostrils. It revived scent-memories of the old family grocery we patronised in my childhood, when all commodities arrived in bulk and had to be weighed and packaged on the spot. An endless chain with spaced arms was bringing up the bales as they were unloaded from the truck. They were unloaded swiftly and those who shouldered them from the lift to the drying troughs were moving at the double for upon this first process of drying the quality of the tea depends. From the moment of plucking until delivery to the factory the leaves begin to sweat and this must be monitored to a precise degree. The bales were emptied into the troughs by the carrier and the leaves evenly disposed to a height of eighteen inches or so by their workers. The troughs, at a guess, were each 60 feet long and about six feet wide. Under each hot air is pumped, or if the temperature rises too high, withdrawn. Three floors of the factory are devoted to drying, thus it has large capacity.

I have a keen sense of smell and have long had the habit of crushing a leaf of plant or tree and, if I knew the plant I was examining to be non-poisonous, of tasting it. I knew that the scent of camellia leaves varied slightly among the species and varieties for I had prepared many cuttings and grafts for propagation. I expected that the scent and taste of a leaf of the tea plant would be distinctively indicative of brewed tea. It is not, and at this stage the potential for one of the world's most favoured beverages remains dormant and hidden. Who is the bright one who first came upon the jewels hidden in the tea leaf?

Mr David showed me leaves affected by blister-blight. Well named, they rest like lesions on the backs of the tender leaves. When dried correctly a handful of leaves pressed tightly in the hand has a rubbery feel, whereas if they react stiffly and are at all brittle they cannot make good tea. The blistered leaves enhance this brittleness, hence the manager is edgy about leaf blister and alert to the level of its incidence.

Drying completed, the leaves move on to the rolling process. They are fed down through great vats onto a circular metal table where the upper part moves over the leaves as they are released, breaking, rolling and twisting them. The name 'broken pekoe' comes to mind and I wondered if it derives from this machine. Mr David could not enlighten me as to the meaning of the word pekoe, as it is Chinese. I believe it is a reference to the tenderest and downiest leaf-shoots of a specific, high class Chinese tea plant and by extension to all teas that lay claim to quality and excellence.

The next process of fermentation takes place in cylinders where humidity and temperature are continuously monitored. During this process the rolled broken leaves blacken and take on the appearance of tea. This section of the building is separated to contain the heat and humidity generated; fans and humidifiers are brought into action. I saw an outsize heavy-duty hygrometer and recalled the dainty instruments we had in our school laboratory so long ago. To the rear of this fermentation area were the furnaces stoked primarily with industrial wastes, mainly peanut shells, which are processed into cylindrical blocks in Madras. In case of a break in supplies there were stockpiles of coal outside the building, also stacks of firewood from forest clearing. Pieces of rosewood among the firewood were put aside and reserved for sale to manufacturers of small items. Rosewood is precious.

One feature which intrigued me was the apparatus which separated the smoke from the heat and pumped it through pipes to a smokestack a hundred yards away. The air is kept pure and no smoky taste is imparted to the tea.

The most visible, explicit stage of manufacture followed, the grading. The installation is a fascinating assemblage of conveyor belts, sieves, shoots and bins for receiving the grades. Tea as we know it — crisp, black and fragrant — emerges at last.

Finally, in the packaging room the graded tea is conveyed past magnets to remove any particles of metal that might have broken off the machinery, or, as I spotted, nails. One magnet is not sufficient for this purpose, there are two. Different sizes of tea chests were stacked about, each with stencilled identification and weight. There were both standard size and small chests. Over many years I had seen tea chests packed with books, clothes, hardware, and on a farm, a box of gumboots. They are the most convenient form of package available and always in demand, but never had I seen one brimming with tea. Here it was in foil and tissue, not just black, crisp particles but black treasure gleaming in its ivory chest.

Mr David picked up a handful of brown springy fibre, like a finer type of coir. This is the waste, he said, that we used to throw out. Now it goes to Nestlé who pulverise it to produce teabag tea. It has a strong colour component. Well, I thought, there is a use for everything. He suggested a cup of tea at his villa. Then one more thing he had overlooked. I had to see the tasting room. This was large and had a tiled bench running the length of the wall. There was a balance where the samples to be tested were weighed and an egg-timer designed to measure the time of infusion which is exactly five minutes. He grinned as he pointed out a battered electric kettle which harked back 30 years if a day. It still functioned satisfactorily.

The tea is infused in china cups which have a section of the rim notched. When infused for the correct period the cup is tipped to rest at an angle into a tasting bowl and left to drain through the notches. A tea taster is the most valuable man in the industry and the international tea brokers employ them as professionals. From samples they can determine if the processing has in any way been defective or less than perfect. The tea may come from too carelessly plucked leaves, the drying overdone, or the fermentation period not long enough or too long. The grading also is assessed. The spray residue percentage is noted. Every aspect which has a bearing on quality is appraised.

Then he proudly gave me a hefty parcel of tea. Later I found it consisted of two bundles wrapped amateurishly in foil, such a quantity. I realised the factory is not into packaging, and the fact he had packed it was touching. We left the building. I had had an important experience. This familiar domestic item, romantic in its origins from the days when tea clippers with raking masts rounded the Cape, took on before my eyes added dimensions on this still, high-country day.

I had traced its journey from the hillside bushes to the tea chests. I had learned that its production was both an art and a science. One other major factor was necessary, the continued mild addiction of masses led by discerning devotees.

We walked over a stile into a nursery holding area where replacement bushes were heeled in. They too were subject to plucking. This section was adjacent to the villa. The garden invited, but we passed directly into the house. First I was offered a brandy while the promised tea was being infused. I could not refuse. Jose, who had been with us as I was shown over the factory, was still on duty and could not return to his charges breathing alcoholic fumes. Mr David poured some local honey into my glass which made the drink tolerable. The bottle was labelled French Brandy, though manufactured here in India in licensed laboratories. I knew its origins lay not in the vineyards of France but the cane fields of India. A small fried fish was an unusual but agreeable accompaniment. Then Mrs David appeared for the curtain act of setting before me a cup of tea with a little vada cake. It was excellent and had a body and taste I had not experienced before. I do not think it was my imagination but I thought there was decidedly a leafy flavour.

JU MARRIES

Baju was to marry Sulekha. I knew neither, but he knew about me and asked his brother Shaji to invite me to the wedding. Shaji I had met at the station farewelling Bharat Singh on his way back to Bhopal. I learned that Baju worked at Abu Dhabi as an executive, he was Muslim and his salary enormous. Shaji was a big, loose-limbed man, warm and pressing when delivering the invitation. The evening prior to the wedding we were asked to attend a stag party, though that term was unfamiliar to them.

Athuba, Shelton, Nixon and I met them first at the Palace Lodge. Baju stood out among the friends — 20 or so. I thought his brother was big but he was bigger still and handsome — a magnificent man, well over six feet, with large, soft eyes, intensely black beard and a measured, commanding manner. His politeness and attention were skilful yet genuine; his attire in casual dress proclaimed his taste, his gold chains, watch and ring his affluence. Elias, his friend, was another big man, also with this grand manner. He had the air of a vizier, and because they were Muslims from the Arab states my imagination provided a background with retinues, marble halls and palace, rather than the more usual abodes of humankind.

Drinks were served. He asked what I would eat and Nixon spoke for me and suggested bull's-eye or omelet; I chose the latter. Plates of diced meats appeared for the others. I was surprised that their preferred meat was pork, which they relished above all. I was introduced to a film actor, well-known in Kerala, who flaunted elegant clothes and rather fawned. We discovered that both of us knew Chandu. Our host took command of the conversation, which turned upon a hypothetical visit to New Zealand. Would I help him obtain a tourist visa? I assured him that no difficulties would arise if he followed with the normal procedures though the New Zealand High Commission in Delhi. He then excused himself as he had to entertain the rest of his friends, and we saw little more of him, Elias or the actor. We stayed on knowing we would all rejoin at the Tagore Centennial Hall, where the decorations for the wedding reception were being installed.

Nixon ordered more meat and a chilli-free dish for me. The instruction was obeyed but the cook compensated for this unheard omission by adding excess pepper. Fortunately I was able to eat a small portion. In any case I was amply satisfied with the three-egg omelet. Nixon, true to his resolution, limited himself to a half-glass of beer. His animation did not depend on his drinking.

We moved into the hall. Inside the vast entrance we had to step over a two-foot wall to enter a smaller room. Only later did I see the door, for this was a cloakroom and the wall we stepped over a counter. There was a long table where Baju's Muslim friends were seated at random and on other chairs towards the walls. They were quiet. There were further drinks. Arshad, a self-effacing man had taken on himself the task of waiter. The silence began to register and it fell to Athuba and Nixon to weld the group into unity — they had natural talent for this office, chatting, singing snatches of song and dancing among us. In the main hall, workmen were busy on the stage where they were constructing a romanticised English cottage and garden. Outside the cottage on the stage the bridal pair would receive their guests the following day. The workmen had just installed a trellised wall, a fancy umbrella and gilded light standards. Heavy rock music filled the empty auditorium.

There was little that could be called action, it was a party and there was conversation, fooling and laughter. They moved back and forth where the drinks were, with Nixon and Athuba pulling in the dancers. Many knew of Shelton's skill as a break-dancer and they urged him on. He responded, looking at his friends as he danced, but kept lapsing as though he did not want to become the centre of attention. Never during the whole evening did he give way to the abandon he was capable of.

One man about 30 was especially amusing. He was short and fat and specialised in a belly-dance, something like the hula, with flowing arm movements and rapid shaking of his belly and laughing powerfully like a hysterical stentor. His laughter consisted of endless ha ha's at differing pitches. This was Thompson.

The hall had many egresses both sides onto long arcaded porches — some gravitated there to smoke, talk and take in the night. It was an evening with no built-in expectation, no posturing or ceremony, and no clearly defined ending. It was low-key and satisfying. I gave no thought as to when we should leave since Nixon attended to such matters, but it became evident an exodus had begun. He delivered Athuba to his home on a borrowed motorbike, returned and handed it back. The question arose how to get a rickshaw. He and Shelton went off in search as the car which was to return and take us did not appear. We waited over an hour before an auto appeared. I was not exhausted and had given no thought to time. Just after 2:30 a.m. I turned in.

The following day we were expected at the hall during the course of the afternoon. The wedding ceremony was performed early in the day elsewhere, and my impression was that it was of a private nature. What we call a wedding reception in the west with set places at long tables and name-cards has no counterpart in the Indian scene. Serving tables are set up and manned by caterers and bearers and food is available over a period of hours. Small tables are set about where the food is taken and eaten.

We arranged to meet up with Athuba, who left early from his office, and again there were the four of us. We had not been in the hall long before Thompson the laughing man joined us. He insisted we go off with him for a peg — five of us in a three-wheeler. The bar had few seats and drinks were ordered. Thompson started up his laugh again. I saw a look of pain on Nixon's face. It had become a little meaningless and we could have done without it. Our response was much weaker. As we left Thompson grabbed an auto and compelled Shelton and me to get in. As we moved off I assumed the others would follow as vacant autos were nearby. Whatever he said to the driver I do not know but he drove off at a mad clip through a maze of narrow lanes, so that I wondered how the others could keep up with us. He explained he wanted to show us his business.

We ended up in a building yard where bags of cement were being unloaded and taken into a godown. The heads of the workers were swathed in wraps to keep out cement dust. We stood about until the truck was unloaded — the men removed their protection and he introduced me to several, happy smiling men.

The auto was kept waiting and with the same speed with which we entered we swept away and rushed back to the hall. Nixon and Athuba asked where we had been and what did we mean by rushing away like that. I could only offer my confusion. Thompson began his laugh again and I looked at him. I was looking on a mask, the eyes beneath held no mirth; before me was spread a stricken ruin. This glimpse was momentary and unpleasant. Nixon, quick in essentials, then offered an explanation of our visit to the main workplace. In Thompson's weak mind he said, were two foolish assumptions, the first was that white foreigners were superior to Indians, and the second that by displaying me to his fellow workers he thereby gained mana. I felt aversion to this stupid fellow, this latter-day ancient mariner outside a wedding feast. On reflection I could not sustain my aversion, for I felt a world of suffering lay beneath the mask and that somewhere, sometime I must enter it as if destined in order to understand him.

The hall this time was packed with guests. Most had done with eating and were occupying the front part of the hall on rows of seats. I was served chicken pieces from a stew; it was good old stew flavour, much to my surprise, neither fiery nor excessively spicy. The hosting families moved among the guests. I was content to gaze upon the array of saris and the overdressed children. The bridal party arrived, mounted the stage and took their seats; was it incongruous that the bejewelled bride, sheathed in gold and eastern flame should sit before a simple English cottage? The groom, in dark western suit was no less distinguished, with male majesty to counterpart her glory.

For close on two hours the bridal party held court, receiving the stream of guests. It was boiling hot there under the lights, and when my turn came to be photographed with them I sweltered. Athuba stood one side of the seated party and I on the other — two guests with non-Indian features. My ten-minute exposure was enough.

One impression I have of this and similar occasions is the casualness. In my country on wedding days, from the heart-twisting moment when the bride appears at the door of the church until she finally waves farewell as she and her groom speed off on their honeymoon, she is the cynosure. Here it is not quite so. This is not to say the bride will be denied her due — lakhs will be spent in decorating buildings with fairy lights, in hiring orchestra, caterers, pot plants, and in obliterating cars, pillars, stage, whole façades with flowers and garlands — large sums will be spent, but there is no attempt to push aside or play down ordinary life and cordon off the occasion as if it were not of this world. Ordinary life is seen to continue in its myriad ways and guests come and go as they please, even during the ceremonies. Thus touches of shabbiness appear, but with a timeless reference and significance. They are necessary.

The wedding petered out late in the afternoon. The few who owned cars drove off, some left on motorbikes, scooters or bicycles, others took rickshaws and those who had walked there left on foot. We four also left and when I got home again and was alone. I felt flat.

JUST SITTING — WOE & MALAISE

I do not go out much. Now and again I go into town with Sojan to do some shopping, and towards sunset I walk to the maiden or temple ground. They do not use that term here but I like the Anglo-Indian sound. The term is still used in the northern states. The Malayalam term is *ambala parambu*. I sit under the banyan. This tree has a four-foot wall around it and the space inside has been raised to the wall level. This provides a seat and it is much used. It is restful and beautiful there. One could unconsciously discount its beauty because the people in the area are for the most part poor, that is in terms of income, though some of the homes are spacious and even gracious. Needs are few and much of the food supply lies ready to hand on trees and bushes or soft plants. Unripe mangoes are gathered for chutney, small berries for various sambals and everyone grows some tapioca.

Last evening I was under this tree. The cricket pitch was in front of me, the lake down a slope to the left, a plantation of tall dense trees to the right. The far end behind the pitch was a high wall overhung by rambling bougainvilleas and spreading branches. A middle-aged man greeted me as he came up from the lakeside. He carried two large bunches of green leaves which looked like silver beet or spinach. He told me it was *cheera* and that they boil it. It grows naturally in several places. He said they did not eat it every day but perhaps two or three times a month. Praveen, sitting beside me, said they had it about once a week. It is a good green, he said, and good for the eyes.

'Then I should eat it, I can't see the ball at all.'

They play on into the dark. I cannot identify the players — the features of their dark skins are rendered indistinct by the slightest shade and now it was dark. All I can make out is the general shape of the body. I tasted the green. It had no distinctive flavour but felt strong and full of iron and would be palatable boiled.

Most evenings I have callers. Kunjumon and Valsan are regulars. I play chess with Kunjumon; we are not good players but enjoy the battle of wits. Valsan, a farmhand, is a silent young man, content to watch. In one way I would prefer to be left alone to read in the evenings, but who am I, a newcomer, to disdain this gift of company? Nixon too and Chandu sometimes call after their work. Chandu takes me for a spin into the country on his Hero Honda and as the light fades and the colours deepen we speed along beside canals under wide skies. It is infinitely refreshing, and for me still romantic to be here in India.

Or Nixon comes on his brother-in-law's motorbike, or when that is not available, by auto — if the latter, his first words are 'Are you ready to come, Uncle? He has the auto waiting. I am always ready to drop everything. We might go into the city where he has arranged to meet Athuba, or to his house, deep among trees, where his mother has made some special dish for me. I tell him that even though we are friends he has no special duty to take me out, and he replies that he thinks I am boring all day in the same place. Bored, I say, and he says bored. He is the quickest learner of English I have come across. From virtual ignorance of the language three years ago when I first met him he can now converse with speed and invention. Occasionally he asks what is the word he is looking for. He is always exuberant and has so much to tell me. Enthusiasm and vitality never leave him.

For three days I did not see him, which was unusual, and when he did come he was apologetic. There had been some trouble with the police. Police? He, Shelton, Paul and about twenty others had gone to a pop concert at the stadium. It was packed. The guest star was Usha Uduppu, had I not heard of her? He did not ask me to come along as he knew I hated crowds and noise and the high-pitched voices. Everybody was singing, dancing and jumping up and down. They were in the gallery and Roy was leaning over the railing thumping a rhythm on a hoarding. The board loosened and suddenly fell down, hitting a small boy below on the arm. The police, who happened to be nearby, rushed upstairs, deciding this had been a deliberate action. Roy spotted them and with his friends close by made off, while Nixon and Shelton, oblivious, went on dancing. The police laid into them and beat them up. For four days previous to this the police had been on irksome escort duty for the visit of the prime minister and other notables. They were frustrated and spoiling for action. Nixon got several blows and one fearful crack on the ear, Shelton fared much worse and was almost knocked out before the police moved on. Nixon showed me bruises on his shoulder and side. He said he was right again. He had been to an ear specialist who said that something was broken inside the ear. There would have to be a small operation if this did not heal naturally. Give it a month, he said, and we will have another look. And Shelton? He was bruised and is recovering. They helped one another home. Young, strong and vital, he will not take long to get right again.

Nixon told me such mindless action by the police is common. There is no remedy, no one to complain to. They are accountable to no one. I am shocked. I read reports of police conduct in the papers continually and am appalled. Deaths occur through their abuse. Rapings, torturing and beatings. On higher levels of administration there are bribes, factitious charges, while the topmost members of the force are in league with smugglers, politicians and business barons, all serving their own ends. It is just one part of corruption in this country. Criminals find it possible to get into power, some into the state, some into the central parliaments. Others direct large business enterprises or the bureaucracy. The country cries out for clean leadership and impartial administration of the law. It needs administrators dedicated to their country, not themselves. Those in office who we can revere may be counted on the fingers of one's hands.

The contemplation of the ills of this country, not just the police, is an exercise so vast and complex that I sink into completest despair. Corruption has seeped into state, national and international politics. Then America, self-serving and arrogant, for instance, is at odds with India because it refuses to submit to pressure. America would like *carte blanche* for her multinationals in this country. On the issue of Pakistan's claim to the north-western states, America has completely and wilfully misread this country. There is not the slightest shadow of doubt that these states of Kashmir belong to India and that this is clearly spelled out in the Treaty of Accession. It suits America to favour the spurious claims to this territory by Pakistan which has waged a propaganda and terrorist war for over a decade. The US has fostered the interests of Pakistan because of its strategies towards other Asian countries. It has turned the screws on a helpless Russia, forcing it to break the contract for the supply to India of cryogenic boosters and technology in this field. It does not suit the US to allow India too much technical capability. And before all this India's leaders remain supine and unassertive. That is how it appears to me.

So many evils abound. One great multi-national fastfood chain has been able to shift the peasants in one state from their traditional subsistence agriculture to the growing of tomatoes for their purposes on a large scale. A subtle bondage will ensue, for the perils of monoculture are not appreciated. Meanwhile the forests, the very flesh of country, are being ravaged by loggers, and the ground scraped by granite-quarrying firms. Only the elephants protest; deprived of their environment, they come down into the villages and towns. The fundamental evil is the irresolute and rudderless leadership which allows that which is greedy, self-serving and devoid of conscience to win by default. So I find it too grievous to read of each and every wrong and scandal that the excellent newspapers so consistently expose. It overwhelms me, so that I seek out the good news — it is not such successful copy so has to be searched for, but it is there, it exists. The contemplation of the bad things going on in this country is debilitating and reduces one to despair, and then indifference, for life itself will not allow one to dwell on it overlong, and one can only take in so much reality. An underlying half-identified anguish nevertheless remains, and I feel it is better, for me at least, not to know too much about it all if it is to lead to paralysis of mind and will, or, on another path, to rage and violence. Gandhiji met his epoch with truth and soul force, and charged head-on into that which was wrong, scrupulous to avoid being tainted by the slightest hatred. This way is still open.

One light-bearer of today, Mother Teresa of Calcutta, deals with human anguish to which she is inordinately sensitive, particularly in its final manifestation as she seeks out and ministers to the moribund victims of chaos. She does not take the fight into the courts and tribunes, but serves in her own way, she uses heart.

There is a happy warrior I find interesting who is dealing blows for the full implementation of law and justice, in the person of the electoral commissioner, T N Seshan, who is determined to thwart corruption and malpractice within his field of operations. He is a disturbing official who dares to rock the boat. Already he has upset many in high places and no doubt they will seek to make him pay the cost.

I have visited Whitefields in Bangalore where the most distinguished and successful godman of the day, Sai Baba, holds darshan, and I have observed the devotion of his followers. There are many Americans and Germans among them, and my impression is that they are over-awed by the demonstration of psychic powers, not the truer attributes of spirituality and sanctity, and they would dearly love to have these powers directed upon them, and the problems of their self-engrossed lives. But in all fairness I must take note of the educational and medical foundations their generosity has made possible. This movement helps us forward. Despite what some would infer and others would question, the enterprise is on the side of the angels.

On this theme of leadership my mind strays outside India to another sprawling world where Rewi Alley poured out his life energies for China. He met the chaos of his times with pragmatic directness and his gung ho spirit was light on dogma and ideology but it released the springs of action which welled up wherever he could inspire groups of people to get together and do for themselves.

Man's yearning is always for catalytic, messianic figures, but these do not appear unless there is an under-swell of readiness. We do well to recognise that many ordinary people are bringing about this state of readiness and receptivity, leading sacrificial lives far from publicity and in small fields where heroism is not a recognisable product. These people are constructing a global network of goodwill. Most do not realise that they belong to this subjective yet substantial network. Its existence must be recognised and its members need to reach out and identify each other. Not only are they drawn from humble quarters, but surprisingly include many in government, commerce, science, industry and learning, and not so surprisingly, from the religious community at large. Collectively they have a tremendous impact on the thought-life and emotional life of humanity.

This concept of a global network is not a grandiose notion ahead of its time, for already we have come to a point where for very survival we must think globally. It is not only the initiatives of the world who are picking up this thought. It has occurred to the generals, as well as relief workers. The group does have a grip on evil, on all the wayward, devious and destructive ways of people, and it will succeed, for it will never let go. Here in India, I am certain, and I am sure, for I meet people of goodwill wherever I go. If I meet such in my small world there must be thousands upon the sub-continent. I would say all is not apathy.

QUESTIONS & ANSWERS

Sojan suggested I take a walk on a path I thought private. He said it was a public path. In fact it was but a track and the better for that. Part lay between thicket fences, then across an open, grassed area of a coconut grove, and finally down to the padi fields where eight or nine women were bent double over the crop. They were too far off for me to see what they were doing, but probably they were weeding. Then I returned, passing the temple on my old route along shady lanes and past many houses. A smiling man stopped me outside his home and indicated to me he wanted me to come inside. The house area was well back from the lane. The path was wide, in fact it took up almost the width of the property. It was swept clean. Immediately in front of the house, the ground looked different as though a slurry of cement had been poured over it. It was a slurry but of cow dung lightly spread and brushed. This combined readily with the ochrous soil and gave a hard smooth finish, far more interesting than dull concrete. His name was Narayanankutty, and later Sojan told me he was our electrician. I had not recognised him. He proudly brought me his little boy, Naveen, who was two. His wife and another young woman were busy sweeping the yard. The little boy was too fearful of the saip with white skin for me to nurse him. I was offered coffee and declined. Tea, then, or fruit juice? No, I had just taken a drink.

Back home all was well, the baby cooing and cossetted; the rice was agrinding and the slapping of garments on the granite slab attested that laundry work was proceeding. In the late afternoon I was reading with windows and door open. All was adrone. I had the ceiling fan on low, lazily shifting the air. Normally I take no notice of the talk on the verandah or inside. It is usually of domestic matters or other things of small consequence which would not bear the weight of translation. Malayalam is such a voluble, excessively polysyllabic tongue that its users employ it with great rapidity in order to cover the ground, so that to an uninformed ear it can suggest alarms and excursions, but never the even tenor of a village day. Today the animation was at a pitch higher than normal and

I was not surprised when Sojan and Mini came to me. Something has happened. Mini looked alarmed and all wonderment.

'So what is it?' I listened to the story. Sojan had been visiting the local policeman, a friend of his, though he was more friendly with his brother, a sub-inspector. While there, this brother arrived. In the course of conversation he said they had received a complaint against Sojan and they had to deal with it. The police had received an anonymous letter, accusing him of having connections with the LTTE terrorists, and of being in touch with spies in Coimbatore and finally of having contacts with many foreigners.

Naturally he was taken aback. His friend said that normally he threw poisoned-pen letters in the rubbish where they belong, but this letter touched on politically sensitive areas, such as security and the Rajeev Gandhi assassination, therefore it had to be the subject of a report. He had not the slightest doubt whatsoever that Sojan was in the clear. This much was deduced as they discussed the letter: the writer was familiar with Sojan's affairs, how two years back he had a soft-drink business in Coimbatore; and he knew there was a foreigner living in his house. The envelope did not show the house name, otherwise the address was correct. This did not signify much one way or the other. All houses in Kerala are required to have a house name. There was a house name but no name plate was displayed.

They had to consider why this letter should be written. Sojan is an easy-going, friendly man whom everyone likes, such is his gentleness and openness. The sub-inspector asked him about foreigners. I was the only one known to Sojan and he told the story of our shared taxi on the way up to Ooty and our subsequent friendship.

'Has he actually done anything for you?' the inspector asked. 'Heaps, he has done many things for me and for others.' He gave a brief account of how I liked India, particularly the friendly people of Kerala, and said I wished to spend the rest of my days here. He inquired about my means and was told they consisted entirely of an Australian age-benefit, remitted every four weeks. This income, of small purchasing power in New Zealand and Australia yielding about 13,000 rupees in India, a princely sum by most standards, but especially when one considers that many families exist on less than a thousand rupee a month.

'It sounds like jealousy, then,' concluded the sub-inspector, 'jealousy of you. Perhaps he has been passed by. Every thing that happens is talked about and enlarged. Perhaps someone believes he has crores, and is sore that none is coming his way.'

So we sat in the room wondering who it could be.

Next morning I had to accompany Sojan to the station so that a report could be made. My passport — well furnished with facts, dates and stamps — was a policeman's delight as it did not call for composition. The policemen asked Sojan had I registered that I was staying with him. Neither Sojan nor I knew of this requirement, as in my travels in India the hotels I registered with took care of that. With hindsight I should have known, for I had had to register with the immigration office when I had lived in a private home in Indonesia. This being so, I had to go to the collector's office and register immediately. The following day there was a further interview with the sub-inspector. In my passport there was evidence of my trip to Sri Lanka a year ago. I went with the express purpose of applying to the Indian High Commissioner's Office for a fresh visa with which to re-enter India. He was not apologetic about his questions. They had to be asked, but he indicated his total disbelief in the accusations against Sojan. His fellow officers were with him in this. There was a further visit, this time to the sub-superintendent's office where again there was much recording from my passport. It was established that I was a bonafide visitor and not in India for any other purpose.

While there Sojan took the opportunity of enquiring about the procedures should my death occur. I had already made a will in India and was keen to make the path smooth for the one burdened with my remains. This was not purely a theoretical concern since two weeks prior to this I had been given evidence that such an event was within the bounds of possibility.

I had been lying on my bed reading one evening when without warning I was seized with nausea and it was imperative I make for the bathroom. I never made it for I had fallen to the floor where, fast losing consciousness, I vomited. Sojan must have heard me fall, but I was too busy to call out, my only thought was for my teeth. The door was bolted as it had been banging in the wind, so he had to kick it down to get in and hurt his foot.

The following morning I regained my senses. I do not say that I was in clinical unconsciousness all night, as distinct from natural sleep. I do not know if they differ because they derive from different causes. I was in hospital, in intensive care and harnessed to a drip-feed. I felt fine and wanted a bed pan. Later in the day I was shifted to a single room on the third floor, not by lift but by trolley pushed up the ramps by three little nurses.

Another friend joined me that day and the night following. In India no one is left alone in hospital if there is some friend or relative who can stay with him. The friend was cheerful Nixon, so solicitous and at the same time joyous — a rare combination of virtues. The previous night Sojan and his cousin stayed in the hospital. They were not allowed to sleep in the intensive care ward but remained in the corridor. It was a worrisome night for them. When I learned of their devotion I was abashed.

The day and evening ushered in a stream of friends. All the evidence I could show them was the drip-feed. I was glad of that for I felt fraudulent evoking so much solicitude.

Back home I felt feeble though in no pain or distress. Give me time, I said. The cause is problematical. I had undergone a similar experience in Kota Kinabalu and the diagnosis was dehydration. It was a proven fact in that instance, but it was not mentioned in this. For two reasons I discounted dehydration. One was that since that first experience I have always taken care to drink at least a jug of water each day on top of my cups of tea and coffee. The other reason is that it is not as hot in these parts as in Borneo; but everyone is an expert on his own condition. I felt it was connected with the blood pressure but was no longer concerned to find out.

The very pleasant hospital doctor on his report wrote that I had hypertension and acid stomach, two symptoms I know I have never experienced. I am not a tense person and the state of my faithful digestive organs has never given me disquiet. I disagreed when I read it but he was not there then. Under persuasion, a week later I consulted a private doctor as I was still tottery. I told him of my dissent from the earlier diagnosis. He was not a listener and wanted to prescribe massage cream for my neck until I told him it was not troublesome. He was reading the first prescription and would have followed it to the letter rather than form his own diagnosis. On his prescription he put disprin, which I told him I was already taking after two heart attacks; he prescribed a pill the purpose of which is a mystery; and he could not refrain from repeating the medicine for the putative stomach condition. I did know that upward pressure from the stomach could cause fainting in some cases, but I also knew I do not suffer from acidosis. He belongs to the hearty sect which declares patients are often as well as if not better than the doctor himself and that all is well. He kept saying all is well. I doubt if he has read the actual words of Mother Julian of Norwich, but in my own opinion, giving him his due, I thought him right. Really, all was well. But I would like it better had he seriously endeavoured to diagnose the cause of all this vexation. Even so, his words were most prescriptive and I thought they could serve with equal healing power on the headstones of his patients. In italic script would be best.

With Sojan on
Noel's 80th birthday.

A SYMBOL IN THE NIGHT

The rich thump of drums puts the night air on alert while the piercing cries of trumpets tear its equanimity apart. What is afoot? I am not primed to go and find out. Of a rash nature, I nevertheless respect Sojan's warning that I must not go out alone at night; the risk from snakes is all too real. After all, he is saddled with the responsibility for my welfare. In deference, I hold my horses and let imagination furnish an answer. It comes sooner than expected and not from the imagination as Kunjumon and Babu sidle into focus from the fringes. They never come straight and direct, but they are direct enough with their summons 'Coming Uncle, you must come and see.' A wave of gratitude arises. Friends and the others, keep me in mind. I put on my shoes and stumble on the steps and arms go out to steady me. I am not basically tottery, but there is a mal-alignment of the neck-bones which at times constricts the flow along the efferent nerves. I suppose tottery old age is similar. Whatever it is, I try and counterbalance it.

Kunjumon, in his mid-20s is the natural leader of the village youth. His appearance is dark and fierce and his voice strong and sometimes scolding. At heart he is gentle and tractable. Babu, much younger, is a dear and I am surprised at his affection. When I first saw him I thought poker-face, hooded eyes and small, pursed mouth. It was only by degrees I learned to read him. He has a mind that runs off to giggles and jokes at every turn of the way. He is a peon, an office messenger. They lead me to the path. I tell them I can manage perfectly well on my own but their arms encircle me. 'The path is humpy, Uncle, and we know the way.'

'Humpy bumpy is the rough road,' I declaim.

'Now tell me, what are we going? What is the procession this time?'

'St Xavier procession.' They can tell me no more. In any case they are Hindus. Years ago the name of this saint had bothered me as I did not know how to deal with the Spanish X. Only after some years I learned that the word was simply 'Saviour', while everyone else knew all along. He was a mighty missionary sent out to India by the Society of Jesus. The local church is dedicated to him and his bones lie in Goa.

The sounds of celebration grew louder and we came onto the procession at the junction of two lanes. In front were devotees in ragged formation, lit by heavy iron lanterns; then followed a swaying canopy of bright umbrellas. They were on stems of about nine feet and formed a magnificent bobbing ceiling. Then more devotees struggled before a blaring banging band, the noise-makers. How the wild discord lifted me and the sight of the players' concentration stirred me! More lantern carriers followed. Finally four smaller umbrellas escort a boy who carried a silken cushion. On the cushion among flowers was an arrow.

'See, Uncle, the arrow is gold.' Then I knew the real nature of the procession. It was to honour Saint Sebastian — the mispronunciation of the word had become in my friends' mouths entangled with the name of Saint Xavier. All is clear. The church of St Xavier had organised this celebration in honour of St Sebastian the martyr. I pictured the traditional paintings of a pretty youth stuck full of arrows as if undergoing acupuncture. I wondered that he should be remembered this moonless night under tropical trees!

Meanwhile fire-crackers exploded along the route. The procession paused at some houses, the Catholic ones, and then the owners set off their sparklers and twisters and cascading fountains. Heads poked through hedges and babies were held up at entrances. It was a wonder and a delight.

Many came to greet me and I primed Kunjumon to whisper to me their names, for in this light I had no hope of identifying dark faces. Though I felt like a curious intruder they welcomed me and were anxious to know if I was pleased. It mattered to them.

'What do they do it for?' I saw money handed over and a receipt written. 'Is it for the church?' No, it is for their expenses.

It went on far into the night and after an hour we left them. A neighbour called out and beckoned us in. A seat was found for me and the women stood as I approached. I told them how in my country it was the men who stand when the women appear. The procession caught up with us for they make a thorough canvass of the village. I gave them 20 rupees and the collector took pains to spell my outlandish name as he wrote a receipt. It was little enough.

So the symbol central to this festivity is an arrow. Being a Sagittarian I took note. I am one, not with the lethal arrow but the aspiring one. What would have been the course of Christianity had it become the symbol of Christianity? The arrow, kin to the rocket, suggests boldness and discovery, rather than submission and sacrifice. Our age is set for new horizons and has done with blind and mechanical devotion. How would the set minds of theologians regard the rebellious arrow and how would the authoritarian leaders retain their hold over their flocks if new worlds come into focus one after another? It is a disturbing symbol.

There is a local legend about St Sebastian. In a community not far from here, and a few centuries ago, the Christians were preparing to stage their annual procession in honour of the saint, as in other parts of the land. But the Brahmin leaders were hostile and stirred up the people so that they drove them away. A week later a case of smallpox was reported, then a couple more. The number of the stricken increased. It reached plague proportions and the people were distraught. When someone suggested this scourge was from God as a punishment of their unkindness to the Christians they seized upon the explanation and turned in fury upon the Brahmin leaders who promptly revoked the ban and made their change of heart known. It was nearing the time for the feast so the local Christians again completed their preparations. The procession, attended by the whole community, took place. It was impossible at first to determine if there was any difference in the impact of the plague. For a while they waited, and all held their breath, but the number of new infections began to drop and most of the sick recovered. They were hopeful and watchful, until the evidence become clear, the plague was abating. It took several months to disappear entirely. By that time all were convinced of the healing powers of the saint and never again was the voice of intolerance heard in the land.

The night following the procession of St Sebastian we were out again, this time to a Hindu festival. I was at a disadvantage, for whereas most westerners including myself have some idea of Christian saints, only ethnologists and a few cognoscenti bother about the pantheon of Hindu culture. One friend was most insistent on the point that Hinduism is not a religion. But has it not gods, I asked, and has it not a rational which brings the phenomenal world into coherence? It certainly unites the community here where I live.

Be that as it may, I attended the procession with the same friends along the same lanes. It was equally entertaining though the sounds and the ritual were different. I could not understand what it was about, except that I knew it was important for each Hindu house to receive these callers.

The following day I related my experience to Chandu and asked him to explain it to me. Before this, with Sojan's help, I had worked out a few things. The lord Brahma is the supreme creative being. He has two co-equals known as Vishnu the sustainer who incarnates as Krishna the saviour, and Shiva, the god of dissolution — Shiva can assume frightening features. When I asked Chandu for more information he launched into an exposition of the festival of Thypooyam Kavadi Maholsavam, which took place a little prior to this. 'See Uncle,' he said, 'it is like this. There is Brahma and Vishnu and Shiva. They form a trinity known throughout India whereas many [gods] have only a local territory. And the second son of Lord Shiva is Subramanya…' He went on to tell me of other members of the family until I sensed we were on the wrong track, but he continued.

'Uncle are you listening, do you understand?'

'I think you're on about another festival. The one I want you to tell me about is the one where the celebrants jump up and down and the bells jingle.'

'Oo, that is Parayeduppu when Velichappadu visits the home. Why didn't you say?' I could see that I was about to receive far more information than I could assimilate, so I asked would he do me a favour and write out what he knew about this festival. Two days later he brought me back some notes and also notes on Kavadi. This is what he wrote down of last night's celebration.

'It is called Parayeduppu. Once every year a procession sets out from every temple on behalf of the goddess Bagavathi. This is led by her representative known as Velichappadu, who will visit each house connected with the temple to collect raw rice. It was believed that, by contributing, each household will receive a blessing and its welfare will be assured.

'The representative of the goddess is dressed in a white dhoti, and a long red cloth is put around his waist. A similar cloth is laid upon his shoulders. In his right hand a sword and in his left hand a Chilambu are held. The Chilambu is an object with bells sewn onto it. He is accompanied by two men in almost the same garbs. Each carries a stick with a bunch of coconut flowers attached to the end. The others carry *chenda* or drums and another a pipe, *kombu*.'

'Each house makes arrangements to receive the group. They will have a *para* — the conventional vessel used to measure the raw rice. Each para will contain 10 kg of raw rice. There are flowers, and candles in an uneven number.

'When they enter a house the representative of the goddess, Velichappadu will shiver with the accompaniment of the drums and Kombu. This shows the presence of the goddess. He will begin to dance in a special way, making loud sounds. The other two men who carry the broom-like thing (a stick with coconut flowers attached) will jump in a dancer's style as they accompany Velichappadu. Later the Velichappadu will stop dancing. He approaches the head of the house, gives him some raw rice taken from the para and says something in a jargon which is believed to be the blessing of the goddess.'

On this occasion we visited only two houses. I noticed the ceremonial group approached in silence, in contrast with the continuous sound of St Sebastian's procession. The leader, the Velichappadu, was a wild looking man with hair hanging over his shoulders. When they had assembled in front of the candles and rice the bearer of the kombu blew the first notes. His pipe or trumpet is circular and the sound which issued was harsh. The drummers began beating, and Velichappadu circled the candle-lit centrepiece three times followed by the bearers of the mop-like objects. For a moment there was frenzy as the leader and attendants jumped straight up into the air, the Chilambu jingling. The noise stopped suddenly. The Velichappadu bent over the rice vessel and scooped up a handful which he threw with bougainvillea petals which strewed the ground. This gave me the impression that the Chilambu was a kind of girdle with bells attached. Some words were chanted in an archaic tongue which, not disparagingly, Chandu referred to as jargon. The ceremony completed, the small group silently took its leave. The household has the blessing and the temple the rice. I had been truly honoured by these kind people for they brought out a chair for me, a spectator not a worshipper, and after the group left I was given bananas broken off an enormous hand along with everyone else. The rice will be taken to the temple later.

SOME NEARBY

I am reading, dimly conscious of those who come and go outside. Most callers bring rice to be ground. The noise of the machine is loud but rhythmical so that over a period I have learned to read or write without the slightest awareness of its operations, even in the climactic stage when the mechanical sieve begins its shuddering. I am aware only when it stops and silence flows in once more.

So this morning I was in my room reading. I was early, a woman arrived and I heard voices. Sojan's mother has a soft voice, she is a good listener but not a gossip. Voices, also, I have learned to ignore, but this morning the hard flat tones of a strong voice were particularly intrusive. I have not the slightest knowledge of Malayalam but was forced to listen. The feature that disturbed me most was the unbroken flow of sound; it was obviously some interminable story and the tone was aggrieved. Why couldn't she shut up and go?! The flow irritated me, and I feel let down when irritated. Had she nothing else to do? Malayalam speech to my ears has no stops or pauses, no inflection and no variation of volume, it can become a trilling monotony, a dreary affront; I was arrested and taken over.

At length I decided I should take a walk. I went out of my room and looked briefly on the face of my tormentor. She was not old, not a virago, and still had good looks. She stood there, slim and graceful in her sari. On seeing me, or else because her spate had run its course, she took her leave.

Later in the day I mentioned to Sojan this woman and her voice. He said, 'You gave her help last year, remember? Her little boy has kidney sickness, you helped pay for the treatment'! I was incredulous. I had forgotten, then remembered. There was a little sister too, with the same kidney condition, she was not so bad. The mother had just returned from the Trivandrum hospital after staying with her boy for the treatment. The doctor said that no more treatment would avail, the boy would die. The family is poor and the neighbours had raised six thousand rupees for the expenses. I asked about the little girl. Yes, she too had kidney trouble but the brother's heart is also affected. He will die. He is ten.

I asked them about the father. Had he a job? 'Yes he has a job. He does tyres. You would not know about this work. When a tyre is finished you people throw it away. 'Oh, you mean recapping and retreading, Yes, we have that too. Retreading tyres is a trade like any other. We do not throw them away. We might have more money but we still cannot afford to throw tyres away, not until we have got the last mile out of them. We will have to help them.'

*

I said to Ranjith, 'What has happened to Sajeevan, I haven't seen him for some time?' I liked this young student. Ranjith's mother boards college students and from time to time he brings some of them to see me. I remember the first bunch he brought along. There were five of them. I found each of interest. They were aged eighteen to nineteen. There was Babu, a tall youth with receding chin. He stood to one side — my memory still has the positions, then Titus the tallest. He was pleasant and exceedingly handsome. By him stood Jayaprakash who was known as J P. I got to know him well later and had a meal at his home when they celebrated the Onam festival. He was well-built but with a gentle sweet oval face that made him look slight. His voice was high-pitched and sounded caught up at the back of his throat. His distinguishing feature was the band across both upper and lower teeth. Then came Santhosh. All I can remember of him was that he wore glasses that made him look like Gandhi and the fact that he was highly-developed intellectually. Finally on the right was Sajeevan — he sat on one of the two chairs. He was short, strong and solid. In due course I found out about his home by a river near a rubber plantation a few hundred kilometres from here. As they were deferential and shy I had to sustain the conversation. I recall telling them I liked Sajeevan best because he was my size and I likened Santhosh to Gandhi with his glasses — light-hearted remarks to amuse.

Sajeevan has heavy features not without charm, and clear modest speech. I was fascinated by the way he returned his lips to normal after speaking as if he composed them. Later, J P told me he came from an extremely poor home — his father had disappeared and his mother worked at a lowly job to support the family and put him through college. He came to see me a few time after this initial visit. I had resolved to help him but had not made my intention known. I had missed seeing him over the Christmas period but would not forget him.

Ranjith told me he had gone to his home near Kannur. He had some sort of accident in a wash-room and broken his leg. He mentioned blood. I could not see how a broken leg could bleed unless the bone came through the skin. I was alarmed. He had been in hospital. I had his address, so sent off a note of sympathy with hopes that his studies had not ceased. Within a week I had a reply. It covered both sides of a single sheet which bore the Engineering College crest. The printing was neat and the layout good. The hand had a slight back slant. This is what he said — it tells his story.

Dear Ginn,

Received your letter yesterday. Thanks for your wishes. Hope that you are keeping well there. I have just slipped down on my knee on 22.01.94 (Saturday) when I was washing my clothes. That time no pain was there and I continued washing. After about four hours I felt severe pain on the knee joint and I was not able to walk at that time. At 2 o'clock we went to hospital by auto. Doctor told that some blood is coated on the knee ball and to remove it by aspiration and I was admitted there. Blood aspiration was on 24th. After two days doctor put plaster on my leg. He put plaster from foot to the top point of the thigh. Now I can't fold my leg properly. I was discharged from the hospital on 27th and I left Trichur on 29th.

After coming home I was suffering from one more disease. Sometimes blood is flowing out of my nose. When I was studying or sitting blood is coming out of my nose. Two days before I met the doctor. He prescribed for capsules and for other medicines. Now I have pain on my foot. Yesterday again I met the doctor. Again the doctor prescribed for some other capsules for the pain also.

Here I have to study a lot of things. My examination is on 21st. But I can't study properly due to these reasons. Now I am always sitting on a chair. As you said, I have pain on the same leg which was affected by polio. Now there is no pain on the knee-joint, but on the foot. The plaster is tight now. I was happy to know your news — when are your leaving Kerala?

Next week I will be there at Trichur. After removing the plaster, I will come to meet you. Actually the plaster will be removing on the 24th. But an exam is starting on 21st. Without removing the plaster, I cannot sit properly on a bench. So I will tell the doctor to remove the plaster before the correct date.

How is your life there? Is it boring? You have got a lot of friends there. Therefore no difficulty is there in spending time. Here my life is boring. I am not permitted to stand from my position and most of time is wasting by sleeping.

Your letter was most unexpected. When I got your letter, I couldn't even imagine whose letter is this because this is for the first time you are writing a letter to me. Here I am trying to complete a new Malayalam poem. It contains a lot of difficult words [some words of the old Indian language Sanskrit can be used in Malayalam] and that is why nobody is ready to publish my poem in their weekly. My poem has little deviation from the modern flow.

Nothing more to write. Wishing you all the best.

Yours Lovingly,

Sajeevan.

There was ample time for a reply from me before his return. Among the things I mentioned was the necessity to avoid learned terms when writing poetry. The words we first learn, the simple homely words, carry most feeling and, used well, can be potent. I thought my letter would help relieve his boredom. So there on the bank of a river he will receive a letter, perhaps on Wednesday.

DARKNESS & LIGHT

The power goes off — a decisive but silent event. We have little use for darkness so everyone looks for a lamp, and for candles and matches. I have a candle on my teapoy — enough to play chess by if a friend comes, but not enough for reading. I sit on my bed well propped with cushions, and look out the window — it is far too early to sleep. Mini brings a plate of rice which is my supper. I am easy to feed for I have rejected all other foods save porridge in the morning, boiled vegetables, midday, and rice in the evening. It could be considered boring but I am content. There is no way I would be allowed to cook for myself. Fruit, yoghurt and tidbits arrive from time to time, chicken and fish at intervals, I learn to appreciate natural flavours but am completely hopeless with chilli foods. They sear my mouth, my nose runs and eyes stream. South Indians use chilli as we use salt, only they are more heavy-handed.

Usually a power cut lasts 30 minutes but tonight it is longer. About nine I reckon no one will come, though Chandu likes to call late. I decide on a shower, and move about in the shadow and half-light of the candle flame. My modest *en suite* is a delightful amenity. The water, from a tank on the roof, is not too cold for a softie. Soon, refreshed and renewed, I return to the bed. It has a wooden base, hence no give. I have a thick rubber mattress and it is perfect. It is firm and unlike other mattresses has the virtue that if there is a cup of coffee upon it and somebody bounces down heavily, the shock is not transmitted. There is a selling point for rubber! Today Mini washed the sheets, the pillow cases and the bedspread, so all is sweet and clean.

What shall I think about? A hockey match has been the event of the day. Cricket is out and hockey in. About 4.30 in the afternoon I walked to the Engineering College grounds to see our village play St Thomas college juniors. I know them well enough now to identify with and am surprised how partisan I have become. They have to be under 19 so Kunjumon and some of the best players cannot play. The walk in the heat is troublesome, even though I have an umbrella. Jose catches up with me, he knows I am going to the hockey and has told me he would bring a letter he wants me to check. We enter the field and stop under a tree. The letter takes only a few minutes and Simon, the umpire, comes over to chat. He is sympathetic with our team which has no coach, no decent ground for training, no shin pads, and unreliable sticks, some actually broken and heavily taped. Only the goalie is well-equipped. He is padded and shielded head to foot so that he looks like an astronaut. In contrast the St Thomas team is smart with top-quality gear. They have a coach and, being hostel boys, can get out on the field twice a day and practice their moves.

Our team is late coming on. Simon said they were having difficulty getting a team together. Two, Kannan and Shijo are little more than children and they play barefoot.

I find the game exciting. Our side has the ball at least half the time, their stick-work is good and their eagerness great. They lack combination skills and I know they will go down. I laugh as the small boys jump high in a mêlée — they are game. They have no ability whatsoever in shooting and are soon repulsed by an efficient defence — if only their mid-field prowess could extend to the circle. The final score is seven zero. I am critical of our goalie, who every time he made a sortie against the enemy, slid onto his back, a result of his charges and skating both feet together, hoping to sweep the attack away with one decisive charge. Time and again he fell over. I say nothing, however. The senior goalie, Pradeesh, is ever so much better. The score did not matter there on the field, only when it is recorded and transferred into statistics will it have any significance.

The power was off all night, so I had no fan to protect me from mosquitoes. I slept well and awoke early enough to enjoy the dawn. It is so different from evening twilight. At first I had a candle on the window-sill. I looked into its fluttering leaf; the central cone had a dove-like shadow while the outer sheath is purest gold, neither pale nor richly brassy but like the clear flowers of gorse. It deserves some notice and I employ the pathetic fallacy to ascribe valiance to it. But what a gap between candle-light and daylight. For that matter what a gap between electric-light and daylight. This is something we could never have imagined, the strength of daylight, never never. Yet we carry the fact lightly at the top of the head and confer significance upon the candle as a unit of luminosity. One candle-power has status and scientists use it to measure sunlight. To the imagination the gap is inconceivable.

The blackness goes out of the sky but not from the trees which hold on, loath to let it go. They allow a suggestion of monochrome, matt and lifeless. The air is still, and does not stir the sensitive tips of the *areca* palms. Today there is no colour, the light has come. It does not call for restful musing but for action.

Nandakumar is a devoted caller. He is a draughtsman and when his work with plans, property deals and permits is over he likes to come along to see me, and is apologetic when days go by without calling. He struggles to express himself in English and has the oddest habit of clutching my hands and jerking them ceaselessly as he makes a point. Today he called half an hour before midday and gradually his intention is revealed as I disentangled tenses and interpreted. He wants to take me along to the boys and then go on to Viyyur where a Kavadi celebration is taken place.

It goes under the name of Thypooyam — Kavadi Maholsavam. They take place each year and are in honour of Lord Subramanya, the second son of Lord Shiva. Lord Subramanya has his abode in nearby Pazhani (Pallani) in Tamil Nadu. It is there where his invisible presence is to be felt. There are Subramanya temples throughout Kerala. One hears the word Kavadi all the time. That is what they call the whole festival but it also refers to the individual constructions which are born in the procession. Originally the ceremony took place only at Pazhani but now they are observed wherever there is a Shiva temple, thus eliminating the need for long journeys. The original Kavadi took the form of a bamboo arch and was carried on the head or the shoulders. It was decorated with peacock feathers. The peacock is the vehicle of Lord Subramanya. It is also adorned with flowers and furnished with offerings such as rice, sacred ash, viboothi and pots of milk attached to each end. Over the years the Kavadi has evolved to become the huge and striking confection of today. Every village or group has its own Kavadis and joins with the others in the procession. I had already been to one Kavadi celebration when Vinod the autodriver had taken me one morning to a small Subramanya temple. There I received the first shock of impact as I looked on men bearing what looked like Christmas trees or great bells of stunning glittering colours on their heads. The bearer revolved, and the hanging branches which ended in bunches of flowers spun out with the motion.

A little farther on I saw another type of Kavadi built like a many-storeyed temple in the shape of a huge wedge, much taller than the tree-type Kavadi. Considered one way, they resembled gigantic isosceles triangles with a five or six foot base and long sides rising skywards ten to fifteen feet. Such pyramidal forms appear in granite in superb temples all over Tamil Nadu, the best specimens I saw being at Tiruchirappalli and Madurai. They have a similar shape, unique and impressive.

Nandakumar and I walked to where our friends were gathered. I was somewhat puzzled as to whether they expected me to walk the whole distance to Viyyur. I have done so before but when I was fitter, and in the late afternoon when the heat was abating. I took my umbrella in case it came to this, but my apprehensions vanished when I saw that Praveen had his father's motorcycle. There were Kunjumon, Praveen, Babu, Vijayan, Kannan and Nandakumar. They were there in their best and sparkled — dark skins, the whitest of white dhotis and perfectly laundered banians proclaimed the greatness of the occasion.

The pillion ride was refreshing as the air rushed by. As we approached the site the number of pedestrians increased until we were in the midst of the fair — for such it was. We parked the motorbike and joined the crowd. The first Kavadi celebrations I had seen had not prepared me for this; it paled into insignificance as I took in the extent of the scene — for it spread over the street and over acres of temple land. First I saw some tree or bell Kavadis, not just eight as previously but endless numbers. The sun bore down on the bearers and they showed no sign of wilting. Soon after our arrival our friends joined us; they had come on bicycles. I had a happy escort as we strolled about, crowding under the shade of our umbrella.

We came on an area where the elephants were being hosed down — one mighty specimen, very black, sucked up great draughts from a drum and dowsed its back offhandedly but effectively. These ultimate creatures of the animal world reduce me to wonder, they have no need of circus tricks to impress. I can only be silent in the face of their magnificence. A little later we saw them being caparisoned, the *pièce de résistance* being the gold frontlet or head-piece which covered the mighty forehead down to the trunk. They deserve all the glory the trappings impart.

We then returned to the Kavadis. There was a bamboo colonnade, all of a hundred metres; it was extremely high, 20 feet or so, and as wide. From the cross-ties hundreds of light green leaf strips waved. These were prepared from coconut leaves. Beneath this the Kavadis were whirling and at long intervals advanced. Each specimen was a masterpiece. I must have seen over a hundred, and the patterns were never repeated. The colours were psychedelic and certainly spun the mind around. The designs showed infinite invention. Each had a dominant colour and in turn one was mesmerised by the glory of deep-blue, light-blue, purple, emerald, gold, silver, red and orange, each bewitching with its mystery. I was able to examine the details — the flowers that spun out were perfect ranunculus, there were strings and fringes of beads, patterns of glass, shells, coloured-thread, glazed paper and various shimmering cloths. One superb Kavadi was like a beehive in shape and stood out as the very spirit of whiteness.

Then we came upon the step or temple Kavadis. There were up to fifteen steps or storeys, each rented out on a daily basis along with two bearers who perform in turn. As the season goes on from October to April their employment is ensured for all that time. There is a whole industry behind the scenes and an entire village — that of Eravimangalam — is devoted to their manufacture and hire.

Chandu had told me that the framework of the Kavadis was of bamboo. That would be for the smaller tree form, but for the tall pyramidal ones the craftsmen used wood from jackfruit logs, while the upper structure was of heavier jungle wood. It is imperative that the whole structure be perfectly in balance, otherwise it would be unmanageable. The four edges have tufts of peacock feathers — I did not think they could exhibit the same brilliance as when displayed on a bird. Whatever I examined revealed craftsmanship, nothing was shoddy or tatty. I found it hard to believe that every day the entire decoration is done afresh.

We drew near to some ornate buildings at the end of the colonnade. From the balcony women and girls in their finest saris were watching the scene. The boys pointed out a girl to me and told me she held special interest for Vijayan. There was much laughter and teasing, for it is very much a segregated society. A music-hall song sounded in my ears, some words.

The girl that I love is up in the balcony,
The girl that I love is looking down on me,
There she is, can't you see,
Awaving of her handkerchee.

The air was alive and packed with sound from trumpets, pipes drums, and — frightening in their proximity — the thundering of strings of bombs. I saw a group of old men engaged in this department, pouring gunpowder into bombs. We were on our way so I learned no details of their activity. We came upon a merry group of dancing drummers. They beat their drums and juggled the sticks through their legs, never missing the beat, then stepped onto the rims. Their cries and laughter sprang from the very wells of merriment, and the young danced around, arms held high. Oh, delight. It was nigh on two o'clock and I had promised Chandu that I would be at home for he was to take me for a haircut. Our way out passed through rows of vendors — a long arcade where all that glitters and excites young eyes was there for a few paise or rupees. There were acres of bangles, it seemed, and strings of beads, cheap jewellery, brooches, clasps and toys of the smaller kind. There were balloons and whistles, a great quantity of nothing I fancied. Nothing.

Praveen took me back. My friends lingered on two more hours, returned to their homes and went again in the evening. At 3.30 in the morning they wearily pedalled homeward. I can well believe it when they told me the spectacle was so much more brilliant in the night light, lit up by thousands of coloured lights. That experience I had to forego. The next day was Sunday. I heard rumours that the celebrations had been stopped by the police. There had been an argument between them and the organisers. A policeman had punched an organiser in the face and an angered crowd protested. As the phrase goes feelings ran high.

SUNIL, & BLACK THOUGHTS IN A BLACK SHADE

There was a sound of motorbikes, then voices outside. 'See who's come,' Sojan called out.

'Come in if you're good-looking,' I called out cheerfully — not altogether an advisable welcome, even though most Keralites fall into that category. Wisdom murmurs about the pitfalls of flippancy.

I recognised Arshad, whom I had met and observed at Baju's wedding. He was the one with the severe look who attended to the needs of all. He is not a smiler but this defect was compensated by the stories I had heard of his acts of kindness. There was Sony, round-faced, spectacled and smiling. I remembered him but not his name. There was another whom I had not met before.

The animated one most eager to greet me I did not recognise, but the moment they said his name I remembered him. It was Sunil. I had only met him once and then among a crowd. But he made a strong impression. There was a gang of us in Nixon's place, the same gang that had celebrated the New Year all-night session, all except him. We were still in celebratory mood. Sunil had befriended me and in no time had asked could he come and visit me to chat as he had been wanting someone to help him out with English. He told me he was unemployed and had thoughts of going to the Gulf. That is about all I recall, except that he was 25 and was tall and — how shall I put it? Endowed with depths of feeling and character. His younger brother I had met on both occasions — the New Year party and the follow-up, but even if I were to see him again I would not remember. He gave me his address. The following day I thought I should drop him a note to suggest he let me know when he proposed to call as I would not want to be out, particularly since he lives a fair way off. I looked forward to his reply but nothing came of it. I was a shade disappointed but thought little about it — any reason that I could think up was bound to be wrong anyway. Whenever there is a turn of events contrary to my expectation, my gift of misjudgment blossoms. I tend to make quick judgments and not keep an open mind. I accepted his silence and forgot about him. I had not judged.

'I got your letter yesterday, Uncle,' he said 'it was waiting for me yesterday.' Six weeks later!

'My letter! Oh, my letter about you visiting me.'

'I went to Bombay after New Year and got back yesterday.'

He had been trying with the help of an uncle to get a visa for the Emirates. He eventually succeeded. It was a free visa, that is one that had no link-up with a particular work contract. A few days later it was cancelled, so he had returned, his time wasted.

Sojan brought in a tray of lemon drinks. The conversations continued about half an hour then they left with the same arrangement as before. He would let me know. This time I knew he would.

I awoke with feelings of indignation over wrongs done, not to me, but to one passed on. Though the events were long ago they still had power and enough vitality to stir me. Negative feelings threatened to take over and I was angry that I could not handle them with dispatch and send them on their way. I have heard a sweet voice that lies and the sounds stay in my ears. It upsets me more than the wrongs of today. I have to get away from this mood, for nothing worthwhile can flourish in its atmosphere. One thing bothers me most, my disappointment at my defences which have allowed this emotion to take over. Had I a better perspective I would have been able to look on this sweet, lying voice with more equanimity, and in time, with some understanding.

I find in my nature an instinctive aversion towards those whose views and outlook differ from mine. I can mention two nations which similarly affect me, though I may not mention the individual whose name has just surfaced from my subconscious. The nations which so upset me are the USA and Pakistan, both blatantly lying over Kashmir and using the lie as a means of political behaviour.

Here it is all too obvious how they are distorting the facts for their own purposes, the one as a means to implement its plans of world dominance of its commercial interests, and the other in a miserable campaign of evil to usurp that which is not its own. The public lie and the private lie are in nature the same.

I wish I had the mental strength to think through this matter of evil right now. The thought of the misuse of life in any shape or form becomes unbearable. It is a thought that contains questions which must be answered — if this is not done the will becomes drained and that is a great evil. Plato says that to become a spectator of time is a cure for meanness of soul. Meanness of soul is what I suffer from right now, it is the correct diagnosis, so I shall have to transfer my attention to world history and become a spectator of time. In other words I must broaden perspectives and reflect upon the long operations and processes of history, the evolutionary triumphs, as well as its still, sad music. This is a bigger commission than I bargain for, but I can interpret it as advice to take the universal viewpoint and work from the general to the particular, the opposite way to science. If this is so I have quite a lot of work to do. In fact I should this moment affix a sign to my door, 'Do not disturb, spectator of time at work.'

IMPRESSION

The day that followed was not entirely devoted to the task of becoming a spectator of time, for time itself drew me into its concerns. It also applied its own salves and lubricants for old pain and rough surfaces, and I knew, not only in my heart of hearts, but in my surface mind, that I would eventually forgive and forget.

Plato's advice on how to avoid meanness of spirit was on my mind, and I pondered his teaching that what we see are but shadows on the wall of a cave cast by figures outside. I saw the need of reverence and respect for a reality greater than we know; but this did not impel me to become a blind devotee of the unknown, rapt in adoration; were I to do so I would become apostate to part of my self; the part that could think was every bit as important as the part that could love and revere. I recognised the need not so much of worship as for meditation. The mind requires it as it requires the working of the subconscious whether asleep or awake. Meditation is a reaching up to that higher form of one's self that one dimly and imperfectly perceives.

My thoughts turned to the first difficulty of meditation, the stilling of the mind from all that is external, namely the stream of communication from the senses. Of these noise is the most troublesome, and then I thought of Ewen. In the 1970s there was a widespread interest in transcendental meditation, and many took to it avidly — it was a time of wing-flexing and soul-searching among the young. I had a friend who was enthusiastic to the point of naivety. It was in Sydney, and Ewen shared a house with the lovely Tricia; he was a Welshman, a painting contractor who had built up a profitable business. He had a wild imagination never checked by reflection, and a gift of mimicry that afforded endless entertainment. Enthusiasm was his way of life and whatever he took up he did so with gusto. His clear blue eyes, auburn hair and magical tongue assured him a ready audience. The thought of meditation fired his imagination and I once disappointed him because I declined his proposition that we wander through Queensland penniless and with a begging-bowl in search of enlightenment. He was a mad romantic.

He showed me an attic he had made into a meditation room, furnishing it simply with a chair and table, and curtaining the window. He showed me the prayer-mat he had purchased with great care, and demonstrated the posture he assumed while meditating. He took pride in his notebook in which he recorded the duration of each period of meditation. He could not meditate without a clock. Later Tricia told me how tyrannous he could be, especially about any noise in the house while he meditated. Once when she started up the washing-machine two floors below in the basement he came raging down in a fury, for she had spoiled his concentration — Christopher Robin was saying his prayers. On some occasions when he had spent an inordinate time meditating and was needed in some way she had found him fast asleep upon his mat. We have regretfully lost contact and I wonder what enthusiasm now is the in-thing back in Wales, for that is where his heart belonged, and I wonder if he is nearer to enlightenment. Dearly would I like to meet up with him again.

I know marginally more about meditation now and realise how common it is. There are many paths, disciplines, and pitfalls, particularly where one voids the mind of mental as well as sensory images, and makes oneself receptive to incoming impressions. How easy to delude oneself that an impression is from a higher plane and fraught with destiny when it is only from the opportunistic subconscious which has rushed in to occupy a vacant lot. The path to self-knowledge is tricky and one tires readily. But who has not at least once in a lifetime received an impression from an inner source in a direct or roundabout way? Its suddenness can startle, and its wit and angle bemuse, or warm with a delight that can hardly be contained.

I waited. The singing birds outside would not go away. They must leave my awareness. One in particular was emphatic that I lend it my ear. It was inditing a rare composition. Its throat genes were akin to those of the skylark and blackbird, I would swear to it. What stunning invention — just as one became sure of the direction a cadence would take, off it would dart elsewhere — what breaks and falls and new entries, what grace-notes and trills, *appoggiatura*! It would be a crime against nature to shoo away such a songster in a bid for some uncertain occult intimation.

An image arose in the stilled mind; it was of a mist rising from the ground, a corny stage mist, but it was suffused unmistakably with joy. An impression had arrived in its own quizzical way. All would work out.

AND BACK TO EARTH

An auto drew up to the sit-out. I could see it was packed as Nixon tumbled out. This nifty three-wheeler with its black Victorian bonnet carried three passengers. The driver was Vinod and the other two were new to me. The greeting formula was the same, I could have said it for him — 'Hello Uncle, are you all right? Are you ready?' It was never as if there had been an arrangement for which I had to be in readiness. Sojan's mother was making coffee and I must perforce wait if only to be polite. Getting ready would take no time as all I had to do was to put on socks and shoes and my newly-cut hair needed no checking.

There was news. Athuba had at last had his application to be posted back to Nagaland granted. He will return by the end of the month, in two weeks. I was pleased for him; he would be reunited with his wife, from whom he had been parted too long. He could not be further away, for Nagaland is a north-east state and Kerala south-west, a train distance of five days. I had helped him with petitions and pleas. These and a gift had been the means whereby the bureaucracy had been persuaded to return him to Dimapur. But I was bereft, and felt I would never see him again. I felt so but the point was arguable. He is so like Nixon, a lively one, a fountain of jollity and the bubbling presence that doubles enjoyment on all our occasions. They had come to collect me and meet up with Athuba in town, so we crowded into the auto and I waved to my hockey friends as we passed the grounds — they would know not to call this evening.

On the way I was introduced to the two others and have already forgotten their names. Why of all Asian names do I find Indian the most difficult? I am up with the Wayans and Ketuts of Indonesia and Malaysia; the Chinese names which are often as not English — Benny, Baby, Sonny and the like. Thai names can be formidable, Somphong and Veera manage to stick, while the Vietnamese names are absurdly easy — Ho Ha Heng Hue (but no Hum).

In remembering Indian names and Indian faces I am a signal failure. The young man on my right was Chandran, a goldsmith, and he owns half-share of the auto which Vinod drives.

We parted. Nixon and I got out and entered a dingy hallway nearby. 'Remember this place, Uncle?' It was the building on the roof of which we had held our New Year's party. It was a labour mounting the stairs and this Nixon did not fail to notice. He wants to take me to an ayurvedic doctor as I have little energy and have become skinny. I have no objection. We went into Javeen's little shop, the depot for his fairy light rentals. Several men were sitting and standing about before a black and white television set which showed a young woman posturing and singing. The sounds were excruciating.

Athuba rushed joyously to greet me. The volume was turned down as we chatted. After many felicitations he, Nixon, Tommy and I left. Nixon had earlier demanded a treat. It caught Athuba on the hop as he had little cash on him at the time. He is all generosity but became thoughtful as he figured out his requirements. We were offering to share, but he wanted none of our help. Off we went to Luciya Palace, Nixon and I by auto, the other two by motorbike.

Set in spacious grounds, Luciya Palace is unpretentious and moderately stately. It has a grand entrance to the main restaurant which is haunted by commissionaires. We went around the side to a smaller porticoed entrance which opened to the heavily curtained bar; I suggested that we not go there but further, onto the outside dining area. Night was approaching and it would be cooler. There were about 30 tables. The garden was enclosed by high walls surmounted by an ornamental parapet; most of them were covered by the small-leafed climbing fig. Beyond were tall trees, mainly palms. The turf was of a springy tufty nature common in the East.

We walked across a twee, arched bridge small enough to be stepped over. It was railed, for this is a drinking area as well as a dining area and its rails might prove helpful to the unsteady. In one corner was a folly. It was a hilly pile of dull-brown stones, featureless save for three small fountains and low standards, bearing lights. The plashing water did something to redeem the ugliness, and the gathering darkness a little more. Were I younger, I thought, how I would relish building another rock-garden. We were early and had choice of place while we were waiting for Athuba and Tommy. I noticed a white cloud drifting past as if from the ground and the scent of incense. An attendant was carrying a large pan of incense-impregnated coals which he passed under each table. There was enough smoke to obscure it and the four chairs for about a minute before the evening airs bore it away. This, I thought, is a true orient touch.

Athuba has a bare working-knowledge of Malayalam, and Tommy a little of English. That most of the conversation was in Malayalam did not bother me for it was light and inconsequential, I had time to observe the setting, and time to eat at my own pace. True to his teetotal resolution Nixon had no hard drink but confined himself to Kingfisher lager which he called a soft drink. His intake was not excessive and the effect not adverse. Athuba and Tommy drank rum. The ice-cold beer exactly suited the occasion, adding a touch to the many-textured night. Nixon plied me with highly-spiced pieces of beef on little sticks. Later a dish of sweet-sour chicken was set before me, especially prepared free of chilli. Any dish without chilli is acceptable to me but I did not regard what I had as a great meal. The fact I was eating indicated polite relish. The sweet of the sugar and the sour of the vinegar had not blended the Chinese way. There was naan, a kind of large, soft pancake, useful as a suppressor of the too-assertive sweet-sour taste.

We talked of Nagaland which has a population of only fifteen lakhs. I had seen many photographs of this friendly, relaxed people, who are mainly Protestant and perhaps a little straight-laced. It is a hilly country with no crowding vegetation as in Kerala.

He wanted me to visit him and his people when next returning to India. I could come from Rangoon, but I had some knowledge of air routes and knew I would have to fly from Kuala Lumpur to Calcutta and thence to Dimapur, which had an airport, unlike the capital Kohima. Well, there were many unknown factors ahead and we must take them as they come. The season would be a big factor because of the extremes of temperature in Nagaland, and also the monsoons are to be avoided. I could see October or November as likely. He told us of Shillong, and the name stirred in me, it was as evocative as Mandalay, a lovely place, Athuba said, set in mountains like Switzerland. It is in the state of Meghalaya, to the south west of Nagaland. It is a state of India I had never heard of. My problem was not the will to visit such places, but the energy. The giddiness that had deprived me of consciousness still lingered and was not to be trusted. The ayurvedic doctor, yes I must see him. The allopathic doctors I had seen were too shut into their tight systems and lacking a true desire to diagnose a non-routine case. I would take up Nixon's offer.

Though I had not eaten in the Indian way I felt the need to wash my hands. There was a porcelain wash-basin against the wall. I had only two glasses of Kingfisher in the two hours we had spent at the table and was not befuddled. Even so, that imbalance and the tufty lawn called for concentration as I made my way. It had been so for many weeks now, far too long, and I must take advice. As for planning visits to outlandish places in the state I found myself, that would be folly.

I had taken no stand in the argument of ayurvedic versus allopathic medicine and felt that to shape up such opposites was to the detriment of the real issues and would invite distortion and wrong conclusions. Some people are passionate in their allegiance. True, eastern medicine appears at first blush to follow a holistic approach to the body's health, while the west appears concerned only with symptoms. That might have been so once, but is it still? I do not think so. Some argue, rather simplistically, that all western medicines are harmful and must be avoided. The more I think of the controversy, the more unprofitable I think it is to pursue it. There is a dreadful field of pharmaceutical politics where eastern countries fare badly in the exploitative grip of western wealth and power. This is quite a different matter. Here, mistrust of western medicine is fuelled by the scandals caused by the greed, duplicity and unaccountability of the multi-nationals.

The physician I met was a qualified doctor in ayurvedic medicine. Nixon had told me he was highly motivated to serve his people. He held socialistic ideas and was also engaged in disseminating his beliefs. He had sources of income which allowed him to offer his medical services freely. I had heard enough to give me confidence, besides, I did not have to know anything about him personally, except the fact of his integrity.

I was prepared for an unorthodox consultation and was not proved wrong. His house, deep among trees, was large and sprawling. We waited until he had finished with a patient and were ushered into a large room with one side open to the yard. Indeed 'room' is misleading, for in the night light I saw other areas into which ours flowed as though enclosed spaces had never been considered.

I thought in the comings and goings of people that the man I saw was an assistant, but when the time came for my consultation found that he was in fact the man I had come to see. He was not tall, more muscular and well-fleshed rather than thick-set, and he wore a drab banian. His eyes were good and spaced well but he had no air of a professional man. There were no formalities. I do not remember that we even shook hands; he hardly looked at me. The doctor, Nixon, Vinod and I sat around a large, deal table on which the doctor placed his elbows as he held his head.

I had briefed Nixon on my disabilities and told him there were two points to make. First, the fact I had dizziness, and low pain at the nape of the head which I felt was connected with a blow I received in my youth. At that time vomiting had occurred and my neck had been troublesome ever since; and second, the utter exhaustion I was undergoing quite beyond the acceptable withdrawal of energies in old age.

Nixon's translation could not have confined itself to these points for it went on for a considerable period. I think the doctor was able to sort it out. He left the room and returned with a plate piled with small, sweet bananas. Nixon peeled one for me. The doctor also brought back his sphygmomanometer. I tested well and he thought my heart system was in good order. This was reassuring, so far so good. He sat a long time as though lost in thought, Nixon told me little: I could not expect quick results with ayurvedic treatment; I must accept the fatigues of age. 'But not the dizziness,' I fired back; the heart was not the cause of my troubles.

He then produced a scruffy notepad and wrote out my prescription. In five days I should feel some relief, in ten I should return to see him again. The visit did not end there, for Nixon was in need of help; he had long had a bladder-stone and a cough. His blood pressure proved high, and he received advice. The scruffy pad was brought into use again. Finally, Vinod told of joint pains which the doctor said would be due to his work as a driver on bad roads which put strain on his joints as he jolted around.

We left. I had offered remuneration and was rebuffed, I was helplessly beholden. On the way I asked Nixon to tell me what the doctor had told him but he said he had forgotten most of it. I teased him on his uselessness, but did not mind, as I knew the essentials. There was an ointment for the head and neck, a tonic, a food supplement which I gathered had calcium for bones and phosphorous for nerves and some pills I knew nothing about. We hastened, for we wanted to reach the ayurvedic pharmacy before it closed. It was large and well-stocked and I was surprised at its extent. Even before the pharmacist had completed assembling my prescription Nixon was rubbing my nape with the ointment.

Five days have passed, three have been moderately good, one bad, one middling. The score was favourable, more than satisfactory; I shall live to see another day. Later, Mini, who had once worked as an aid in a hospital, suggested the black pills, which had no explanatory packaging, contained iron.

LACRIMAE RERUM[*]

I was later than usual this morning, the editorials were meatier, and then I did some copying. Usually I keep watch on the time — I like to catch the freshness but today was sidetracked. Besides, it was cloudy, it would keep, I could still go out. Turn right, it will not be far. I'll wander along by the temple, then see how much further I want to go. Mostly I concentrate on the sky, where it meets the treetops. It extends me, I get the feeling of extension. I did not expect to find anyone around at this time as it was Sunday, but was greeted with a shout by Shajo, the one they call Beef. This liveliest of youngsters ran to me, 'Uncle, come, Uncle, come.' He hurried towards me, took my hand and led me down towards the lake. He watched my footing as I clambered down the outcrop. It levels out to a grassy slope before the low embankment. The lowest part of this strip is permanently under water — it is not a swamp, for fresh water seeps from higher ground. Grass grows through it and often the hockey or cricket balls fall into it, followed by a charging player.

Babu was standing by the water with a long pole 'Snake, Uncle see, snake.' It took some time for me to focus where they were pointing. I saw a ripple then the head, or something horrible which should have been the head. It looked like something smashed or eviscerated.

Until I could make it out I was revolted. I was looking for a head but there was none to see, for the object terminated in the rear of a frog and two splayed legs. Even when I knew what it was I was revolted, but the emotion was changing to fascination. The legs were moving feebly.

'Is it poisonous?'

'Not water snakes, not poisonous.'

'Most are in Australia — there the water snakes are dangerous.'

'Not dangerous, this one.'

Babu worked the pole under it and goaded it into action, he deftly balanced it and swung it out of the water onto higher ground. We watched in silence for ten minutes as the frog slowly disappeared down the lubricated gullet. The swollen section slowly increased until two small feet

---

[*]tears for things

fluttered a last farewell. Then Babu whacked it, three swift blows to break the back. There was violent movement and then the barest twitching. The frog was disgorged. He picked it up on the pole but it was all but dead. By this time Kannan had joined us. He realised what was going on and grabbed a pole. We four stood watching.

'Oh, why did your kill it? You didn't have to kill it.' Even now the snake showed signs of life until Kannan fetched a couple of blows which ended all movement.

I walked back thoughtfully on this lazy morning. The air was still as fresh and cool and the shade as inviting, but my cosy mood had gone. It was as if the earth had stirred in its sleep to remind me of something, something I was not wanting to hear.

We revel in nature's changing forms, we watch the light playing on hills and mountains. It dips into its airy palette to touch the vapours that form a rainbow; with a breath of air it catches the russet on the acacia pods, and it strays into deep, moist places to twinkle on gossamer and dew-fed mosses.

The changes delight us and we who grow plants do not mourn as the cherished flowers are transferred to the compost-bin; we endorse the transformation to sweet, friable soil.

It is only when we get to the animal kingdom that these changes come a little closer to the bone, and delight becomes tempered with second thoughts, and when we see such things as a frog in the throat of a snake we are seized with horror. We are not prepared to consider this type of transition, for it bears the name of death.

In this term, which we use for both the animal and human kingdoms, we do not recognise transition. We make it a full stop, a fell termination. That is our gross error. In mitigation we grant poignancy a perpetual lease and write poetry about the tears in things. All because we reject change and transition, all because we do not understand the energies that substand the form.

TUESDAY IS SATISFACTORY

The last game of the series was played today and I was asked by several would I attend, with the implication that I should. Our team was playing the veterans. Kunjumon came towards midday. It is a while since he has paid a midday visit, though I see him most evenings when he calls or when I go on my walk. We had a game of chess — it was at least two weeks since we had a game and after such a break we did not play with zest. Still, it was a tussle and the old game asserted its fascination.

Praveen called for me late in the afternoon — I was prepared to walk to the hockey grounds, but was overruled. I took advantage of the scooter to post a letter I had written to Pranob. At the grounds Praveen wandered off to the dressing shed to see his friends while I took a solitary walk around the field. We were early; the game was to begin at 4:30 but I reckoned the starting time would be five; as it happened it was 5:30 as the veterans had to wait for some players to come from work. Our senior team was to play them in the finals.

I sat for a while on the concrete surround of a great tree which had already cast half this end of the ground into shade. Two students wandered over. They were polite and smiling and wanted to talk. Mechanically, I answered the stock questions. They introduced themselves.

One told me his name was Joseph, named after the father of Jesus Christ, and the other had the unusual name Raldo, made up from Raphael and Dominic, a rather inspired fusion. I looked on their young, intelligent faces. They were gentle — harmony rules their backgrounds. They were engineering students, the most favoured discipline, the second being that of computer science.

They were keen to know why I came to India. I told them of the two years I had spent in Bangalore with side trips to Kerala and my more permanent shift here. I told them I had found a niche which gave me the proportions of solitude and freedom I desired. I had made more friends in Kerala than Bangalore; in fact looking back, I found Bangalore as friendless as any large city I have been to. Here, friendships come easily, in the big city one has to work at them.

I was asked my opinion of India and I said, 'What should I say of one-fifth of the world? The world is both good and evil and the mix is uneven. What I find here is intensely interesting. As an islander my values were imported from our motherland, England. A new set of values is emerging as a native product, but I was always looking across the sea. Islanders have a compulsion to travel. You in India are self-contained. You have had your values from old, from way back.'

In such answers I stress their accomplishments and achievements, and inferiority attitudes must not be allowed to harm their self-image, as India's gift to the world is more than she realises. The arrogance of white people who once usurped their land must not be allowed to engender sentiments of inferiority.

The game was faster and more spirited than those I had seen of the juniors, especially in the second half when our team had put on four goals, winning 5-1. There were thrilling moments, but as the light faded I could not see the ball and relied on Praveen to tell me what happened. We did not linger after the final whistle. On the way back we made our way round an elephant that carried a load of coconut branches, for it commandeered the whole road.

About nine I had just finished showering when Kunjumon arrived to see me. With him were Valsan, Vijayan, Rajendran, and Nandakumar. Two things I mildly suggested: one, that they talk in voices more suited to a room than across the hill-tops; and two, that they talk in sequence. We were tired and it was a last get-together for the day. I have a long mirror on my wardrobe and each in turn is drawn to it to examine hair, clothes and general appearance. In this evening hour each wore his best clothes — or dress as they call it. Vijayan asked had I any hair-cut catalogues, he wanted to study hair styles — he is the most handsome one.

I was filled in on the points of the game I had missed, how the goalie had fallen over and damaged his leg, and how Simon had created an uproar by bringing the handle of his stick backwards into an opponent's body. Kunjumon did not like this man who was a coach and umpire playing today for the veterans. He said his umpiring was biased. I know and like both Kunjumon and Simon and was forced to consider this might be so, I said it was a pity, but I would continue to like him.

JOSE

Jose has been visiting more than usual. He is always welcome, being such a personable and interesting young man, forever busy with his studies and projects. I too, have been busy with things I want to do. These visits hold me captive, I give my time. Yesterday, for instance, Kunjumon popped in for a game of chess at midday and I relished the break.

After my meal I have to take a rest of at least half an hour. Fatigue collects in my head like a sediment and a siesta gives me a chance to wash it away. I had just reached that point when Jose arrived. To my shame I felt dismay, I did not feel fully committed in the attention I was giving him. There were pauses and silences, he imagining I was pondering deeply upon his words, and I with just one thought predominating — when will I sleep? At last I told him I was overtired and must take a rest, and he took his leave.

I met him two years ago when on a visit here; suddenly I found I was without any reading whatsoever and felt desperate for a book. Sojan said he had a friend, a student, who had some books, a lot of books, and he would take me around to see him.

I could see the household had never been touched by the constraints of poverty; the airy sitting room proclaimed the comforts of the middle class — the furniture, old and substantial, scorned time and bespoke order and repose. There were several people present when we called and I was introduced to each in turn and was told briefly the connection, whether family or friend, information that could remain in my mind no longer than a butterfly remained on a petal. I did note, however, the tired father and the still-active mother. He had been a banker and she a schoolteacher. They were up in years. When the introductory necessities were fulfilled Sojan indicated to me one of the group and pushed me towards him, for he was the one I had come to see. I told him I was in a bad way for lack of something to read. He replied that actually he possessed few books and most were of a technical nature. I registered his solidity, the intense gaze of closely-set eyes, and the full attention he was giving me. 'Come, I'll show you my room, you shall see.'

He kept his room locked which surprised me, and once inside he showed me a pile of books which he described as English lit. They consisted of school texts, many obviously second — or third — hand for they were heavily annotated by different hands. In my day I had similarly defaced French and Italian books, and regret that I did so, for I deplore the habit. I selected a couple of poetry anthologies and a copy of *The Scarlet Letter*, a novel I had not thought of for yonks. It would do very well indeed, I would like to read it once more.

There was a model aircraft on his table. He had made it. There were also his sketches of luxury motorcars. He told me motorbikes and cars had always held his interest, as well as aeroplanes. I told him that Murthi with whom I was staying in Bangalore was formerly an engineering foreman in the Benz works in Germany and had similar interests. I would tell him about Jose and his wish to contact a fellow hobbyist.

We were together there in the room up to an hour; part of the time a youngster was also present. Our chat was congenial. He told me something of his inner life and I was surprised how one so young and vital could have such tension and frustration. He told me his parents had no sympathy with his studies and hobbies, and no understanding of his philosophical nature. He lived a stranger in the house.

They were a Catholic family and Jose despised them for narrowness and set ways. He scorned them for the smugness and superficiality of their religious belief. He had stopped going to Mass and said his prayers alone in his room.

I was drawn to him, so passionately honest and so desirous to enter the wider world of ideas and thought and true living. Already he had made clearcut decisions as to what he would or would not do. Sport was a waste of time, he said, life was too short for it. He had resolved never to touch alcohol or drugs; he would marry but not allow any children to come into such an evil world through his union; that would be the worst possible crime he could commit.

I had forgotten the vehemence of youth, where issues are simple and judgments absolute. I did not think there was any extreme that experience could not temper. The fact of feeling intensely on a number of issues was indicative of a fiery spirit, and far more important than the holding of so-called correct views. Wherever he was, he would be on the barricades.

On parting he asked could he write to me, could he correspond. In the letters which followed he allowed deeper entry into his life — he told me his disappointments and aspirations. There was one sorrowful story of a teenage romance between him and a schoolgirl three years before. When the tender idyll had been discovered by the parents of both sides it inflated into scandal, branded as immoral and ruthlessly destroyed. He was still bitter over that event.

He was the youngest member of the family and between him and his next sibling there was a gap of twelve years. Both brothers were married and held good positions and his only sister had also married well. His brothers had no love for him and despised him; they put him down as a rebel and non-conformist. In such a tight circle of their small society there would be no place for him. They were unable to gauge the extent of his intense, wide-ranging mind. Over the course of our correspondence I was able to send a few books as I came across what I thought might be of interest. One was *A Brief History of Time* by Stephen Hawking, and another about his life. He had heard of Hawking and was ready for him.

I am ever appalled at the woeful libraries I have visited. The State Library of Karnataka which I visited in Bangalore was stocked with antiquated third-rate books from the turn of the century. The original cover had been replaced with uniform black bindings and the titles were hand-written on the spine. I think of the excellent libraries down under. My heart, if it knew how, would bleed for the deprived intellectuals and readers of this country. That library in Bangalore is housed in a splendid domed building of architectural distinction. The library here in this town has an abominable collection, enough to imprint on a young mind a life-long revulsion for libraries. It also has a splendid dwelling-place. If ever a revolution is needed it is in this strategic field. I speak out of a limited experience, but from what I have seen in particular I fear in general.

I say a word in favour for the British Library, which I joined for a limited period. Though in the literary section it is behind the times, it houses a fairly representative collection of books printed in England and receives funding from that country. Its main feature is its collection of technological works, but of that field I have not the slightest competence to make a comment.

Now that I live here more or less permanently I see much of Jose and on our trip to Mannur he disclosed a spontaneous care-free merriment as he joined in the uninhibited dancing of Nixon and Athuba. One day he gave me a letter he had written. He had found an opportunity he wished to follow which would start him off on the path of independence. He had a friend engaged in electronic and circuitry work who was manufacturing audio units and walkmen. There was a proposition that Jose buy the parts and the circuitry which he could assemble and market independently. In his letter he went into careful detail as he costed each item of the project, adding a modest profit of a thousand rupees. He felt he could market a product of better quality in tone and which would sell below the market price.

In his letter he asked would I be able to lend him enough money to manufacture the first unit, and he outlined how after a few sales he would be able to repay me. The sum was not high and I readily agreed, and told him I did not need repayment. The project went ahead according to plan and I soon learned of his first sale, sharing his elation as he made his first thousand rupees of profit.

This project was not to become a full-time activity but was to go towards his maintenance expenses during study. It could lead to self-support. I saw him less often during the following months as he was fully occupied with his studies. The project was halted for a period as his supplier had encountered temporary difficulty in acquiring his basic material. Apart from a general desire to see Jose prosper I had given little thought to his venture. There had been one time when Jose told me he thought his friend had been playing games — some other friends had dealings with this same man.

The visits had been more frequent of late and there came the occasion when I had to ask him to let me take my nap. The next occasion we met I was fresher and able to give him full attention. He was dispirited. He had many causes for this but fundamentally it was a lack of love on the part of his family. He spoke with frankness. He had not been a wanted child from the start. His mother had observed traditional practices for birth control, but twelve years after the birth of the son who was to be the last, the precautions had failed. He was a mistake. His parents had performed their bounden duties by him but had manifested little beyond criticism and disapproval. He was an intelligent, bright boy, ahead of his peers, but his parents saw this as a fault and he was upbraided for thinking too much, for his wilfulness and predilection for books. This was surprising conduct from a schoolteacher mother and businessman father. They never took interest in his original mind as it unfolded. He was passionate in his denunciation of his parents and said he hated them. I was uncomfortable with such words, I listened with pain, but he continued with his vehement attack. I was wondering if there was lack of objectivity and a strong element of self-pity, and was inclined to believe him without hearing the other side. This in any case, would be something that could never happen.

When the flood of his outburst had abated and held no more force I diverted our talk to other matters. He soon regained his calm. I asked how the matter of his audio systems project was proceeding and was surprised to learn that far from having difficulties in obtaining supplies, his friend had disappeared not only with Jose's money but that of three other friends. They were on his trail, however, and would not go to the police for there would be nothing in the case for them. They would take their own measures.

'Measures, what do you mean?'

'Thirty rupees it will cost.'

'Meaning?'

'He must be taught a lesson. We will deal with him.'

'Will you beat him up?'

'Thirty rupees is the cost of a tube of super-glue. You know how dangerous it is and will stick surfaces and skin together so that only surgery will be able to separate them!'

'Yes of course I do. But what will you do?'

'He must be taught a lesson. You have only to put it to your eyes and the lids will be permanently sealed.'

'You surely wouldn't do that! Not seriously.'

Thirty pieces of silver for all his ideals, I thought.

'He must be taught a lesson.'

'Who do you think you are? Do you think you are God?'

A chill went through me. Such things do happen and the young can be merciless. There is much to think over and much to discuss. His imagination must be awakened.

POSTCARDS & A VASE OF FLOWERS

John has written and enclosed two postcards of Dunedin, one of the law courts and railway station and the other of the St Clair and St Kilda coastline. They cause much interest here. Everything is so clean and uncluttered with the period buildings settled into time as permanent residents — calm, order, beauty. They contrast with the central area here; I can imagine nothing more different, but of course I am comparing a still photo with a living scene where heat is the major feature, followed closely by the traffic and jostling people. From what I can gather Trichur has one to two lakhs (200,000) of population, roughly the same as Dunedin. This might be an under-estimate for Indian people are uncountable. In New Zealand we are population conscious and use such terms as surpass, close on, approaching, as if the achieving of numbers is important. In India no one thinks this way, as even the villages are overflowing. A news item recently referred to a 'tiny town of 50,000 in Gujarat.'

The place is saturated and inescapably populous. A recent report said that in 1992 India passed the 900,000,000 mark. Moreover, in this hot climate the people are visible, whereas in Dunedin they remain largely indoors. I see New Zealand as a landscape where weather and wind are the animating feature, with the movement of clouds and mist over land and sea, the rest is a slow-moving dream.

He also enclosed a plastic-coated postcard of one of his paintings.* It is a flower-piece, a gem. The colours are strong and muffled and the shapes cunningly careless; impossible flowers assemble to form the archetype of all flower pieces. What makes it so endearing is that it is an ordinary bunch of flowers, not a grand and lavish composition. It is ordinary, and to be shifted about as one does the dusting — plain flowers in a plain vase, and lovely.

I guess that John dashed it off in minutes — I have seen him at such work — yet years of discipline have gone into its creation. I look for the signature — *John Robinson*. It is not there: sign it, John, it is a masterpiece!

---

*Used on the cover of Noel's *Dweller on the Threshold*, see page 256

MEA CULPA

I have been mortified, accused by implication and by my own conscience. I ask few questions here, as exact answers are hard to get, considering our language barrier. Many things of a minor nature are continually happening and I do not know, nor do I need to know, about them. For instance, I did not know exactly what was happening over the farewell we were to give Athuba. I voiced my misgivings and uncertainties to a friend, and he immediately retailed them to the person concerned.

He had told me once before never to tell him anything in confidence as he would be unable to conceal it. I could not believe that anyone would have so great an insensitivity and down-right stupidity as to pass on what I mentioned in private, straight back. This was done with neither motive nor malice — but as mindless news-mongering.

The person concerned came to me and clarified the doubts that had been in my mind, and I believe in his probity, but no longer in mine. I am angry not only with myself but the gossiper as well, and shall have to reassess our friendship, and learn to know him as he really is. I am a gullible person and readily make assumptions that because I think and act in a certain way then others will be working on that same basis and act in a similar way. It is an erroneous and problem-engendering assumption.

The truth is that in personal matters we sail dangerous waters and most of us are thoroughly incompetent at navigation. At the personal level we are self-serving and self-oriented by nature and must be extremely careful. We are only safe when we examine our motives scrupulously and remain on guard that we are always harmless. Harmlessness is not a mild virtue, nor is it a minor virtue, for it has its origins in the soul or conscience. We must as a foremost rule of conduct think and relate to the higher-self of others, and see and think no evil. We must not listen to evil and never allow the tongue free rein for it is the most treacherous and disloyal organ we possess.

I am lashed and lacerated that I have hosted misgivings and criticism. It will take exertion to rehabilitate myself and re-establish where I would permanently be — on the highest level I know, never leaving the side of love and wisdom for any reason whatsoever. Only then will the crass behaviour of others be denied fuel from me. They will have to find other sources.

I worked hard that abashed and disconcerting day, not in penance but for distraction. I chose to answer letters I was stalling on and gave of my best. The pain would go and in a few days would show as a temporary dip on the graph of my days.

I sat on my bed by the window and was working away when a smile and large shock of hair appeared unexpectedly outside. It was Sunil, joy leapt up; only this morning I had been considering his silence and his absence. He was accompanied by a plumpish man introduced as Shanavas. He was on holiday for a few months from his work in Qatar, where he worked with cement and there was a swimming-pool. I could not work out the connection but I did not press for clarification. Sunil's joy was equal to mine. He had received my letter and drafted two in reply but felt he could not post them. I upbraided him.

The visit was short as they had other calls to make and then a journey of 40 kilometres on the motorbike. Sunil asked had I any elementary books on English he could borrow but I had nothing. I would try to find something locally, or if unsuccessful, I would send for material from my sister in New Zealand. We would meet the following evening at the railway station where we would be farewelling our mutual friend, Athuba. As they left they embraced me the Eastern way, or was it the Muslim way? Shanavas gave me a small phial. It contained scent.

The clouds that had held the day in sombre check now parted and a grave beauty shone down. The day held two more episodes. I had taken my meal on the sit-out, Sojan sat there. He and Mini had just returned from the hospital where a girl had been born to a cousin's wife. It was in an incubator suffering from jaundice. I listened to this news.

An auto pulled up. The arrival was of the one who had injured me; He brought me a belt as he had seen that mine was broken. I had bought it on the streets of Bangalore for 20 rupees. It was not a peace-offering as he was unaware of any breach. The coals of anguish still burned and I was numb as he enthusiastically demonstrated the patent catch. I could not chide this warm-hearted blunderer. I just wanted to go away and be alone.

After his departure there was still enough daylight for a short walk. Curiously I thought of Sir Walter Raleigh, imprisoned so many years in the Tower of London. I remember seeing the passage along which he took his exercise, the one who wrote a history, a giant of those days, one who walked for sanity. I came to a corner with a slight slope and a man of about 30 came towards me driving a flock of goats and kids. He was walking up the slope. He looked up at me, head tilted back he looked at me, his whole glance hung upon me as though to rest for a moment the burden of some nameless grief. In that look was all humanity. I thought how can sorrow have such depths.

THEY ASK ME TO AGREE

'You must agree,' they say, 'that the world is getting worse. There are crimes and violence as never before, sexual vice, drugs, war, corruption in high places and new forms of wickedness. In every way the world is going to the dogs.' I stand there in the doorway, wondering what to do about all these evils. I also ponder how to handle the opening gambit, for I know what is coming. This happened in Dunedin but is so vivid in my mind today I must give it expression. Depending upon which sect is witnessing, these door-knockers, who have agonised in private over the plight of the world, now agonise in public. Some believe that retribution and vengeance are soon to come from the hand of an affronted deity and that the great clean-up is nigh, but there is a way out and they have found the key. Or they are not so heavy on the vengeance angle but seek to share the personal salvation they have experienced since meeting face to face with the Lord. Have I been too insensitive towards their sense of mission and destiny, their deepest truest feeling which has been decked out by their leaders in simplistic propositions and remedies? I fear I have been. They stand there, well-dressed and idealistic, and they are good.

Once I opened the door to a couple of fresh-faced students at the back door while I was busy cooking. I told them their zeal was better than their creed and packed them off as I could hear someone ringing at the front door. Bless me, if there were not two more missionaries who had come onto the property by another entrance. I felt besieged. They were not young, in fact they were an old couple, probably married. As soon as I ascertained the nature of their visit I scolded them — what right had they to invade privacy in this way, it was an affront; if I felt I had the need for religious instruction I knew where the various advisers were to be found. They were so humble and meek in their apologies that I was smitten. My self-righteousness had no stamina and gave way. I apologised also, and there were the three of us all expressing apologies, and ever since I have felt that I had been scolding angels.

But is the world really going downhill? I have been living most of this century and can't help thinking that the exact opposite is the case, it is getting better. Yes, I'll stand up and say that. A longer look at history than that afforded by the sensational dailies gives ample evidence to support this view and it is clear to me that something good is happening on this planet; something is very much afoot. Millions more than ever before are literate and are thinking about world affairs. There is education and knowledge as never before, health surveillance, environmental concern as never before. For the first time in history there is global awareness that never existed before. There have been vast empires in the past, but never world organisations. Is this not an advance from the self-preoccupation of individuals and groups?

When first I went to school I was taught pride in our native land and loyalty to the British Empire; let the rest of the world go by. Is that so nowadays? Very little, I guess. The emphasis is upon the world as a whole, our planet in space. The vision is more often shifting from the particular to the universal. Donne would be amazed at the success of his phrase, 'No man is an island,' which now has world currency.

This is not to deny that this century has seen wickedness as never before (the phrase is pure Ezra Pound). Everything is on a greater scale; if goodwill is in evidence as never before, so are destruction, selfishness and greed. We are clearly engaged in the most intense uproar of contention and argument since humans first became articulate. The protagonists are emerging painfully from the crudity of physical combat onto the mental plane, but much remains obscured by the pea-soupers of the emotional life, the vapours and mists of greed and bigotry in all their swirling variations. Obsessive cries are heard everywhere, but also are heard sane, informed and sober voices, and they are many. Events such as the struggle in South Africa provide a glass to show how sanity is gaining ground.

The century has been one long, agonising and atrocious gestation, and now that the birth pangs of a new age have begun, thousands of world-servers are about the task of building, healing, teaching, monitoring, smoothing rough places and battling for the dispossessed. Quite observably the old world is lumbering onto a new course and tearing the heart out of ancient evil.

Evil is still monstrous and manifold and its stockpile of lies endangers the nations, but its hour has come; too many tumours afflict its substance for it to flourish as before. Its decline, though slow, is assured; something is unquestionably afoot, and I am more than positive that we have gained ground over this appalling century.

AVE ATHUBA

The air was thick with heat, and an energetic wind moved it about as if moving coals; it was not steady and predictable and one could not come to terms with it. In its lighter movements it was wilful as a puppy and grabbed papers and small objects, then suddenly discarded them. I decided when I settled to read the paper and then do letters and to pay the obnoxious intruder no attention. Surprisingly, neglected, and given as cold a shoulder as one can manage in Kerala, it sulked and then went away. So there was some merit in the ostrich technique of ignoring what is troublesome, It does often go away. This counsel of evasion may not be applied to all problems, as some may not be evaded, but it serves admirably with trivialities; by not energising them they deflate and retire into oblivion.

So the morning advanced to midday, and then Kunjumon called to play chess. He is ever welcome but I still had things on my mind and did not attend to the play, consequently losing two games one after another. After good starts which gave me an advantage I found my queen whisked away, or a rook. I was glad for his sake as I had been winning every game over the last fortnight. I said this but was not truly noble, for I would never lose if I could help it. We then played two quick games which I won through the sheer force of hurt pride, but even then had only passing satisfaction as I was still preoccupied. As we had played quickly there was time for a tie-breaker. Kunjumon was keen, again I began with promise and again nemesis delivered a blow for lapse of concentration. It was a passing blow. I was able to work a draw.

Later in the afternoon Jose called to return a magazine. Its major article was devoted to the story of the way the USA had fought a proxy war in Afghanistan through Pakistan. The article was prompted by the chilling exposé of the nuclear race in William E Burrows study, *Critical Mass*. I was fascinated and horrified by the revelations and by the realisation that international affairs have no input of idealism or morality, but are governed by the play of the forces of naked power with little consideration to the effect on the mass of humanity.

The aspect of the story which impressed Jose was the drama of Casey's four clandestine trips to Islamabad in the huge black Starliner furnished like a five-star hotel which was refuelled in flight to arrive incognito in darkness. Heady days for those involved.

Athuba's train which left from Kochi (Cochin) was called the Guwhati Express as it terminated there in Assam. It was scheduled to leave Trichur at 7:00 p.m. This was the official time, the unattainable ideal. There were many factors which had a bearing on such a journey which would take up to five days, counting the extra journey from Guwhati onto Dimapur in Nagaland. For instance, the week before there was sabotage of the track in Assam. Today (we learned later) there was a bandh protest in Tamil Nadu that had upset the slatings. We knew before six that the expected time of departure was five past seven, a later check was even earlier at 6.45. So we arrived in good time to spend at least half hour with Athuba. We checked again as we passed the enquiries office and found that the departure time would be 11:30, five hours away, a different story. Athuba and Nixon were standing by his luggage. He had seven items, some of them sizeable bales sewn up tightly in scrim. Arshad and Sunil appeared, Sunil beaming with joy to see me and Arshad characteristically grave. The delay did not faze Athuba for he was on a high; the day so long fought for and planned for had arrived. Other friends came by, Jose and Rajan. Rajan also worked at the khadi office with Athuba. He too had a transfer and in three weeks would leave for Calcutta.

Athuba was telling of a letter one of his clerks had written in English and brought to him for signature; it finished with the phrase 'Please reply recently.' Nixon said he should have written 'Please reply suddenly.' We enjoyed this, particularly Athuba and I. In a way laughter is unfair, for few who have English as a mother tongue would care to come to grips with the intricacies of any Indian language and the rigours of nuance.

Jessy and Catherine appeared, friends of Athuba. Catherine has the Tibetan cast of feature and comes from Nagaland; she looked quite fair with her yellow skin against her dark Kerala friend. She is a doctor of veterinary science and is doing further studies here in Kerala. Conversation was difficult, for a nearby loudspeaker poured out Indian pop music.

Sunil and Arshad took their leave, they had two Malaysian friends to meet. After about an hour Nixon, Athuba, Sojan and I left the pile of luggage in the care of Jose while we sought out a restaurant. Up the hill and past the parking lot was a superior place called Aramana and there, upstairs we had our last meal with Athuba. It was a joyful occasion. Sojan and Athuba had rum and I Haywards as Kingfisher was not available. In the heat it was refreshing. Nixon remained true to his abstemious vow, not even 'soft drink' this time. So hot and the nearest fan so slow to turn our way. I did not care to pit my tolerances against Kerala soup, nor was I venturesome enough to explore the menu. I settled on a sandwich and was entirely satisfied; it was really too hot to eat.

About 10:30 my friends decided to send me home. I was not tired, inert would be a better way to describe my lack of animation. I took their decision with indifference and made my farewells. Nixon drove me back on the bike. Sojan did not return from the station until one the next morning — the train had left well after midnight.

So now he is on his sweltering way, some of his seven bundles stowed about him and some with his motorbike in the brake-van. He is in a first class compartment and this is locked overnight. Even Indians, the most inured of travellers, find this vast journey across the sub-continent exhausting and they draw heavily on their reserves of endurance. I shall miss Athuba. While I did not see him more than once or twice a week he loomed large among my friendships. He is pre-eminently a happy man. His most engaging qualities are his naturalness and directness of manner. We have sworn to correspond. For my part it will be easy to keep that promise for I have time to write, but from him I cannot expect a heavy compliance. He will have to visit relatives throughout the state; they must find a house which they will buy and then set up home; above all this, he will be a working man and this will consume the lion's share of his time and energies.

Nixon and Sojan gave him a large box of halva for which Kerala is renowned; it is not available in Nagaland. All I had to offer was a small pot of sandalwood paste, a modest gift even though it is an incomparable product.

It occurred to me I should write straight away considering the long time it takes for mail to reach Dimapur; yet it seemed foolish and excessive since I had seen him a few hours back, but this excessiveness would fall away on the long journey. I began in a light vein — 'Dear Athuba, the trees have lost their leaves, the flowers have all gone black and tears are falling in Trichur.' He enjoys nonsense and knows we will cope well without him even though we do care quite a lot.

Wrong Again

Exchange rates are kind and there is quite a surplus in kitty when the cheque is cleared. How I bless the Australian government as it arrives on time every four weeks without fail. It has afforded me security and more in this poorest of countries, and self-interest is present as I examine the financial indices. For months now the Indian rupee has kept at the same low rate on the world market in order to favour the export figures, whereas it has been appreciating in real terms so that as a result of this disparity I receive from 1600 to 1800 rupees extra when the rupee is thus protected.

I was able to hand some over to Sojan beyond the usual amount. Mini was with him at the time and remarked enthusiastically about the purchase of a gold bracelet. I was not so enthused for I felt that there were many necessities lacking in the house and these should have priority. No more was said and I did some reflecting on the difficulty of helping people, and what a clumsy instrument of good intention money can be.

I remember once when my father had given me ten shillings. I was 14 and it was the time of the Napier earthquake when Napier and Hastings were reduced to rubble. My father had business interests in those places, mainly with the furnishing and carpeting of hotels. Three days after the disaster we drove through to the scene. It was my first sight of devastation and I recall the rubble and water pipes and half-demolished cathedral. I saw the harbour-bed which had been raised so that small ships were sitting on what once had been the harbour bottom; I saw the hill that had slipped to the sea and buried people. Already relief measures had been taken (later our family billeted two school children for some months). I was interested in a temporary shopping area that had been opened — a long row of makeshift booths — among them I saw books I desired. They were extremely cheap and I bought five with my ten shillings. I recall only four: there were volumes of Keats and Pope in a similar edition, one of Poe's *Tales of Mystery and Imagination* and an attractive book with soft leather binding of Carlyle's *Heroes and Hero Worship*. I had these books for many years. I showed them proudly to my father, my treasures, and I could tell at once that he regarded my purchases as wasteful and frivolous. He said nothing and I thought what better could I have done with the money he gave me, they were classics.

Sojan and I decided to go into town to enquire about a small table I needed, and to look at bookshops; I was wanting an English textbook for Sunil. Our first stop on the way was at an office, a financing business. There Roy worked, the one who was so disconsolate the night of our party. He told me a little about the business and I concluded it was much like our building societies where regular contributions were paid in with periodic draws for the free (or low interest) loan. I saw Sojan hand over a bundle of notes which I thought were for the investment. As we left he showed me the gold bracelet he had redeemed. Mini had given it to him many months back and he had hocked it to meet some emergency payments. On our return Mini was all smiles to have her bracelet back. She said her family had continually asked when she was to get it back.

The bookshops are disappointing, all except one which had good presentation and display. I soon examined the stock which was meagre and was sorry I could find nothing there for my immediate purpose. Three others we visited in turn. One was devoted entirely to books in Malayalam, fair enough. The main bookshop is a repellent and congested muddle with books in stacks on the floor and the stock poorly classified. Some areas had no access unless one were bold enough to step over scattered stock. Customers had no passing-space and were waiting for others to move. I saw some English textbooks — dreary publications that would entice few takers, and they were, to boot, full of errors, for I riffled through their pages. I could write better myself, I thought, and even entertained the idea of doing so. But the labour would be great and I am not a trained teacher. I would ask Nixon about my next move, for I was keen to help Sunil.

We visited a furniture factory, for the slum we entered was technically a factory. I could not tell where the rubbish in the lane of approach left off and the rubbish of the factory began. Inside was a shambles but a far cry from The Shambles of York. The products were reasonably good, however, and the quote for a small table satisfactory and much lower than that I would have to pay in a retail shop.

Our final visit was to the mission hospital to see the wife of Sojan's cousin and the baby girl who had hepatitis. This hospital, like the one at Angamaly where Mini's baby was born, is also run by mission sisters.

When we entered a religious service was being relayed in overpowering volume throughout the precincts. Inside and outside the buildings there was no escape from participation. The general impression I formed of this hospital was consistent with the drab, crowded entrance yard. It did not seem as clean as its Angamaly counterpart and it was overcrowded, even the corridors were lined with beds. The baby was lying by itself on a bed in a small room and Raisa lay on a bed opposite. It was now six days old and out of the incubator. The little one was fast asleep in the long dream of its first days on earth.

Back at the house we saw the joy of Mini with her bracelet restored. I thought how wrong I had been about her wish to spend money on a new bracelet; she only wanted to have that which was hers returned.

This was not my only mis-reading of the last few days. For instance in the matter of the rice-straw for the roof of my room to keep the heat down, I was also far out. Nandakumar had told me, as I thought, we would need only a couple of bundles and that they would cost a few paise each. Sojan told me that at least 50 bundles would be required and they would run out at a rupee apiece — and there was a further piece of misinformation I had acquired. I put it down to the large role guesswork plays in interpreting faulty English. I had also understood that Arshad was the owner of a restaurant near to the station where we once met him. This is not so. That he belongs to a wealthy family and has no need to work is correct. Actually he is unemployed and the fact sits heavily on his mind. There is some talk of his going to the Gulf to work.

So I have to be careful in interpretation of all that is said to me in broken phrases. To my many questions or statements the word *yes* follows. It is a holding word to sustain the rapport and is not primarily involved in matters of truth. Wrong information leads to misinterpretation; misinformation to judgment, vocal or unexpressed, and both can prove as awkward as mines in a minefield.

JOSE ET AL.

Sometimes I feel too vulnerable to interruptions and should issue fiats and lock doors. Callers are not what I always want, but is that the only way to look at it? When I say to myself I want solitude, do I not put a wall of separation between myself and reality? If I were to screen all those I would see would it be wise? Or sensible? Unpatterned as my ways are, I do have a goal of sorts and do feel it is worthy of protection and pursuit, but one has need of life's raw material. It comes and goes and is weighed and tested — there is always the obligation to choose and to pick a way through the crowding moments.

I have known about Jose's north Indian penfriend from the start and he has told me of her letters and shown me several. He wants my opinion on the latest, and my advice on his reply. I devote myself for an hour on that which the two must work out themselves. Hers is a lyrical love letter and Jose asks me what it means. I say to him, the language is no longer that of a penfriend but one of a lover and that you two have built up images of each other as lovers, the answer to the innermost dream. What she means is love. You accept her interest and the endearments and reply in a similar way. Then you ask me what does she mean. You say 'she doesn't say she loves me, the actual words.' You're hedging and there's a little part of you that's dishonest. If you want a love relationship you must recognise the fact. If you want something slightly less you must examine your phrasing. Are you leading her on just for titillation, relying upon the fact she had not written the three specific words to provide you with an escape?

He is high-minded and innocent and in the early stages of self-knowledge. He needs to be made aware of what is happening. Both have been sharing a mutual love to which each has unevenly contributed. As we say in our know-all way, she has been taking him seriously. I guess Jose is overtaken by surprise as he gets my interpretation. He thinks up a succession of objections to my simple interpretation. I promise to help him draft a reply and ask him in the meantime to try and think exactly what he wants their relationship to be. Poor Jose, in confusion and alarm, poor Sheela who is so clearly a beautiful young soul.

Well then, back to what I was doing. Jose goes off and as if on cue from the wings another arrives — a fresh personable young man.

'You know me? I'm Liju's brother from college at Erode. I'm Siju.' He is Sojan's cousin.

'Yes, of course I remember you. We went to see you there once, and you came back with us.' He is studying for a degree in business management. Liju is the brother who is up north beyond Patna at university, and Biju works here — he is the one married to Raisa and father of the little girl.

'So, how's things?' It is the way to open a conversation. I gave it as much support as I could but found his loud voice a surprise. It has a flat harsh sound and would need no amplifiers on any political platform. I imagine him later in life delivering the annual report to shareholders. Arrival of food mercifully delivered respite, and a little later I told him I must have a midday rest. 'You take a nap,' he boomed, this Indian stentor with a herald's voice.

It was Friday, the day to revisit the ayurvedic doctor, I thought with Vinod and Nixon in the auto-rickshaw in the evening. Instead Nixon arrived about three on a borrowed Enfield. 'Are you ready, Uncle…?' It was hot and he took the full force of the burnt air as we drove the twelve kilometres. The roads made smooth travel impossible even on this well-sprung bike, otherwise it was pleasant travelling through open countryside alternating with leaf-enclosed lanes.

The doctor was away at a wedding and would not return until six. Two hours to wait. We went to Nixon's grandmother two kilometres away. The grandchildren met us at the gate — Jackson, a tall 14 year old with a head of wavy hair any brunette in the west would give half her salary to possess; two small boys and a smaller girl.

The grandmother was a big woman, badly out of shape and carefully contained by her clothes. We sat down to rest after the ride and exchanged family news. A dish of small bananas appeared. Happiness and order reigned in this congenial household and everyone loved the grandparents. We went to the rear where the grandfather was cementing. Nixon said they were building a woodshed. What I saw was a noble pavilion with four corner columns and a flat roof. It was a stoa and was extensive, with open sides. Grandfather and his brother were working — strong men with gentle faces, and they remembered me from an earlier visit. Nixon disappeared for half an hour, as he had to phone his mother about the delay in our return. I transferred to the verandah and watched the children playing. Grandmother brought me a glass of black coffee. On Nixon's return he told me we would go to visit a friend of Athuba — Athuba being still on the train. After a false trail we took another route on poorly defined roads, almost tracks and eventually came to a small settlement. He made enquiries and was directed to a large two-storey structure set in high-walled grounds. It was a residential medical college for women, and the one we were to see was Wendy. We made ourselves known at the gate and she met us. She was of similar Tibetan colouring and feature to Catherine whom we had met at the station, and of similar bright presence and humour. She invited us inside. We walked through a formal garden in the last stages of degradation; garments and cloths were spread over many of the low dead bushes to dry, cere-cloths I thought.

Wendy was joined by her friend Ranjuka. She was from Mizoram and her friend from Manipur. We entered a graceless concrete building and sat on hard chairs. It was refreshing to talk with them after the limited conversations possible with most Indian women — they had no constraints of sex and caste and were highly intelligent and strong in character. They were in the second year of their medical studies. The conversation flowed and gurgled as we were happy with one another. We learned a little about their small states away up on the north-east of the country, where each had its own language.

By this time the doctor was back — he stood outside as we turned in and I thought how handsome he looked and well turned-out in white banian and dhoti, a much better impression than on my first visit. The examination and consultation were much the same as before, that is completely unintelligible to me. My blood pressure had changed. I thought it very low but was at the fag end of a busy day. He assured me it would come up; the heart was tapping out a healthy message but the energies needed building up. He prescribed slightly different medications.

Nixon had his turn; he has a troublesome cough complaint and his BP needs watching. Darkness had arrived by the time this amiable doctor finished with us, and the air was much cooler. I was shielded from its full impact by Nixon; he complained of the cold. Night had me lost and there was little that I recognised.

On the way Nixon said 'Elephant before.' At first I could not see it but then saw the high stern with a red reflector attached to the uppermost part of its tail, it was confirming to the law. On its forehead it bore a clear reflector, again we headed for the ayurvedic pharmacy. It was interesting to watch, with the young dispensers moving about energetically, counting out pills, assembling orders and wrapping them deftly. I was desperately tired when I arrived back and was heading for the shower, my hair gritty after the ride, when Kunjumon with five of his friends arrived. I both endured and enjoyed their company but after an hour indicated that I must turn in.

Another day, and if not another dollar, another day to do what I wanted. The interruption had set me back. Once more I was to be hindered, for Jose was free on this particular morning. I told him I had not time to write the draft of the letter I had promised and detailed my interruptions. I told him that before I slept and in the watches of the night I had shaped up a few thoughts.

He told me he had a phone call from Sheela the previous evening, an STD call from 3900 kilometres away that would set her back 50 rupees. He gave a blow-by-blow account. First the voice was sweet and very beautiful, asking for Jose.

Jose replied 'I am Jose.'

Then a long pause.

'Are you there?' he asked.

She said, 'I want to speak to Jose' again.

He said he was Jose, and she laughed for ten seconds. She asked if he knew who was calling and he said yes, it is Sheela. The line was silent, then she said 'I'll call you again in five minutes.'

The connection was then cut. No second call came through.

Jose said that as he took his hand from the phone it was sweating. He still could not accept that she was in love with him and pursuing him. We went over the ground previously covered and he said he still was not sure what she meant.

'Then tell me why else she would pluck up the courage to ring you when she had never met you or heard your voice? Would you be pleased if she landed on your doorstep?'

'Oh, God, have I really made her think that I love her too? I've never actually said so. I'm not going to sell my soul for her.' He was disturbed more than before, and I was reassuring him that we would clarify it in the letter. It was an awkward affair and each was finding out more about his and her self and the self of the other. Suddenly I felt anguish for them. It was affecting me too.

QUESTIONED

In this night of surreal images and uncountable hours a restless spirit hovers like a mosquito over my pillow; it is brooding over the life that once flowed in childhood, in the home of my childhood, once so rich, now vacated and abandoned; it drags me there. The house was substantial, or so we thought, we had no gauges, and now it is modernised and others live there. The house has carried on but is no longer my childhood home.

In the obsessive way of night-thoughts it becomes imperative to have certain information, and on this occasion the focus is upon the kitchen.

'Ah,' says the Freudian, 'the soul of the home is the hearth,' That may be, but prosaically it wants to know about the bins in the pantry.

'Ah, that too can be explained, as the riches of childhood are contained in treasure chests.' Explanations are too forthcoming. The thought is ingenious and pat but an unlikely association; any way the contents of the bins helped us to grow and the sugar rot our teeth. I remember those bins, a heavy piece of furniture of four units, so balanced that when full it took a hefty pull to swing each one open. It was painted green. So much was painted green, like the long stool and the outside chairs.

This information did not satisfy the night spirit and I had to declare what the bins contained. Gradually I worked it out. There was sugar, oatmeal, flour and bread, a bin each.

'Did it have potatoes? One did, you know.'

No, vegetables were stored in the wash-house. It was better there for they smell, particularly if there is a rotten potato in the bag.

The inquisitor wants more information, first about the pantry. Half remembering, half imagining we make a tiki-tour. The pantry is long, about fifteen feet by six, so is really narrow. Straight opposite the door are the cookie jars, the best-remembered the one for peanut biscuits I always make for after school. Oh, there are so many things — stacks of dishes, cups on hooks, jugs, gravy boat, casseroles and dessert dishes, and at least a hundred jars of jam and preserved fruit, nectarine, peach, plum, and my favourite apple and blackberry. There are jars of pickled onions which an aunt calls violets on account of their effect on the breath — I do not see that as very funny. What else? Split peas, dried peas and beans, a bag of hundreds and thousands, packets of candles and matches, which were called waxed vestas, tins of pineapple, salmon, and sardines, scales (both balance and hook), tins of golden syrup and treacle, and stone jars of salted-down beans, and in a dark corner a lurid, menacing purple bottle of castor oil.

'What about the kitchen, the stove?'

It is black and shiny with Orion on the oven door, a wonderful installation when going. Oven cloth at hand, stand by as hot air rushes out with a tray of date scones. On the top of the stove my mother is making gravy, she is always making gravy. The smell of roast beef has me lingering there.

What else then? Nothing much, it is an atmosphere, not a period collection. Strips of flypaper hang from the ceiling, and Daisy Fly-killer pads lie about the place. They are marked POISON. That is all. Well? The walls are match-lined, and varnished brown, and the floor has linoleum with squares and curves. We do not polish it for that makes it slippery. Satisfied?

My parents are of no age. They are always busy, a fact of which we children are unaware. Our world is a closed one, theirs is another, and is uninteresting.

I do not want to go on about the past. A glance of tenderness, another of gratitude, should suffice. It does not do to live there, as some would have us know — the very word past indicates we have moved away. Others would say that the past is right here, contained in the present. Be that as it may, I am here with the black bolsters of night around me; it is possible to establish some facts about the bins, the pantry and the kitchen, and I have done so. All so crazy. The Visitant after all might not be witless. In his oblique way he is propelling me to consider the struggling journeys we are making through life, sometimes hand in hand, some times alone. We dawdle such a lot. I look out the window onto the daisied lawn. All too soon it needs mowing again; my father says that is my job but I hate mowing lawns. I prefer to look at the daisies, they are really so pretty.

IN THE CIRCLE & ON THE ROOF

I have a commitment to go with Chandu to a movie. He tells me it is not in the main cinema where the sound system is always switched on high. A few months ago he was hanging about a film production unit at Ernakulam where a film star, Mohan Lal was starring in a movie. This notable makes more than one movie at a time, a scene here, a scene there, and they are sorted and pieced together in the studios. Chandu has aspirations to get into the industry and he has been seeking a job — with a thousand others I suppose — as an extra. I imagine it is a matter of toadying and dancing attendance on the producers. He succeeded to the extent of a single appearance where he drives the hero up to a building on his motorbike. Among the locals such an achievement is a wonder and a matter of comment.

This is the day when the rice straw arrives; It is not easy to procure and we have made several enquiries. We have decided to spread straw on the roof of my room as the days become increasingly hot. One day when it was 32°C in my room and 35°C on the verandah I placed my small thermometer on the ground in the full sun. In seven minutes the mercury had reached 50° which is the limit for the instrument, so fearful lest the glass should break, I removed it to safer quarters. The straw has arrived; instead of buying 50 bundles at a rupee apiece which we reckoned on, we have had to settle for 25 larger bundles at three rupees apiece. My friends will come this evening and spread it for me. Meanwhile the hens are greatly attracted and are busily disintegrating the bundles in search of an overlooked grain of rice. We shoo them away.

Chandu arrives on time and we go to his house and sit in his room. His mother brings an omelet and a coffee. As the film is in Malayalam I ask Chandu to tell me the story. This is a labour, but he is keen to tell me, and I follow convoluted English. I pay close attention as I do not want to flounder in too much ignorance when we see the film. He is thorough and painstaking and soon I feel equipped with the plot. On his bed was a large old volume, one of a series, on the life of Mahatma Gandhi. I spend some time looking at photos of his boyhood, youth and early manhood. I was fascinated with his calm and beautiful face. I was surprised to find that he was 80 when he was assassinated — I had thought him to be in his late 60s. I would never have the patience to read such a many-tomed life.

To my dismay it was to the noisy cinema I had proscribed that we drove into; we went under the building to the parking lot, again I had misinterpreted Indian English. We had dress-circle seats but they held no comfort as the upholstery, faulty in the first place, had worn. I find myself incapable of sitting for long on hard surfaces, the tone of the gluteal muscles has gone, and they are no longer equal to their task.

To my further dismay the volume was excessively loud, and, since the sound producer of the film had no understanding of the usages of silence and variation in sound, I had to submit to two and a half hours of accumulating *fortissimo*, so that well before interval I was in pain.

I was grateful for the briefing Chandu had given me. The males in the film were in their 30s or 40s; none, including the star, could be called handsome. Yet the state of Kerala abounds in handsome faces. The great hero, Mohan Lal, has a face like Wallace Beery. I readily concede his presence and charisma but do not care to look at his face with the thoroughness the numerous close-ups invite. On the other hand the faces of the women were uniformly good, some were lovely and the camera several times discovered and enhanced an angle, a pose of eternal beauty. The 'character' actresses also, the confidante, the servant, the ageing mother, were convincing and full of reality. The voices were always loud and contentious. The filming had a minimum of Indian clichés — youth chases maiden round a tree or a well, that sort of thing. One silhouette by a lake had all the makings of one as two women confided in each other, but though no feature was discernible the effect was of delicacy and restraint. The climactic scene where the female lead ran from a would-be raper, followed by rescuers, up and down the floors of a building in construction was so old-hat that I was relieved when it ended, with the collapse of a floor. The next scene was doubly explicit when the lead appeared bandaged head to foot in a ward where the lights over the entrance spelled *Intensive Care*. There was no doubt about her serious condition, not a shadow of doubt. There were a few intrusions of scenery for its own sake that had no business to be included. The grounds and interiors of luxurious residences and buildings were presented with mastery and at times the screen held the rich colourings of Rembrandt paintings. Needless to say in this Malayalam film there was much footage of natural scenery, particularly of banana palms. Several fell to the raging anger of the hero who chopped off their crowns. Perhaps when trees become eligible for Oscars this photogenic plant will be considered. But the noise — against it I had no armament — just as I have no armament against chilli. I thought I could sit it out.

Some time after the interval I saw Chandu on the wide screen sweeping up to a grand building on his Hero Honda with Mohan Lal on the pillion. The great man dismounted and Chandu swept away as gracefully as he came. It was his moment and we laughed in delight. We agreed that the shot was a little blurred. For Chandu's sake I sat out the rest of the film, finally staggering away with the exhaustion that follows pain. I am not given to vows and absolutes but am near to a decision that I shall never enter that ear-tormenting hall again.

It was 9:30 when we arrived back at the house; the stack of rice straw was no longer on the ground but in place on the roof with coconut leaves placed on top for weight. My friends were sitting on the verandah: Kunjumon, Valsan, Babu, Nandakumar, Vijyan, Rajendra and his cousin Kannan. Like me Sojan had been absent when the work was done. Before leaving their work they watered the straw, the correct procedure. Their voices were loud and they were all talking at once, *fortissimo*.

I thought it was my bad luck to walk out of one tormenting situation and enter another. It was not for long. I was able to quieten their lusty voices and they began to think about moving. I was truly grateful for the work they had done. Murthi told me years before that Kerala people think and work with maximum group consciousness and this was one further demonstration that this was so.

Today is another swelterer. It is 30° in my room as against 33° yesterday and it is just as hot a day outside. I am sure the straw sheathing is producing a good effect. After all, 30° without the fan is tolerable. I shall survive. As for my gluteal muscles, they need not be downcast, they gave of their best and may have the next of the week off.

TRINITY

I have been trying to measure precisely the difference between the temperature of my room and that of the sit-out. I have taken them at various times throughout the day and it varies between 3° and 3.5°. I realise I have not been taking all the factors into account; I have had windows open various amounts and when Valsan called with four others for a game of chess the door was wide open for an hour.

At 5:30 I am at it again with the thermometer in the declining heat. My conclusion is that if I were to seal my room there would be 4° difference. It has been more than 36° in the shade today. I stay outside, giving the thermometer time to react. It is truly oven-like and I look forward to a shower, but defer it until after my walk for I will only have another meltdown.

There is activity outside. A house is being built next to Laju's house and five men are unloading bricks from a ten-ton truck. The temperature they have to contend with is close to 40°; they wear lungis only. Two stand on the deck passing bricks to the three stackers, they work fast. When the bricks on one half of the truck are unloaded the driver turns it round. Before it is unloaded a second delivery of bricks arrives and has to wait in the roadstead. On the broad panel above the cabin is the word *Jesus* in large lettering. The first truck moves off and then I regret I had not looked at its panel to see what it was called. The thought taunts me but it has moved on, I shall never know.

A third truck arrives and I keep watch to see if it is equally holy. It has turned and I see it belongs to the same distinguished company. It bears in ornate lettering the name *St Jos*, so both are of the same household. The springs are down and on the uneven ground it lurches dangerously. Sojan told me the actual load would be fourteen tons.

Pictorial religion comes often into the Indian workplace, unlike our country where we are shy and private about our religious adherence, and it comes with tolerance. Vinod's auto-rickshaw is decked out in Catholic art and possesses a small crucifix. Its owner acquired it fairly recently and though he and Vinod are Hindu they have not changed the décor in honour of their own tutelary deity. Besides the Christian gods might be offended.

I take a stroll for the last half-hour of daylight and am more conscious than usual that all is leaves and trunks, leaves and trunks. The tall slender *areca* palms bound to such a height for so small a crown. I am dreaming. I think there is no way I will find out the name of this first truck; this member of the Trinity will have to remain anonymous. Could it be *Mary* or perhaps *St Thomas*, their very own apostle? But there are too many letters for the panel; yet they could contract it to *St Thom*. The shadows which had been crowding the wings have now all come out and joined hands.

To my surprise the men were still unloading bricks, the fourth load. Could this be the original truck? It was facing the other way. Sojan, on the verandah, whose eyes are sharp would be able to read it when it turned to go — it was almost emptied — but he was on the point of leaving. There was only one thing for it; I slipped on my chappals and went over to the exit path and walked about. I did not have to wait long. The truck swung around and came towards me. I could easily make out the florid printing. It was *Paul*. Our family was complete.

St Paul, who was obsessed with sin, the man who had a thorn in his flesh, and who wrote a marvellous letter about love to his friends in Corinth. I had been down the stone well where he was imprisoned in Rome — there was a little trickle of water running into a channel, and very little room where he could lie and I also saw the cave where he stayed while he was in Malta. It held a small vase of soleil d'or jonquils, and the scent pervaded. Outside, very near, was the deep blue green Mediterranean.

I walked about in the dark, lingering, loath to go inside, thinking about St Paul, his staunchness. He was impervious to vicissitude; a mighty idea had rendered him dauntless.

VIVAT NIXON

Kunjumon said something about Nixon. I caught the name in the flow of Malayalam. He then repeated in English that Nixon was in hospital. He had the news from Shelton. He was in the hospital where his sister worked. I was alarmed but not surprised for he called the evening before and could hardly speak, for his sinuses were blocked. He had nasal drops which he had been using before work but was not able to continue doing so during the day. As a travelling salesman he was always in a hot breeze, which he said affected him. The ayurvedic medication had not yet had time to work. This news I received late on Thursday. I would be able to visit him the following day. The next day Sojan and I decided to visit straight after lunch — he had to go out in the morning and would return at midday. I washed out some T-shirts and a few things, but not without protest from him and his mother who thought I should not do any work. I was just settling down to read when I heard an auto. It was Vinod who had come to tell us the news, not knowing we already knew. He wanted to take me there and then and I thought it a good idea, which would save Sojan taking me later.

On the way he told me he was not seriously ill — that was good to hear — but as Vinod had no command of English I could gather no more. When I asked which hospital he was in he said 'Okay, Uncle.' When we entered the room he was sitting on the bed. He looked much better than the last time I saw him, two days previously, so I knew he must be over the worst. He had been admitted in the middle of the night as he was struggling for breath, a frightening experience. He had an injection as soon as he arrived, followed by medication. He was sitting, waiting there for the doctor on his rounds, and expected to be discharged that day, even though his head was still aching and stuffy.

Vinod took me to see a friend a few room away. He had been run over by a jeep while riding a motorbike. His thigh was bandaged and a metal contraption was showing. It looked like a clamp with a screw. He explained that the thigh-bone was not broken but split. He was not in pain. It was unfortunate for he had just received his notice to join the police force and begin training. He did not lose his great chance, however, as his call-up was deferred for six months.

Back in Nixon's room we weighed ourselves on the scales there, and the surprise was that Vinod who is six foot tall weighed only 52 kilos, two fewer than I. I knew I had gone down in weight for flaps were hanging on my arms; I should be nearer to 60.

We left at twelve and on the way back called in at Chandran's house where the auto belongs. His was a goldsmith family and four men sat working on the sit-out. We went inside and roused Chandran who had been sleeping. Brothers appeared from all directions. One I kept looking at, his classic features and liquid eyes were altogether too perfect. He was robust, however, and curious about me. Another brother asks about this brother's hair: 'What about his hair, Uncle, is it like Michael Jackson? 'It was a bit, I told them, it was a fraction better — they had their enthusiasms and models. His name was Haresh.

Back at the house *St Jos* was just departing after bringing another load of bricks. It is hotter than yesterday but a breeze is starting up high in the trees, soon it should come down to our level, I invoke it, to do so.

IT IS COOLER IN KERALA

As I took my walk Uncle who usually ignores me caught up and began talking. It had been six months since he last spoke, and I was glad as the animosity of his household had gone on too long. He asked me how far I usually walked. I said, that depends how I feel and how much shade is about. How many kilometres, he persisted. I gave him a precise answer as that was what he wanted. He has a style of speaking, quite characteristic. 'For instance...' he begins as if there has been a preceding conversation whereas there has been nothing of the sort. Whenever he speaks to me he expounds and lectures.

He now tells me how the two months March and April are the hottest, but I must not suppose the climate in India is uniform. In the north it gets to be a great heat but we in Kerala have the benefit of the equator which passes through Trivandrum, and this keeps the heat down.

It is true that temperatures in the north attain fiery heights far higher than here in the south, but his explanation is novel. Trivandrum is not on the equator, I knew that and upon my return from the walk, checked it on the map and found it lies north of the eighth parallel. Kerala is coastal and rises from sandy shores to the moist western ghats which form its boundary with Tamil Nadu. Because of the long season of monsoonal rains it is heavily forested — all these factors have a bearing on the climate. Those parts of Tamil Nadu on the same parallel are hotter being farther inland and somewhat arid.

When I first came for short stays with Sojan three years ago I met Uncle. He is in his 60s, usually bare-chested and forever working on his property. He is bald with a shiny brown nut of a head which I often see bent over a small fire as he crouches and feeds it. He is of medium build with fine and firm musculature. His wife whom everyone calls Auntie is the sister of Sojan's father who died when he was three. They have a good, well-treed property next door and his son, Saju, and wife, Pele, live with them. There is also an elfin little boy Akhil who is three. Sojan's mother had spent her widowhood in a small half-built house and I guess had been supported in many ways by the well-off and intact family next door, as well as members of her own family. A small flourmill to which people from around bring their rice to be ground, has yielded a meagre livelihood. The constant trickle of customers has been the means whereby I have met several young people, among whom are Jaison, Jayaprakash and Praveen. I would be on the sit-out reading when they called with their bags of rice and while they waited we chatted, trying to hear each other above the pounding of the mill.

I had three visits to this place, each lasting a month before coming to live more or less permanently. At first Uncle would tell me at length his difficulties with the pension authorities. I could not follow his exposition but could see how important money was to him, even though he has substantial investments. Auntie had no English so we could not speak but we exchanged guarded nods and smiles. She is a solidly built woman with dark heavy features and she moves majestically.

Each time I visited Sojan and his mother I was able to effect some improvement in the house; the well had to be deepened and a well-head built; the floor of the house, of unsmoothed concrete, had to be completed with shiny black finish. When I came to stay more permanently the mutual nodding with my neighbours tapered off. I did not mind as in any case they had not come into my life. Mini, the new wife had arrived. The place had to have water laid on and a pump for this purpose; a tank had to be built on the roof.

I did not notice any distancing of our relationship until Mini indicated one day that they were 'jealousy' of Sojan and his family. I was astounded as I would have expected their approval, if not pleasure, at the arrival of some basic amenities. It was a puzzle to me as they had infinitely greater possessions. I figured out that Sojan's mother was becoming less dependent upon her erstwhile benefactors. No longer did she have to borrow their electric iron, or draw from their well when hers ran dry. The role of poor relation was eroded, and because of this, I thought, Auntie and Uncle were angry.

This came to a head when my room was being built. In the approved plan there was provision for a toilet and shower room on the outside wall. I heard much argument and commotion and by degrees learned that Uncle had forbidden the building of this facility jutting from the outside wall. When Sojan told me I laughed, for the matter had nothing whatsoever to do with the next-door property. Regulations had been complied with, and the toilet would have been on the diagonal, 30 feet distant from the neighbouring house. In any case Sojan's house was set further back from the lane so that his house front was in line with that of the rear of the other house. Moreover a substantial coconut palm with a thick mantle of pepper vine stood in the line of sight of the proposed toilet. I found it incredible that objection should be raised. It was a demonstration of malice in action.

The voices were angry and vehement night and day. In the end the modest en-suite was transferred inside the new room, considerably reducing its area. They had prevailed, though Sojan maintained that this was a temporary move to be rectified at a more propitious time. I could not follow his reasoning. There was nothing else for it, I had to accept the defeat with as good grace as I could muster. This victory of Uncle and Auntie did not reduce the ill-will and one-way criticism, but I was well shielded from Auntie's voice by the fact I could not understand her native tongue. Gradually my sense of injustice and interference subsided, yet each time that some new item for the household arrived Auntie would raise her voice. She could not endure the acquisition of electric fans, and an electric mixer. When the painter of the new room had finished, he was painting the four folding chairs the same bone colour, out in front. Auntie stood watching in disapproval and spoke to the painter, to ask the cost of the paint.

A second climax was reached the evening when the refrigerator arrived. We decided to have a small celebration and to that end a few of Sojan's friends were invited. A table and chairs were set outside and pappadums, nuts and chips placed on the table with the drinks soft and hard. Soon dishes of beef and chicken followed. I heard a flat voice of continuing flow from afar. It was a lamentation which became more and more noticeable and cut into the flow of conversation. It was the voice of our amazing neighbour who stood formidably and menacingly like Cassandra on the boundary, with folded arms and majestic defiant stance. It was a denouncement, a magnificent flow of rhetoric which continued for half an hour. Not pots of acid but living thunderbolts were hurled. At one stage Sojan answered back. She had demanded to be told if this was a bar and had we a licence. Sojan answered that we had just been to get one. He would have continued but his friends restrained him from such a fruitless engagement. I knew later that she had said shameful things which no woman of good feeling would ever utter.

I could not be angry, as the poor simple woman in her jealousy and rage was reacting primitively. She did not know how to rearrange her world, and her outlook was affronted by the changes. The advent of the saip had blasted her little world apart.

Sojan and Mini explained to me how petty and jealous villagers could be and that I so far had seen kindliness and neighbourliness. The contents of their mental world are few and far between and the tittle-tattle of mutual observation is the major source in its furnishing. Somehow I can only admire Auntie's lack of dissimulation; she has not reached the stage where she can recognise jealousy and therefore had no thought to conceal its demeaning symptoms. She has no repressions, is utterly forthright and in her own way is a force of nature. By projection and extrapolation one can began to understand the field in which demagogues can flourish, at times this is all too evident in the east. It can be frightening.

Uncle, much more intelligent, had played a supportive role. His stubborn and resentful opposition had a more tangible target, that of resisting the toilet unit, while his wife had been tilting at insubstantial windmills; whatever the conflict and whatever the odds her guns would go on blazing.

I could see no way to repair this situation. Sojan's mother and Mini had played no part in this altercation hence there was no difficulty in their visiting Auntie's household as before in order to watch television or listen to the radio. I learned to endure my ostracism, as I had offended deeply. It was no great matter for me, who had lived in cities and known their impersonality. I could look in their direction and smile and their blank look would never meet mine. After all I did not know them and had never set foot in their house. They were strangers.

But today Uncle spoke to me and revealed that the equator makes it cooler in Kerala; but today, to the contrary, I had detected a slight degree of warmth and felt good about it.

BRIEF ENCOUNTERS

Nixon was well again. He called and we went into town, he wanted me to have a change of scene. We went again to the lawn restaurant of Luciya Palace, as good a place as any, though Nehru Gardens would please as well, but I believe that the gates shut at nightfall. I must find out.

He feels well after the hospital treatment, but is tired, as he worked hard the following days. This is the month of March when the books closed, it is the last chance in the year to boost figures. Today he worked hard also, the sprint must be maintained.

We missed the company of Athuba and were hoping for a message any time though he would be frantically busy for a while, settling into his new office as superintendent, and with his wife, seeking a house to live in. We would have to exercise patience. His absence was a little death.

It is the end of Ramzan, what I knew of in Indonesia as Ramadan, and I looked at the new moon among the palm leaves. It is tiny, the smallest I have ever seen as though through the wrong end of a telescope. For a moment I invested it with loneliness, certainly it looked wan and remote. The Muslims will now be able to eat in daylight, Ramzan has been of 50 days duration, whereas in other countries I have been it is ten days shorter.

On leaving we ran into Roy and Suresh and for the first time I remembered the name of Suresh. He is a pleasant happy man whereas Roy remains under siege to some secret melancholy; in his late 20s his days are clouded. I caught his face at an angle which revealed how he would look in his old age, bleak and gaunt.

We wandered on. Nixon had in mind to meet his student friends who usually ganged up at a certain place of an evening. He maintained they were keen to see me again, but I had another opinion, that I was boring and had lost any novelty for them. For I had been bored with them as they peppered me with questions as though I were answerable to them for all things in my life. I had to give and defend all opinions on the questions propounded. I saw no merit being present at an autopsy on my life. Why should I endure this? Their approval or rejection had no bearing on any purpose of mine and I wished to deny myself such a gratuitous ordeal. Friendships are made in more informal ways, unexpected ways, and with no onus to befriend, entertain or become acquainted. The last thing I want is celebrity status and the second last to show myself as canvassing such a spurious classification.

We did not find them and then I felt I had been churlish and should not blow such things up. I was like a needle on a dial that fluctuates wildly for a moment before settling down to a true reading. How can I ever give a true reading when feelings and mind persist in moving? For me a steady reading is a goal, an ideal. We wandered a little further and then decided to pick up an auto and return home.

The following morning Jayaprakash visited. I had not seen him for all of two months and knew he was deep into his studies. Mid-April is the beginning of examinations and in the student world every thing focuses on that time. The day before I had been thinking of him and today he appears. This sort of thing happens so often, not only with me but with others, for are we not all in a minor way psychics?

What a serene and gentle youth he is — his quality and quietness pervade as he sits there with me. He is still working on his project which requires him to make regular visits out of town to an engineering works, and his work is shaping up well.

He asked me had I heard about the elephant that had been killed yesterday; he had passed the place where this had happened but was on a bus so could not get down and have a look. It was at Wadakkancherry and that was four or five kilometres further on from our ayurvedic doctor's village. It was not at the railway crossing where we waited while on our last visit but the next crossing on. These gates are operated automatically.

There had been the usual queue of buses and other traffic which everyone finds so irksome. So I can understand how those waiting felt. The mahouts knew the district well and they must have known that two trains would be passing within ten minutes of each other. They also knew of another place a hundred metres down the track where they could cross, so they and the elephant made their way there. As soon as the Bangalore train had passed they would cross.

There were two mahouts, one of whom, Balan, sat on the neck of the elephant, and the other, Ramakrishnan walked alongside with his guiding pole. Out of the blue the Alappuzha Bokaro Express appeared and was immediately upon them, just as the elephant had stepped onto the track. It stood motionless as if stunned. Balan tried to urge it forward while Ramakrishnan was prodding it to reverse. The train struck it full on, tearing three feet of its side apart and knocking it over. Poor Balan was thrown clear, but he had also been struck. The train carried on another kilometre before stopping with a jerk which startled the passengers. Had the driver applied the brakes immediately on impact carriages would have derailed and passengers been injured. The body of the elephant had become entangled in the engine as it was borne along and it was mangled hideously, parts of its flesh, tusks and trunk were scattered along the track. There was a photo in the newspaper the next day showing workers pulling ropes attached to the body and others levering the carcase with poles, easing it off the track.

One could see the great gash in its side and the cascading entrails. Balan was rushed to a near-by private hospital but died of his injuries soon after. Ramakrishnan, though involved, had never been in danger.

I looked long at the photo. Beyond the track was a plantation of young banana palms. Passengers stood around watching. The elephant was twelve years old and bore the name Gopalankutty, and Balan was 34. That was the scene; a wide white sky rode high above and it was nine o'clock in the morning.

PINNED

Nandakumar and I played two games of chess which I won but did not deserve to for I played quickly, not prepared to settle down and study the positions. We are roughly equal and there is an easy rivalry; he has such a sunny chuckling nature that win or lose he laughs for the whole thing is a joke.

Then Kunjumon arrived. I was tired and did not want to play any more so they played one another. They also are equally matched. Nandakumar operates intuitively and is quick, disconcertingly so, while Kunjumon is the thinker and plodder who builds up his attack with care.

I decided to have my shower and prepare for bed, and was even then ready to put the light out and call it a day. Three others of the gang arrived; Babu had some skin gashed off his heel, it looked raw and nasty so I dressed it as best I could and then found the bandaids were old and would not stick, so we thought it better to leave the wound open to the air. I told him to take the antiseptic cream home with him.

The non-players chattered, mostly in Malayalam and I was content just to sit and enjoy the company. Their voices are loud, however, and when raised become unbearable in a small room. Kunjumon and Nandakumar were arguing a point. The issue was whether a pinned piece could deliver a check at the same time as it was pinned against the king. They asked me about it and my contention was that the pin freezes movement absolutely and the piece is deprived of its powers so it cannot function in the normal way; it is immobilised. In such a case a king could move within a rook's normal range and suffer no threat, it would be powerless to check it. I explained my point of view and said I was sure I was right. Nandakumar did not agree and shifted the pieces about in demonstration of his viewpoint, with Kunjumon loudly delivering his idea. I explained the effect of a pin several times. Nandakumar kept arguing and we were all talking at once. Voices were raised and the non-players also had something to say. It was pandemonium, like the whole pack of cards flying up into the air in Alice in Wonderland. Really Nandakumar was obtuse. It was his inability to hear me out that got me rattled and I told him he was being dense and stupid — it sounds bad on paper but was only one small voice among many that constituted the din. In the end we suddenly stopped. Nandakumar was smiling away as usual as he returned the pieces to the box. I was glad when they went, for the sake of quiet and also for the ignoble reason that for the moment I detested him and his voice yet possibly he was the one I was closest to, together with Kunjumon.

I went to bed in this disgraceful state of mind. I know I was rattled and angry. The point of issue was not what worried me — it could be settled when we manage to find a book of rules — but the fact that I had lost my calm, in that I was very much in the wrong. What in my nature made me react in this way? Anger is a removal of the mind from conflict and being a mindless state justifies the old saying that it is temporary madness. It is many more things and they are all regressive states. I find it hard to think in abstracts any time and decided that falling asleep time is quite the wrong time to work out the philosophy of anger. So I dismissed the subject — it must not be allowed to surface the way it had.

I found a way to do this by switching to the thought of conflicts, a much more amenable subject to ponder. I hate them and have had many in my life, but they are part of the air we breathe, and reluctantly I recognise that it is the only means by which we can reach harmony and equilibrium. In fact it is the way through which we can get to know each other and without it we would never have evolved. We hate it because it brings tension, but, when we have worked through it, strangely we find we have a better understanding of ourselves and a better grip on things.

The following evening Nandakumar was on the doorstep, bright as ever. I told him of my introspections and contrite mood and he laughed and went to my cupboard where the chess set is kept. He is a stunning friend.

A TIME TO DREAM

I am not given to planning for old age and should not think about it; I allow no high-rising dread to block out the light, nor any foreboding to have me packing and planning for an insurance-protected pension-sustained haven where I could sit all day and wait for Godot.

Some perversity has discouraged me from living prudently. On the other hand I have not been reckless, indeed, necessity has held the whip for most of my days, but when at last I was free I travelled, for strong as a homing instinct, was an urge to see England. At length I saw it and loved it and found it alien! I had a hard lesson to learn. The magnet that drew me belonged to an interior England, an England of values, literature and dreams, and I had confused this with the physical reality. The distinction is crucial. Now I have it clear, that though I would like to see England again, I have no obsession.

The thought of England brings an image of cosiness, and suddenly I feel a desire for a place of my own, I allow myself a fantasy. I am being disloyal, I know, towards the monitor in my nature, for I know it is not to be, but for once, just the once, I want to set down a few notes about this dream place. I have to be brief, and have only time to tip it out on the page, but no longer, for the monitor will foreclose and bring me back to earth, he wants me there and not in any fancy place which leads to regression.

I want a cottage. It must be in some secluded and slightly unusual place, close to nature, so that I must watch my step lest I stand barefoot on clover. It must have some notable feature, mountain stream or sea, with sky and distance in abundance so that their austere communications may descend; and there must be a chance to own or make a garden, well protected, and stocked with plants for which I have affinity. I have had my time chasing horticultural exotica and now revert to simple plants without pretension. I want no breeder's *tour de force*. My garden would be a jungle with a minimum of order, and enough access to get through, with twists and vistas that surprise, and garden seats waiting in nooks out of the wind. There would be rocks and stones as honoured guests; and a couple of terracotta pots as though forgotten near the back door. But I do not go into details for dreams deal only in impressions. I think of it as all there with plants I love in place. I want a hedge of *abelia*, not the variegated form which is miffy, for its elegance and elusive fragrance; and honeysuckle for basic rural intoxication; I want a *buddleia*, the bumble-bee bush for its rough disturbing scent; an *eriostemen* would be there, for to crush its leaves is to release dreams; I would need roses, scented roses, for they convey that which is unutterable; if possible I would find a place for a *prunus*, one of the single species but never, never one of the double confections, let others drool and photograph. It will be planned to function with a minimum of attention, that goes with out saying. I would encourage a monitored wildness and allow nature scope for her exuberance and invite riotous behaviour.

I have not mentioned herbs for ailments, though more to provide pungency to food. Some will pay their keep when I tread on then or brush by and release their scent. I have the thymes and mints in mind, others like sage must bide my mood. Nor have I mentioned vegetables, I want to gaze on water drops balanced like mercury on a cabbage leaf (though I see them here on a leaf of a plant like *allocasia*, but only in the wet season); I want to gaze on the red flowers of a bean rack, a story-book colour. I would not aim to be self-supporting, but it would be nice to cosset a few rows of potatoes with selected flavours, and I would like to follow a few tomatoes from the first two leaves right up to bounteous fruition, loaded as a Christmas tree. I now mention a quirk. I want to grow horseradish, not only because providence designed it specifically to go with roast-beef [others need not know, but for me it is an ordinance], but also for the memory of witch-like Minty Arnold, an eccentric English friend who regularly supplied me with horseradish sauce. Her maiden name, need it be said, was Lamb. Allow me.

What do I really want from this garden? I want the unexacting companionship of plants, many of which have befriended my ancestors and all of which have given delight and solace. I want to see healthy leaves as well as the bloom. I want scent above all. The sense of smell is mysterious and scent gets to me deeper than form or colour. The clean eager colours of sweet-peas for instance delight me as nothing else in this world, but ah! their scent ravishes me.

Of daphne, I am in two minds, it disturbs me, and as a poet friend told me, is a symbol of unholy enchantment — how right he was; of lilac whose scent has power to tip the scales, I have no misgivings; and if I could get a plant of *boronia* to flourish, I would risk death from excess inhalation. I would not overlook scented geraniums, and I would allow wallflowers to seed every where, especially in limy places. Wherever I have been I have longed for their scent and their tawny, poorly-designed flowers. Oh yes, give me, give me wall-flowers! I want some grasses for specimens too, and there must be shivery grass.

Is the dreams complete? It will do, though no thought has been given to the cottage, outside or inside. This does not bother me for I accept what comes, except there must be no latticed windows. I can make whatever offers yield delight, even through Ruthless Measures, but generally I would go along with what is there.

That is the dream. The reality is that I am far from the subtleties of a cool climate and the flora grew up with. I find delight in other subtleties and other forms. Today I sit like a dish in a slow oven, but it will cool, for night is dependable and will turn it down when it comes. I am content, and, beyond any understanding and desert, am wallowing in contentment. Is not that enough? I think so. Now is greater than forever, for it is in possession.

I must leave this garden; it is not too much of a wrench, as I feel that in time its cosiness would pall. I am not the only one to relinquish a cherished garden, for did not our first parents, who had a fabulous place, find that in the end they had to move on? Their circumstances were different and times have changed, but they did set a precedent, and came out of it, as far as I know, reasonably well.

CATHERINE, PIGS
& A TRANSFORMING TOUCH

The sun stretches its strong thighs to put its stamp upon yet another day; already its vigour and strength have touched the life below so that crowding trees and plants reach up in response, while the forms of life endowed with mobility crawl, walk, cycle or fly in the new light — all except the ruminants which bow, maybe in reverence to the scrubby pastures which afford them sustenance. Only the weak things of earth cower and seek to evade so rude a touch, as they make for holes, crevices, pools, or places where only light that is divested of heat can penetrate.

Among such am I, so mindful of the leaf-laden shade-gathering boughs that my progress, though defined by lanes and tracks, is nevertheless erratic as I follow the shade and puzzle the observer. I have come to respond to pools of shade automatically as a navigator responds to dials and signals. I enjoy my walk.

Later though, I must brace myself and walk where nothing can shield me from the sun as it turns its hot hydrants upon the earth; even though I carry an umbrella the heat will rush through. Nixon and I have motor-cycled six kilometres the other side of Trichur making the ride twelve from base. He suffers from the hot air we push through, while I am largely protected by his body. We come to Mannuthy where the veterinary college is sited; we have come to see Catherine and Jessy. The college, which in the map of our minds is a pinpoint, now expands to a widespread campus of over five hundred hectares with its own network of roads leading to buildings, farms, hospitals, library and various headquarters of other disciplines. Fortunately the administration building is readily identifiable and Nixon enters to make enquires. We go to a series of buildings by bike in search of our friends. Finally we locate Catherine; she is in the library and I wait ten minutes while Nixon goes to fetch her. He reappears with Catherine.

How like Athuba she is with the same direct manner and open gaze and Tibetan looks. Immediately she plunges into our day as though she belonged there all along. What is the word which would describe her best? She is so real and practical. She asks would I care to see the library, saying that it is not large. I readily agree. What I noticed immediately on entering were the signs for silence just like the libraries of my youth when even a whisper came under interdiction. The building was modern and spacious with a mezzanine in the main body of the library. The stacks were metal and modern and I noticed the large number of scientific magazines and papers.

In spite of Catherine's apologetic remark about the size of the library I thought the stock considerable, given that it was to service a college, not a whole university. We walked through the rows of separate tables where students male and female were in contemplation deep over tomes, writing pads and notebooks. I was an intruder stumbling upon an arcanum, where light and knowledge poured down into young receptive minds.

We had at least two hours at our disposal and could not hope to explore the many farms. As it was we walked long distances, past the poultry farm and the rabbitry and headed for the piggery, for Catherine thought we would prefer to see the pigs.

The main road leading into this zone was lined with jackfruit trees. I was struck how strong and tall they grow with their knobbly, awesome, bomb-like fruit attached directly to the trunk itself. Something stirred in my memory. Did not these trees belong to the same family as the stinging nettles, the urticaria? What a family with such odd and ranging talents Sojan's mother gives me some segments of jack fruit from time to time. They have a slightly fetid smell not unlike the durian of Malaysia. Once I overcome this I find the taste more rewarding, but by no means delectable. Nixon says this fruit is not good for the stomach, Sojan says it is heating.

I know this college was established well after the demise of the British régime, probably 20 to 30 years ago. It is a point I meant to ask about. What prompted my speculation was the amount of building construction still under way. On one side of this jackfruit avenue was an area of four or five acres where work was going on; and, as the piggery buildings were adjacent, I assumed this was to be an extension. We came to the main gate which led to a maze of paths, sties, low walls and sides, otherwise it was open and covered by two enormous roofs.

The smell was foul and pervasive though the place was clean and well-maintained. We saw only two breeds of pig which surprised me, so used to various breeds at our agricultural and pastoral shows. The main breed was the White Yorkshire which adapts well to Indian conditions. The other breed is the small, somewhat stumpy black Indian pig whose shiny piglets are ever so cute. Research work is being undertaken in crossing these breeds with the purpose of combining the merits of both. Nixon was over-awed. Many urban people never see a pig in the course of their lives unless they visit one of the few zoos. He was fascinated.

Each pen has an iron piping about two feet from the wall and eight inches above the floor where the piglets can huddle in safety from the crushing bulk of their dam. I could see little variation among the pigs in the dozens of pens we examined but each was documented and the subject of experiment and research. Catherine's field is medical, it was in medicine that she gained her doctorate; but the constant walking and gazing as well as the heat did not provide the proper occasion for asking about the nature of her work. My energies were concentrated on stumbling up or down the occasional steps, or the more uneven ground of the paths, and on keeping body and soul together in the midday furnace.

We made our way to the 'Ladies Hostel' where we met Jessy, so pretty in a diaphanous pink sari. Her feminine ways contrasted with Catherine's no-nonsense directness which had naught to do in the glamour stakes. Her beauty was strong and lay as much in her character. We sat in an open entrance hall on badly upholstered couches. Catherine produced a dish of oranges which she delicately peeled for us, and a jug of chilled water.

Nixon did most of the talking and Athuba provided most of the subject matter. He had just received a letter from him written a day or so after his arrival at Dimapur in Nagaland.

A third friend arrived. She was Catherine's room-mate, tall, thin and lovely in a glowing white sari. I did not get her name and would like to see more of her. In the final period when we were standing about to leave, she and I were to one side and she asked many thoughtful questions, which revealed as much of her nature and mind as I guess my more explicit answers did of mine.

Catherine told us there were many breeds of rabbits and we must see them next time — there was much research in this field for their meat potential as well as their fur. Among the breeds was a specimen of New Zealand White, this is the name they give to it. We agreed this visit must be considered but introductory, for there are many farms to see.

A large framed and faded photograph of a woman was on the wall behind us, I gave it no attention, thinking it to be of the founding principal. On a change of angle where the glazing did not shine I saw that it was of Indira Gandhi. Thinking later about this I concluded that the college was built during her heyday. As we rode back in the blaze Nixon told me that next visit we would arrive early. I thought, even so, me would be returning in the heat.

I cannot say I learned much, for a superficial survey will not implant the learning that the students in the library are acquiring so arduously but I did get an insight into the sheer number of workers who are toiling, teaching and researching in this field. Allowing for all manner of wastage and misapplication of discoveries the people of India are being steadily enriched in knowledge and expertise. The land that is India may appear to lie exhausted and effete under a stupefying sun, or pullulating in the steamy monsoon, but there is plenty of intellectual activity, and the rewards when they come will not be a trickle but a spate, for India's potential is yet to be realised. They are not to be measured by an outsider's discomfort or the degrees registered by his thermometer.

One place which I would like to visit, much more than a College of Veterinary and Animal Studies, would be an agricultural college, much closer to my interests. Techniques with plants and crops which have proved so successful in my country are not necessarily so relevant here.

A surprising and pleasant change of direction is taking place, an event which will change the face of India. India has suddenly found she has many things in common with Israel and Israel has the same awareness. They are teaming up, as they can do many things together. They have found an ease in communication, with common knowledge of English, and legal and administration systems not too dissimilar, as well as trading systems like those obtaining in Europe. Compared with China, India can be penetrated much more easily. Hence Israel sees in India an enormous market for her wares and also as a possible partner with India in marketing her produce in the world markets.

Be this as it may, by far the largest and most dramatic turn of events lies in the field of agriculture. Where Israeli aid and expertise are already being applied; the expertise that has transformed Palestine's arid land into a fertile zone is being applied by Israeli entrepreneurs to the desert of Rajasthan. Israel leads the world in the field of water-management and aquifer control in arid zones. The benign partnership will help green Rajasthan and show the way for new approaches to old problems.

In a related field, Israeli is making competitive bids to install desalination plants for regions such as Madras. India, of course, has her own expertise in this field. This is the Israel we like to hear about, managing resources, greening the waste places so that the hills clap their hands. India can be transformed, she knows it, and Israel will show some of the ways. Is this not good news?

EMPTY SECTION

Late this afternoon Sojan left me at a place in Viyyur while he went off to buy kerosene. There were houses all about, but this property of about a quarter acre had only a couple of brick sheds. It contained an astonishing sight: two elephants, the nearest one so gigantic that I stood in complete awe.

They were temple elephants and the property was temple property. Sojan was given the nod by an old man in the yard that it would be in order for me to wait there. Besides the old man there was another old man, the master mahout, Balan, and two young men. I was offered a seat on the side of a square concrete trough.

The elephant's back foot was chained to a tree, long since dead, and it was surrounded by vegetable rubble, mostly half-rotted chunks of palm trunks. The other elephant at the bottom of the property was smaller, I gave my attention entirely to the larger one before me.

It stood there swaying rhythmically, its trunk ceaselessly combing the rubbish or picking up a switch for a half-hearted flagellation. The great ears were also in continuous motion; they are too large and specialised to be called fans, but the alternative word with Miltonic flavour, vans, is too archaic for us to use. What shall we call them?

The first old man sat beside me and asked a few questions. He told me about this larger elephant. It was 75 years old and would live to be 120. It had no teeth so they supplemented its intake of a few leaves and banana-palm pulp with rice and jaggery.

One of the young men carried three loads of palm leaves to throw in front of the further elephant. The other produced two vessels, one as large as a cauldron. Each contained rice and jaggery. He added three buckets of water and then began kneading the contents with his hand. Evidently the rice was lumpy, or more likely, the jaggery, for he did this for a quarter of an hour. The other young man joined him and worked on the contents of the smaller pot. They carried the heavy vessels and placed them before the elephant, too far away I thought, but I had not reckoned on the great reach of the trunk. Though watching I was not clear how the bulk of the food was sucked up through the trunk, for the elephant scooped up only two or three helpings to swing into its mouth. Yet the vessels were empty.

The smaller elephant does not have to be fed in this way. The old man asked me had I heard of the accident on the railway-line, and I knew he referred to the elephant and mahout who were killed. That elephant, he said, belonged here where their mahouts worked. I asked about the surviving mahout Ramakrishnan. He told me he had gone into hiding from the police. I was puzzled at this but was told he caused the accident. I had given no thought to this aspect of the tragedy, all my attention had gone to the tragedy itself. Yet it was true that the mahout had broken the law. I learned that the true name of the man who had been killed was Balankutty, not Balan.

Sojan returned to watch with me. The young man had slashed the trunks of banana palm which he tossed to the elephant. His trunk ranged over the offering until he found the piece which met his approval. He put his great foot down to crush half the thickness and separate it, then lifted it to his mouth. This fibre did not have to be chewed.

Sojan told me later that the value of the old elephant was five lakhs, and I worked it out in our currency to be about 30,000 dollars. I gave it one last look and noticed the great hollows either side of the eyes. The eyes themselves were half hidden. I supposed they were relatively small to avoid damage during their main occupation of tearing down branches. Darwin would know.

Granted they are noble, magnificent beasts, but they are disturbing, for they place us among the Lilliputians, and all our ways and habitations are tiny and quaint, picturesque but slightly ridiculous.

FAD

When it comes to a matter of one's own ailments there is an alertness for remedies, and when success follows their application they have lifetime advocates who are aglow with missionary zeal. Not for them the caution of the true physician, but a blind health-giving faith that can remove tumours. It has ever been so and the contributions of the mind in effecting a cure remain unknown and unassessable to this day.

Many wonder remedies have appeared from time to time. Once it was yoghurt for longevity and a host of ailments; then cider vinegar, yeast or garlic, ginseng or celery; they have not had their day, I am not going to claim that, for they have large followings and the considerable support of evidence. Further, one might generalise and suggest that since these are natural products their concentrations are not dangerous — it is a poor debater who does not stick his neck out. My feelings lie very much in favour of all these wonders and I would use them merrily if someone would undertake to assemble them and keep me supplied — I might be excused the yeast and cider vinegar, for they have already had a turn.

My news is that a new wonder drug has been announced, it has surfaced here in India, its credentials are high, it is readily available, and, among many other accomplishments, it can reduce the amount of cholesterol in the blood mainly by checking its flow from the gut.

This is heigh-ho and bully for me, for I have grave suspicions from my reading of superficial articles in magazines that I have too many platelets in my system, and of course, too much cholesterol.

I have gone so far without mentioning its name — inadvertently, I have no design to delay — the wonder drug is turmeric, the yellow-red powder we use in curries, from small roots of a plant much like ginger which I first saw growing in Malayattur. Scientists have turned their attention to this herb and are discovering its many therapeutic properties. The list is impressive and long. I shall name a few, confessing that my information is from an article in the *Indian Express* by Ramadasan Kuttan. It is anti-inflammatory and said to be as good as aspirin. It can inhibit the growth of the fungus — a real bad one — *aspergillus parasiticus*, which causes diseases such as liver cancer; it can inhibit the progress of liver fibrosis caused by alcohol; I mentioned the cholesterol, so much a factor in heart diseases; it kills parasites inside and outside the body and protects the coconut trees from white ants; it is found to inhibit the growth of cells produced by carcinogenic chemicals. My list ends here for I do not like the sound of the diseases I have omitted.

The fact is that turmeric is claimed to be a panacea and for those who are given to excess when into a drug, it is non-toxic in itself. I enjoy its earthy flavour, halfway between pepper and — I suppose — curry.

THEY RAISE THE ROOF

It is Sunday evening, nine o'clock. Sounds of building can still be heard from nearby as the workers prepare the boxing for the roof by the aid of lamps. The moon can help to only half of its capacity, for it is seven days to the full. The most persistent noise is the ceaseless hammering on the steel reinforcing rods as they are straightened. Tomorrow will be the big day. The bamboo poles are in place and all is ready for the pouring.

I have not felt all that excited about the owner. He is a man in his 30s with two children. I see a contentious side to his nature and a jeering note creeps in to his voice when he is arguing in Malayalam. To me he is ingratiating and given to expressing inanities.

I will be sitting on the verandah reading the paper when he arrives, and I look up and greet him. He says 'You are reading the newspaper.' I answer 'Yes.' He will then look over my shoulder and ask do I like the newspaper. I answer that I find the main papers good. He stands there thinking and then asks me what is in the news. I say I have yet to read it. He will then ask me if he is stopping me from reading and I suppose that he is, but I've got all day. It is quite a while before he goes.

Or I will be writing a letter and he asks me am I writing a letter. When I confirm that I am, he asks who am I writing to. I tell him. This interchange was fast becoming a pattern until one day I gave him a good-morning nod and reverted to the paper as though completely immersed. He waited for over five minutes before moving away. By my rudeness I have safeguarded myself from inanities and the weariness of spirit which descends whenever he appears. Many of my friends are simple people with less mental ability than this man, but they do not bore me. In fact they have an opposite effect and I take delight in the things they tell me. The injunction to suffer fools gladly is something I cannot obey. I am judgemental but do not want to be known as such. I would worry if people thought me terse or proud. But I know I have put this man down and that I will have to do better than this.

He called a few hours ago with his brother-in-law, whom he introduced. I recall his name, a triumph for me. It is Sachidananda.

I remember it because we had an Indian at our college who came from Fiji and boarded at the hostel. His name was similar. The Ananda part has the meaning of happiness. This man has quite a different manner and his English is much more comprehensible, so I was not surprised when I learned he works on a ship, an oil tanker, and he works eight months at a stretch followed by four months leave. His wife and family live in Calicut and he had come to help his brother-in-law with the pouring.

He was interesting and told me of his work as a technician. When he was told I come from New Zealand he was keen to tell me he had visited there several times and liked the country. He found it cold and mentioned the snow at Whangarei where they unloaded. I was surprised for I knew snow never falls in Whangarei, which is more or less the same latitude as Sydney. He had his wires crossed, and he began talking of the snow at Rotterdam and Turkey at the same time. I conceded it can be cold in Whangarei especially when temperatures are down and the wind is blowing.

His crew is Indian, his manager English, and the company, he said, was American, in fact a multinational. His base is in Bombay and whenever his holiday is over the company flies him back to his ship. That was the sum-total of our conservation as they had too move on. I hold hopes of meeting him again.

*

It is the next day, cloudy with promise of some relief from the sun. The work begins at nine when 30 workers appear. All is done by hand. I will not see a concrete-mixer. They start late but will work until the job is completed, whatever the work demands.

I look inside the house, it is a forest of bamboo poles, the first supporter until the hardening concrete finds its own strength. It was in Portugal where I first saw scaffolding with wooden poles and I recall my amazement at the primitive nature of their building methods. Since then I have come to appreciate their efficacy. I have seen the sea of poles in many-storeyed buildings; from knobby, crooked and feeble sticks a modern, slick, and sophisticated building emerges.

Large piles of sand and chipped granite are in front of the house, a barrel of water drawn from our well stands nearby and bags of cement arrive periodically in a three-wheeler truck. The house has a large well but as yet no power, while ours has an electric pump and a long hosepipe.

The men wear coloured lungis and white banians with coloured cloths on the head, while the women are in their saris, also wearing cloths over the head. The scene is colourful with so many moving about the site.

Now the first of the cement is mixed and a relay forms from the ground to the roof. There are ten in the relay, maybe more as I could not see beyond the edge of the roof. The cement is mixed with the multi-use manvetti and the pile of wok-like dishes, or chatties is filled. As each is filled it is lofted and I was amazed at the speed with which it floated to the ladder and levitated over the four heads of those on the ladder and onto the roof; chatty followed chatty, I saw fifteen empties returned to the pile of cement and just managed to count them before they were drawn into service again. The clouds dispersed and the air boiled, but the flow of chatties never stopped. Looking so as to mask all but the chatties from my view they sailed up miraculously. Looking on the workers was like watching eurythmics. In succession the relay members bent low then hoisted high. All was vigour and efficiency. It was shades of the relay games in our school days.

The day grew intensely hot and I made for my room where I spent most of the day. From time to time I watched the workers, who never flagged. They were like the pictured pyramid builders I saw as a child in H G Well's *Outline of History*. We must not forget that great constructions like dams are still being built in many parts of the world with a maximum use of labour.

They left, most of them, about 5:30, and I noticed each of the women carrying a pile of chatties on her head. So here where there are few modern tools the workers bring their own. A few workers remained to clean up and complete the operation.

Before darkness fell they were all gone. Most went on foot, a few on bicycle and motor-cycle. The animated scene had changed to stillness and isolation as night folded in on it. It would remain so for fifteen days while the concrete hardened.

A few days later I went inside the empty building. I was looking for a piece of thin wire to clear a blocked tap. It was eerie among the poles. They were not all the same length and were packed with two or more layers of bricks or wedges of wood. Some were bowed to an extent I would have thought ruled them out for use. The bulk were reasonably vertical but some were as much as two feet out of perpendicular. Say they gave way and the roof fell! We are aware of such possibilities as we follow the course of construction and illogically feel safer once the props are removed.

That evening I smiled my greeting as the owner passed. He asked me what I thought of the Kerala summer. I said it was muggy. He said Kerala had the best climate in the world. I said it was cooler in Bangalore and asked if it could rain. He said he thought so in a day of two. It was five months since we had rain and the wells were getting low.

I awoke in the night. The fan was making a louder sound than usual. This I attributed to the power surges. I was drowsy and turned it off, as the switch is near my pillow. The sound continued — perhaps I had only tripped the switch and not turned it off properly. I then realised that the switch had no effect on the sound, the noise came from outside. It was raining!

What a glorious realisation. I pushed the windows wide open and listened to its music. No orchestra could have played more harmoniously than the rain as it fell on the ground and on my very being. I was one with receptive earth and leaves. It was heavy and descended with long unbroken strokes. I was willing it to continue like that for an hour, a whole day. I watched and participated for half an hour, when it began to thin and I fell onto my bed into slumber again. That last sleep was the finishing lap of the night and I arose joyfully to smell the new earth and breath the new air. It was, I know, the same old earth and the same old air but freshness had renewed everything.

As soon as I was free I took my walk. The size of the puddles confirmed the heaviness of the fall. The sky was clear and the early sun strong. As I turned from the main road back into the lanes the new neighbour came towards me on his Honda.

'What do you think of my prediction?' he called out triumphantly.

'Bang on, wonderful! You sure are a weather prophet.'

He was gone. I had ended my rudeness and no longer gave him a cold shoulder. Hopefully he might now have some notion that I am basically friendly but with some peculiar reservations.

CONJUNCTION

The day has been ruinous and unproductive. First Jose calls and I understand his state of mind. I try to encourage him for he is on a punishing schedule of study in which he works for six hours and sleeps six hours, day and night, studying; he changed to the six-hour stint from the four hours he first set himself. His examinations are in three weeks time and his face is drawn and eyes red. He is unshaven.

He is alienated from his family and leaves his room only for meals; and when really desperate, to visit me. The fault lies with him for he measures them against his own strong powers of intellect and they fall short. He regards their conversation as trivial, they talk only silly things, silly things. It will be some time before the tree of understanding in his nature blossoms. He will grow out of this, he must, and during this period it will be hard going for them.

He is hungry for diversion and seizes on the newspaper, then magazines lying about. He has escaped temporarily from the prison of his self-discipline. He is a strong character and will win through. I hear him out, though I too am immersed in my own little world; I cannot shut the door. I objectify the scene and see two people with their worlds lightly touching in bright recognition. We like each other and have this knowledge that there is an invisible bond which will hold, come what may.

He has a material need which he lays before me. I am touched in two ways, for his is a proud nature and fierce independence is his goal. No help can come but through me in a matter of supreme importance to him. Help is possible, though not convenient — I shall have to adjust. He spends an hour with me, the maximum his discipline will permit, then leaves.

Chandu arrives just before this, so a coming and a going overlap. Chandu's circumstances are painful for him and they pain me too. I know just how far I can be drawn into the whirlpool of another's woes. My affection for him is strong, so we talk awhile, then go to his house to see his mother. She, poor soul, is beset with cares, as well as her own health — there has been a swelling of the arms and legs. I nod to his mute sister. We have a sweet coffee, then he takes me to one of the town's two supermarkets. Though small they are similar to those of the west and I feel that I am in familiar territory. I still long to be let loose in a decent supermarket, but realise I am in another world.

We arrange the plastic shopping bags on the bike and return to my place at midday. I will soon take my meal, then join the rest of the world in a siesta.

I had barely settled down when, after knocking on the open door, a smiling young man walked in. I called him Ranjith, he was not dissimilar but knew I was wrong. He was Sudheer, a new friend. I had been walking one evening when he caught up with me. He wanted to make himself known. He lived nearby Jayaprakash and said he knew all about me from him. He pressed me to go to his house. His is not a poor family and as far as I could tell there was no adverse factor so often the case in many of the homes — a sick child with kidney disease, a sick parent or drunken father, or widowed mother. His father was apparently a good wage-earner who worked in the railways. The house was spacious, airy and exceedingly clean. He showed me his room — chair, table, bookshelf, clothes on a rack — but no bed. Like most people in India he slept on the floor. A woven mat would be unrolled on the shiny black floor.

Since that first meeting he had visited me with Jayaprakash, and on that occasion had asked could he call to see me for conversation.

I felt cheated of my morning, half-resentful yet knowing it was not essentially without purpose, though not my purpose. It was not easy maintaining a conversation so we settled on a game of chess during which we chatted freely and I checked his phrasing and pronunciation without too much pedantry. The English he learns from me will be learned inadvertently, it will rub off. He was a smart opponent and we played three games; he specified they must be quick. Before he left I took the precaution of telling him that I was too busy to have callers in the morning.

The heat grew steadily and forced its way into the consciousness. Trying to ignore it worked only to a limited extent. I settled down again. Some village women gathered on the verandah and began an interminable conversation. This was worse than the heat. Mercifully it was conducted in Malayalam so I was spared he urgencies of village trivia. I closed my door and turned on the fan.

The power failed. For the remainder of the afternoon I concentrated on a news magazine until the mail arrived, welcome as aid-relief. It was a good mail and the day regained buoyancy. Tomorrow surely would treat me with more consideration. I would be more amenable and tolerant. When the women departed I saw their faces, sharp-features with a touch of beauty — my one-eyed interpretation of their chatter called for revision. It was now around four o'clock.

Earlier in the day I had heard repeated swishing, dragging sounds which could come only from palm branches. Sojan's mother had evidently found a rich source, an invaluable contribution to our fuel. She is always active while others rest in the heat, a true gatherer.

Though it was hotter on the sit-out, I sat there now it was vacated. I wanted the openness it afforded. I looked at the deep living curtain of the plantation and it did not register correctly. I was cock-eyed seeing it differently. Although it was a tangle and jungle of trunks, I felt something had changed, a palm tree was missing, the crooked one which parted from the perpendicular three-quarters of the way up. I had often focused on it and wondered what had caused the change of direction. By God! There it was lying on the ground. I had not heard it fall — its stiff branches would have prevented a thud and the trunk would first have struck the low earthen wall. Already the fronds had been removed. I recalled the sudden violent gusts of wind that had been a feature of an otherwise still afternoon, they were quick and furious. These squalls and a darkening sky had brought portentousness as though some drama was brewing. I wandered over to the fallen palm; a barbed fence preventing me from going up to the base, but I could see nothing of the root system; it had not been uprooted, in fact there was a short length of the trunk intact. It had not been chopped for it was a source of income. It was rotten, chewed out by white ants, the first I had seen. Now I was aware of the value of the white stockings of bordeaux and lime with which so many trees in the district are painted. In this area there was neglect, there was no disfigurement by paint, hence no protection.

As night fell the raiding gusts were joined, then absorbed by steadier currents which tamed the mad bucking airs. There was more purpose and urgency as cool air rushed to replace the hot rising air. Flashes of lightning started up, across the sky like the flutter of fluorescent tubes when first switched on; the growling thunder skulked on the horizon.

The flashes followed so swiftly, one upon the other so that for an hour the sky was light more after than dark. I had rarely seen such fulsome displays. The dull day was fully redeemed by all this airy drama. In the midst of it all Sudheer arrived, with Jeevan who at long last had returned to his house. They wanted to sit in the room. Jeevan was unshaven and said he had decided not to shave until his exams were over. Of the two, Sudheer had the better command of English. He was two years older.

He picked up a letter from the table and I said he could read it. It was from Unni, writing from his unit in the army, I knew not where, as his address was coded. We spent some time on this letter as I commented on the phrasing and choice of words. The power failed and we lit a candle. Then Sudheer produced a three-page story he had written. He wanted comment and correction.

It was a sweet little story of his love for Vitya, a little girl from the time they were nine years old. He would call at her house and they would walk or play by the river nearby. One day when he called he heard raised voices and Vitya crying. He was told he may no longer see or speak to Vitya as she was twelve years old and grown. He asked why and was told not to ask questions as that was the Indian culture. He then hated Indian culture. He left the house, walked along the river bank alone, crying. Then he added: many years later he had met a foreigner who came from New Zealand and he had taken him to his house. After he left his mother said 'Who is this man?' as she did not want ideas of western culture brought to this house, as it was bad.

I asked if his mother disapproved of me and our new friendship and he laughed and said only in the story. His mother, he said, really liked me and approved, but he had altered this to show up Indian culture. I was uneasy but he reassured me and said I must visit again.

We corrected the errors which were mainly of tense, and the use of *he* and *she* had to be mastered. Jeevan wandered outside and reported it was not just the wind but rain that was making the noise. It gathered strength and rapidly became a tropical downpour. They decided to go as they had been here an hour.

They took my umbrella. I could not see that an umbrella would keep then dry in such a turbulent deluge but they did not care as it was not cold. I returned to the sit-out to enjoy the rain. It was forceful as it pounded the earth, so receptive and accommodating. The blackness beyond the porch light was impenetrable. I fancied I could hear noises, wild noises.

Suddenly three figures burst into the light together with two umbrellas. The bodies were naked but for loincloths and were streaming wet. It was Kunjuman, Babu and Valsan in a merry mood. They danced wildly in front of me. Kunjuman was the most dishevelled as the rain had matted his long hair. He rolled his eyes as his legs and arms made demonic movements. It was a fitting touch of madness to cap the evening. They would not come in, not even onto the verandah, they had just come to greet me. Babu grabbed my hand and made as if to bite. Then in a flash the three bodies and the two umbrellas were gone. It was still raining heavily. There was weight in the drops.

GOOD FRIDAY

Today is Good Friday and such is the prevalence of the Christian community that stillness descends. When I took my walk I saw no one except a hard-case little boy of about six who always climbs up a bank to come and shake hands with me. He stretches out his hand as soon as he spots me, and holds it out until we meet. His teeth are wide-spaced, and straight hair falls down his face. He strides forward with old-fashioned manliness. I shake his hand and give this grinning gamin a hug and he asks me how old I am. This question is the common greeting of children who try to speak English. It has no other meaning save greeting.

I saw one other person, a woman sweeping the lane beside her house. She was smiling so I smiled back. It is unusual for women to acknowledge strangers so I am happy. She has seen me many times on my walks.

The air hangs still, resting after its excesses of the day before. The sky is overcast. Mary, Sojan's mother, is away early to church. She looks beautiful in a black and white sari but though gravely beautiful she is not preoccupied with her appearance. Her face is worn until she smiles. I fancy I see the same pensiveness in her baby grandson, the same sweet sad smile. There is no Mass today but devotions continue nevertheless.

Religions festivals, Hindu or Christian, are highly extrovert; everything that can impress the eye and pound the ear is brought into service. Loudspeaker recordings, bells, drums and fireworks play their part while banners and ceremonial umbrellas appear on special occasions. Everyone is on deck to watch or join in, but today quietness prevails. It is the day of immolation. I see in the paper a photo where an artist has drawn an image of the suffering Christ on the road in front of the cathedral in Kochi. There is a dish where the faithful can shed a coin.

I do not feel critical about such celebrations, whereas in my youth where Protestantism prevailed, such a carry-on would have created a scandal. I am no longer shocked. Somewhere I read that travestied truth remains unsullied truth on its own plane — as true and profound a statement as ever I have heard. I try to remember a phrase of Gerard Manley Hopkins where he writes that all bears man's smudge and shares man's smell, but fail. No, it is not an equivalent statement for it is entirely pessimistic and puts man down. It is a cry of pain from one who despairs. I wish this moment I had a copy of his poems.

He stood in my mind for beauty, passion and gloom, whereas William Blake brought in joy and sunlight. One a seeker, the other a knower.

Back home again Mini brings me payasam, the celebratory cup of coconut and ground rice, with many other ingredients. I find this cloying. This was followed by slices of mango. I do some reading of a philosophical nature; it is hard going to get a grip on these 26 pages; it is not as difficult as when I read them the day before. I do want to get the hang of it and my brain tires and pulls back from the effort.

Jose was to come at five when we would go to his house and he would take me around the trees. I had seen this well-stocked garden before but somewhat hastily as night was falling. It was a quarter to six and I had given up waiting for him and set out on a walk in the direction he would come if he came at all. Sure enough I had just rounded the first bend of the path when he came towards me on his bicycle. He locked it and drew it to the side of the lane and we headed towards his house. What had delayed him, he said, was the Good Friday procession. He stood as a spectator whereas his Catholic friends were thinking he should be with them. We passed the hockey players battling away — one was detached enough to give a wave. As we approached the main road he told me the noise I could hear was that of the procession. What I was to see would be the tail-end. I was a little disappointed in this as I wanted to see Sojan's mother. Her sweet, deeply sincere piety would have moved me, I knew. I saw several hundred people of all ages walking slowly on both sides of the road. A van was directly at the point where we emerged from the lane and was broadcasting a hymn. It was low-keyed and murmurous and fitted the sorrowful occasion. Many sang, singing from printed slips. Most were dressed in white; some carried a black wooden cross. A boy bore his cross casually trailing it as though it were a walking-stick.

I looked at the faces. The women appeared deep in sorrow, identifying with the suffering. The men, particularly the middle-aged men of successful standing, as indicated by their girth, looked self-conscious and secretly gratified by their grand gesture. They accounted it a credit in the ledger. The faces of the old men were moving. No asset-attachment or pride could be read from their bent shoulders and lined faces as, skin and bone, they shuffled along. The music ceased and the man in the van broadcast a prayer — it was in Malayalam. Everyone knelt where they stood. Traffic was sparse and the way difficult but it slowly worked through the devotees. They knelt on spotless saris and dhotis. I looked at the man leading the prayer from the van, he did not appear to be a priest. Perhaps the priests were at the head of the procession.

It ended with a large truck painted every inch a dull black — a lugubrious spectacle in this colourful land. On the back a coffin was mounted, on top of which was a draped body with only the face showing. It was high up and I could not see the face. I asked Jose was the dead body real and he said no, it was an idol of Jesus, and I commented that they turned it on rather thick. He said it was all a vain outward display. I could not agree as I saw the unifying power of a common belief. The sense of a fellowship of mourners was undeniable. There was no ostentation, for grief predominated, and those who did not grieve did their best to enter into that emotion.

Jose's house was nearby, behind a high wall. There would be barely time to see the trees properly. Christopher, a tall young man with glasses, and Pranjit, had joined us. Pranjit had a massive physique, bidding fair to increase by working out regularly in the gymnasium. Once when walking I had felt unwell and he had brought me back on his motorbike.

Jose had studied botany for examination purposes but confessed he had not the slightest interest in the subject. In this he disappointed me, yet he could change. He was young and high-minded and his proneness to extremes would modify as he met the complexities of existence. Extremism is characteristic of immaturity. He said he never walked in this densely canopied garden, not even as a change from study; it interested him not one whit. He proved right in his ignorance of botanical names, though he knew the Malayalam equivalent and also something at least about the properties of the trees and the purpose behind their planting.

Later, thinking on his indifference towards nature, a subject so close to me, I recognised that he was engrossed with other things — he had a colossal knowledge of cars, motorbikes, aeroplanes, of recording apparatus and western pop music, all of which left me cold. There was still truth left in the cliché that one man's meat is another man's poison. Reality is so vast it has to be so.

As we wandered, examining the trees, an interesting fact emerged. I expressed surprise at the poor condition and sparse leafage of the tamarinds which, though well-shaped, looked particularly bare. Jose explained that in the dry season up until June which they call summer, leaf-fall is common with a number of trees in order to conserve moisture. We have the reverse situation in cold climates where bare trees characterise winter. This gives food for thought, I need to know more. The equation is not quite as simple, as I had already observed a banyan tree devoid of leafage in November and now in April it is dense with foliage. The same was true of the cotton tree, *ceiba*, about November, when the rains had ended, it was in a sorry state so that a tyro in the matter of Indian flora would have deemed it to be dying. Now four months later it had leaves, large leaves but not in great abundance.

I smelled crushed leaves, some I tasted; I smelled crushed bark, pure spice; I tasted many varieties of small fruit, mostly of a crisp, tart nature, with the exception of the tamarind pods the flesh of which appeared like mashed prunes coating a hard seed and having a sweet-sour taste.

One shrub delighted me — an old friend which I had grown in Brisbane. It was the curry bush, *duranta*, with its musky scent and which I had so often used in cooking. I wondered how long it would be before I could claim familiarity with the wide range of trees I saw in this garden. The recognition and identification of plants as I wander in the wild is a passion with me. Again darkness defeated our inspection. Jose and Christopher walked the whole way back with me in the dark lanes. I deplored the absence of books on trees and the absence of botanical gardens. Where were the lovers of trees and the devotees of horticulture who could impart to the Indian people an enthusiasm for their amazing flora? I have put it on Jose to fossick around and find me books and information on local plants. In my own searching all I have found is a botanical census, comprising many volumes at high prices. This work, a basic study, is for botanists, and cannot help the amateur. I do not need specialist knowledge to that extent — no more than I need a knowledge of anatomy when looking upon an elephant or tiger. Jose explained this gap of facilities for the studying of plants being due to the lack of interest. I said precisely, there is a vague love of plants among the people and this must be intensified and transformed into a living knowledge of what the plant kingdom is about. Then not only practical information will become available but a general raising of the aesthetic consciousness of a lively, sensitive people. I tell him I come from a country which has an awareness of horticulture and agricultural matters and that this knowledge plays a significant part in its economy.

ANOTHER DAY

Having made an early start I have accomplished by 10:30 what usually takes the whole morning. I find I am in an vacuum — what to do? A plate of sliced mango and two bananas appears. I pour coffee from the flask and consider options. The fresh scene is inviting, it is not too hot for a short walk. A frisky little breeze is sporting like a puppy. In spite of the sun I walk to the temple ground. It is the swooning, pausing time of the morning and there is enough shade to keep my head out of the sun, though I would have done better to have taken an umbrella.

I turn the corner and a palm branch crashes on to the path, then dead stubs of branches. Unnikrishnan is up a coconut palm; several coconuts fall heavily. He descends to my feet in a flash and gives me the friendliest grin. His manner of ascent is like this. He puts a cloth on the opposite side of the trunk from which he climbs and holds each end — the cloth is just above the flange of a tree, the place of branch severance. By pulling on the cloth he has enough support to bring his whole body up as far as possible. His feet are inside a loop of cloth and he presses his feet outwards. Each time the foot cloth is put in a new position it uses the slight purchase of the branch scar. A practised climber ascends the loftiest trunk in seconds.

A slasher is tucked in his lungi, and with this he cuts off dead or dying branches and detaches the coconuts. He is incredibly nimble and in the space of ten minutes dealt with three trees. My aimless walk is rewarded. Clouds dimmed the sun as I turned back — it was as though I had attended a command performance, the timing was perfection. A little farther on and I looked on a grove of palms of all sizes so that green wings spread everywhere. It was an open cupboard of wings.

I had hardly settled into my walk again when Vinod and Nixon arrived in Vinod's auto. I was able to show them Athuba's letter as well as that of Unnikrishnan — not the tree climber, but the friend who was in the army. I had a third letter from Anand in Bangalore, written after his honeymoon. Anand was in fact actually that moment in the air en route from Bombay to Dubai when his letter arrived. He had accepted an inviting offer from

Sony Gulf to join their sales department — a position requiring specialised knowledge. At first he will be allotted bachelor's quarters. Uma has to remain behind as she has to take her MBA examinations in sales and marketing management. By the time she joins Anand he will be allotted family accommodation, hopefully. Then he says, he can invite me to stay with them. I am touched by his enthusiasm. Never would I have thought to go to such a place, but why not? The determining factors would be health and money supplies. Life in Dubai is almost entirely in air-conditioned flats and offices, and all the shopping and entertainment areas are similarly made habitable. The chances of my visiting I would estimate are 20 out of a hundred. Or less than that. They came to remind me that tomorrow I go to Nixon's for the Easter meal. I had not forgotten.

Sojan returned mid-afternoon from the spiritual retreat near Idukki. He said it was attended by two hundred men, and the purpose was mainly to cure their addiction to drink and smoking. Sojan rarely did either and I asked what vice he had to be cured of. He said laziness. I did not have all his descriptions and impressions as it so difficult for him to communicate. They had to listen to twelve lectures over the period given by priests in brown habits.

'Franciscans?' When he nodded I said, 'Franciscans, they are good.'

Memory still preserves the moment I passed through the large gateway of a Franciscan friary with a Catholic friend as we began a retreat in Auckland. The high walls enclosed spacious grounds where beauty and peace reigned, and I felt a rush of romantic excitement on seeing medieval monks in brown habits walking in the gardens solitarily, with a breviary or prayer-book in hand. Sons of the little man of Assisi, a man so charged with other-worldly love that seven centuries later the radiance was still shed in a place like this. The monks were modernised, their habits were tailored and laundered, and they were educated and refined. Poverty is a word they love but their order is wealthy and their properties vast. They followed, but from afar.

The fellow retreatants were so average and earthy. My friend pointed out one who was a bookie; and I recalled how they guffawed during a sermon in the exquisite little chapel when the priest referred to Elizabeth the Virgin Queen. 'Believe me, my friends, she was no more virgin than our friary cat.' The coarse laughter in the beautiful setting shocked me. Ancient hatred still smouldered.

I was shocked also at the hectoring tones of the priest who scolded us in advance lest we place a niggardly sum into the contribution box. These little things remain in the mind — also the silence in the refectory as a priest at the lectern read to us from the lives of the saints.

Would I like to have been with Sojan at his retreat? It was not considered. In my case the services and lecturers would have been in Malayalam. Besides I had no special interest and had shown no leaning towards the faith here in Kerala. Yet the setting in the high country and the chill air would rekindle my love of this wondrous man.

EASTER DAY

Nixon and Vinod arrived early in the black-bonneted auto-rickshaw, but I was ready. The day before, Sojan had given Nixon his old denim shorts which he admired. They were faded, unhemmed and ragged in the approved way and he chose to wear them on this holy day. In his hand was an opened bottle of Kingfisher, which he called a soft drink. He was his usual merry self, celebrating the day as he did every day. He had not been drinking, but would, and it was part of his honesty that he should display to one and all what he did.

Vinod switched on a western ballad as we rode off. It was rowdy and beating, but I softened as I heard the words confidentially crooned. They bore a simple measure and though based on romantic love extended a love to all people. He called it revolutionary music. It is, I suppose, in the ears of revellers who would not listen to the same words stated perhaps in a church. They joined in lustily — no effort was made to observe the proprieties and we rattled on like a drunken boat. Nixon was happy as a lark.

First we went to Shelton's house where friends and neighbours were gathered on the sit-out. A little drink was there, chilled water, soft drinks for the vodka, and plates of meat were set before us. I enjoyed the spectacle. These village houses, though partly fenced with plaited bamboo through which creepers wandered, had intermingling common ground, all open and swept. Some of the friends I knew, and — miracolo — remembered their names. I was no longer an overwhelming novelty and was at ease. But I was in a flat state, curious because I had looked forward to this occasion. Later I realised it was not moodiness but apathy brought on by low blood pressure — I thought it was a thing of the past.

Noise is the basis of such gatherings and the cassettes followed one upon the other. There were loud and singing voices and a man unknown to me was showing interest and wanted to know where I was from. I told him and he shook hands. This he kept doing, so many times I concluded he was drunk. Even in the noise his questions kept coming. Shelton noticed and in his splintered and husky voice became fed up and began half singing half shouting 'Where are you from, where are you from? You keep on asking him. He is from the uterus.' It was the definitive answer that passed almost without notice.

Nelson was there, Shelton's younger but bigger brother, and I was happy chatting with him. He is gentle and thoughtful; both are handsome and I saw their looks in both the parents. Later Nandakumar told me they were twins — he said *tins*, could not say *twins* — he was at school with them. I checked and found they were a year apart in age. Sunil arrived with Arshad. I was busy eating two drumsticks, unbearably fiery.

It was a brief visit and we left these neighbours and wandered along to Nixon's for the meal — Arshad, Sunil, Shelton, Nixon and I. After our meal, beautifully prepared, others arrived and we crowded into Nixon's room to talk against the music. Arshad is soon to go to the Gulf. He has a job with a petrol company. His reserve is almost impenetrable. There is something hostile about him — yet that would be an unfair reading, for I had seen him working and waiting on others at Baju's wedding, and Nixon told me of several acts of his kindness. No, hostile is the wrong word. It is more like a fierce privacy. He tells me he is unemployed. I know that his family is immensely rich. Subsequent to our first meeting I had taken care to be friendly in greeting, not knowing what was going on in his mind. Nixon said he was by nature reserved and on top of that was an added shyness because he could speak so little English. There is in India an insistent apologetic streak about this, which I can understand only to a degree, for no one need be ashamed of their mother tongue. There are advantages a knowledge of English confers, but essentially it is an alien tongue fostered upon a cultured people. With Arshad there is more than that to his aloofness, even if he were fluent his conduct would remain the same.

The room was crowded. They were shifting about and Arshad came near me. The young never fail to compare skin colour. A white skin is quite a phenomenon in a provincial town. They compare the colours, of hands and feet. Mine are particularly white — against the almost black skin of some South Indians the contrast is striking. Sunil was examining my hand, then Arshad took it. He was playing with a ring on his finger. He had taken it off and was putting it on mine. He was seeing what it would look like. I said I never wear rings because my fingers are not slender. I made to take it off but he would not allow me. It was, I thought, most elegant and a handsome stone was mounted on it.

'See, Uncle, it is violet,' Sunil said.

I would have said clear, except for flashes of pale pink on the way to violet. I was confused, our relationship was tenuous and undefined. I was surprised by his gift. I had no doubts that it marked an attitude and gave no thought to its price. It was a valuable stone, though I am an innocent in such matters. In fact I loved it and saw much to admire in it. He wore other rings and a striking gold chain with Muslim emblems.

Sunil drove me back on a borrowed motorbike. The noise and celebration would continue and I was indifferent whether I stayed or not. There had been something happening behind the scenes between Nixon and his mother. Whether his wildness had upset her or his hatred of his father I had no knowledge. Shelton was scolding him. It was not for me to take in.

To arrive back home from any celebration in the afternoon is a mistake. It is deflating and my dispiritedness had not changed. Later I wandered about and passed a throng of people standing under the banyan. Some of the boys came over to me. I asked what was happening and they said a wedding was going on. Someone said there had been some trouble, another asked where I had been and where was I going.

That evening I was still enjoying the novelty of a ring on my finger, and still admiring the lights, noting how the subtle violet had changed to golden in the electric light. Pleasure was mine and the enigma of Arshad very much in mind. Jose arrived later on and told me it was a cheap ring and the stone was plastic. The mounting was loose and cheap and he could see what he called holes in the substance of the stone. By that he meant bubbles formed in the pouring of the plastic onto the mercuric oxide base which imparted brilliance. He knew so much that I was crestfallen that this object, precious to me, should be the subject of appraisal. It was I who had made the assumption of genuineness and Arshad had made no great matter in transferring it to me. Jose's brother had a lot to do with jewellery, hence his own knowledge. People are jewellery-conscious here and they would know its value at a glance.

Its intrinsic beauty remained — how should marketability affect inherent beauty and the play of lights? Once the word plastic is pronounced, how is it we lose our ability to appraise the virtues of an artefact? In Arshad's mind there was no thought of a valuable topaz, but just a trinket he could let go and give to me — after all, he himself had been wearing it for a long time. I shall treasure it.

For three days now we have had respite from the succession of scorching days. Those who know the climate say this is unprecedented. Rain has fallen with intensity on Kerala for three days around sunset. The meteorologists tell us there has been an increase in summer cloud resulting in prolonged displays of thunder and lightning. Also they tell us a low pressure has formed over Sri Lanka, touching parts of the southern peninsula, our part.

I have increased the distance of my walks, attributing this extra energy to the ayurvedic medicines; another factor could well be the drop in temperatures. Today has been the dullest, coolest, most agreeable day this whole summer. The sun has not shone. What I thought an early morning mist persisted until midday. It has lifted but there is a feeling of cloud every where — it is like being in the high country of Ooty or Kodaikanal. The clouds are both vertical and low. I do not know if we'll have late thunderstorms, but I expect rain. This monsoonal weather will persist for a week, the oracles foretell, then back we'll go to hot days and clear skies; we'll be refreshed and all the better for the respite. The grass that has miraculously greened in hours will be hand-cropped by tethered cows and what is left will turn to brown again.

In my walk I saw Kunjumon and asked him about the wedding the day before. I asked why the people remained outside the temple during the ceremony.

'Not all,' he said.

'And what was the trouble Praveen mentioned?'

'It was illegal, illegal wedding.'

'How come? Was there a child bride?'

'Not, not child bride. She was under-age.'

'How old was she?'

'Seventeen. The law is 18 for a girl, 21 for a boy.'

'And the boy — how old was he?'

'Eighteen.'

'Well, how was it they allowed the wedding to go on?'

'No one made a complaint.'

The air becomes heavier. Rain will surely come within the hour. I decided to go out while I had the chance.

'Take an umbrella, then,' Sojan called. He was inside playing with the baby. Random spots were falling even as I set out but not enough for me to unfurl the umbrella. I went on an erratic route and along the way

I thought to call on Jayaprakash. They told me he had shaved his head and I wanted to see what he looked like.

Sudheer was in the lane as I reached his house. We chatted and Jeevan joined us. His exam paper had gone well enough, he thought. I learned that Jayaprakash was out of town on his study project. I did not want to linger so pushed on. Enough raindrops were falling to warrant opening the umbrella, but by the time I reached the main road it had eased off so I furled it.

Nothing happened until I heard someone running behind me not long after I had turned off the main road. It was Jayaprakash, his face beaming. He had just got off the bus. I had timed it well. He wore a cricketer's cap.

'Well, let's see,' I said

He took off his cap. The new hair had sprouted so he did not look at all bald. His head shape is very fine and I thought of photos of Negro heads I had seen.

'But why did you do it?'

'Because I was hot.'

We went our ways. The raindrops had not wet the whole surface of the tarseal but they continued, a little thicker, perhaps, so I took cover again. I had hardly been in the house five minutes when the drops lengthened, fattened and in no time formed a steady rain. I watched blissfully until I noticed my towel which had been drying on the line; by now it was quite wet.

St Thomas Gets a Drubbing

I am in Malayattur again, sitting under a nutmeg tree. It is not as quiet as I planned, but the sources of noise are at a tolerable remove. The main one is radio pop, annoying but unavoidable. The other noise is more in harmony with the exotic setting; it is from the chatter of Sini and her two friends who sit plaiting bamboo mats beneath another large tree.

I came from Trichur with Johnny this morning. After all the rain, the heat had gone and the air came to us fresh and clean. Johnny had surprised me when he arrived at dusk the evening before, he said to take me back with him immediately. He is Mini's half-brother. He had asked me to visit several times but I demurred, not feeling up to it. Now I am stronger. There had been a difference between us for I had helped him to my limits in the building of his house, and he kept on begging for more. I had already stated my limits, and they were true limits. His last letter angered me with its insistence and I sent back a blunt reply. I like him, of course I do, but there is some ambivalence. He is inclined to take me over — oh, that is enough, I do not want to write about it. A new baby has just arrived as if to augment his bargaining power. His needs are real enough. He is frail and cannot do much physical work. There is perpetual or partial unemployment for such as he in this rural district; his low income background does not foster niceties of behaviour, and diplomacy is not in its narrow curriculum. One big factor remains; he is part of the family which has adopted me and I want to help him when I can.

Our greeting was unconstrained, then when the others had gone inside he told me he was sorry for his conduct. This was good. I said not to worry and that I had a lot of time for him. I knew he had come to make it up, and then to take me back, though he added two inducements. He wanted me to see the great festival of St Thomas, and the other was that he was now in a position to commence building and wanted me to share the excitement of the moment. The first was no great lure as I could not go to the mountain and climb up to the chapel, but I would be able to see the large Portuguese-styled church at Malayattur in the height of the festival. I pictured the lavish caparison of lights and the crowding devotees.

I would not agree to return immediately, it was too late for me. Besides, Sojan was out at the moment and I should not leave in such a casual way. He stayed the night and we set out fairly early the next day. Sojan lectured him severely on my welfare — it had sounded like an argument so I had asked for a translation. It looked as if the rains were over but I took my umbrella in case. The rough bus ride did not bother me and within an hour we were at Angamally, the place where our baby was born. We had to change buses there but first took the chance to look up Siju who was working at a fruit-shop. It proved a bright clean place with a sizeable ice-cream and soft drink parlour. Siju, Mini's brother, is a shy, likeable youth of 20 with the same captivating and half-deferential smile as his sister. He is not at all like his half-brother, but is tall and strong. His skin is marred by acne but his looks are salvaged by the dazzling perfection of his teeth. Johnny's father had a large family by his first wife and Johnny at 32 is the youngest. Of the second marriage Siju is the youngest. His siblings are a sister Sini, 21 and Mini who is 23. He is a delightful character. From accounts I have of him from Sojan and Mini he is the provider, he is the worker. These virtues go unnoticed as he has a self-effacing manner that takes him into the background; the father shares this characteristic. I have noticed such ability before, it was evident in a Laotian man I met in Sydney who in a roomful of people would seemingly fade into invisibility. He was delighted to see me and made his happiness evident as he touched my shoulder. He diverted attention to a fellow-assistant called Jiju whom he introduced. He was a schoolmate and a neighbour of the family. I had previously met him. They worked seven days a week at the shop for 30 rupees a day. This included board and a place to sleep in the house of the owner. We took the second bus which delivered us a kilometre from the family house. It was warming up and I was glad of the umbrella even though much of the lane was in shade. The greetings were pleasant, but I had been thinking to see Jessy and the new baby. I had forgotten that she was now living at her parents' home, as custom prescribes.

After lunch and a rest, Johnny chose this place for me under the tree where I now sit. It is a magnificent tree in its prime. In spread and foliage it resembles a beech and its fruit are like apricots just before the honey-green colour changes to sunset hues. It is in fact a great green umbrella. The leaves on the many horizontal branches are numerous so that when a sudden shower descended a few moments later not a drop came through, I was protected. Johnny hastened to take my chair inside though I was of a mind to sit it out. I wish I had, for now it is all over. The return to the house was compensated by a cup of coffee. While we sat there a three-wheeler truck with six bags of cement arrived. They stacked it on the verandah. This was about four o'clock. By this time thunder-clouds served clear notice of further rainfall, and when it came it was heavy and prolonged into the night so I was defeated in my intention to visit the site of the new house. I slept in Johnny's room. It was dark and inconvenient. I was on the wooden-based bed and Johnny slept on a mat on the floor. I could get no comfort and had a disturbed night. The following day was Easter day and he was off early to Mass and was away a long time. I took a walk, pleased that the half-grown dog chose to accompany me.

I examined the foundations of the house. The bricks had been delivered. I know by now that three types of brick are available. The cheapest are what they call clamp bricks. These are not fired to the same degree as the kiln bricks which have the benefit of high-temperature burning, and consequently require plastering. How much more picturesque the houses would look if not disfigured by the plaster! The kiln bricks are smoother with keener edges and are not affordable for the lower-income people. The other bricks are more like blocks, and weigh, according to one I asked, about 20 kilograms each. So they are large and heavy, each one costing on site around four rupees. They are hewn from laterite quarries, slowly and patiently cut out of the wall, brick by brick. The colour is iron red, sometimes pale, sometimes very red. The country abounds in iron as the ubiquitous red soil attests. Johnny's house is to be of laterite brick. It requires plastering only in the inside, so I am pleased. The almost venetian red against the emerald of banana leaves is pleasing. In New Zealand I have not seen laterite; whether it exists or not I do not know. At first I was comparing it with scoria rock so common in the Auckland region, but the style and feel are different. For one thing the laterite is softer and can be cut accurately to size by the adze-like tool used for all digging, hoeing and shovelling work. I have an idea the laterite slowly hardens on exposure to the air.

The day crawled, for I was not happy. I had a pain in the nape of the head, ever my speciality, a disappointing state that disturbs concentration and thought. My only reading was *News India*, a weekly patterned on *Time* magazine format and somewhat larger. It is a splendid and authoritative publication largely devoted to political and business affairs — in this it does not really meet my interests. There is a section on the arts and

Indian literature but it is not large and for me quite esoteric. The cinema section has more generous treatment and there again it is esoteric. I need a supplementary magazine that gives world news — *Time* is the only one offering and I find it expensive. I begin to think like an Indian.

So I am alone and purposeless. Johnny is away counting the bricks and later told me that according to his tally, there was short delivery of a hundred. He is thorough as step by step he organises each stage. I am alone in the house, for it is drizzling lightly. Had I a purpose I would readily go out. It was mid-afternoon. I admitted it, I was bored, a most unusual and unacceptable state of mind. I was glad of his return but when he announced that he would be out the rest of the afternoon at a prayer meeting I began to regret my visit. These prayer meetings were monthly occasions of two hours, held in private homes on rotation and led by a priest. All must attend. Why, I thought, had he invited me only to leave me hour after hour in an empty house? I had come at his insistence so when he asked would I be okay on my own I voiced my objection and asked why then had he asked me to visit if most of the time I would be on my own. He asked me where I wanted to go and I said he should decide, for he was the host. It was a protest delivered mildly but I was inwardly frustrated and ashamed to be at the end of my own resources. I know that he had given no thought at all what to do with me once he had made the big effort to bring me here. He was completely caught up in his own affairs despite his good intentions. The following day he would be equally busy with the start of building. I was a problem for him and decided to make it evident. He became aware of my situation and said he would go to the prayer meeting and come back after fifteen minutes. We would then go to see his wife and family, and on the return see the great old St Thomas church in festive mood.

I was agreeable and grateful and decided I had no reason for shame having diverted him from his vague routine. We had an option, to visit Jessy first, it was farthest off, and cross the Periyar by ferry to get to the church, or go first to the church, and if the weather permitted then cross the Periyar and go to Jessy that way.

We walked some distance to the bus stop for we live not actually in Malayattur but in a village called Neeleswaram five kilometres from Malayattur. The sky was clouded and we thought it as well to be prepared. At the stop the buses which went to our left would lead to Jessy's place and those to our right the town of Malayattur. We waited and waited.

There were many buses but only in the direction of the festival. On asking a driver Johnny ascertained that they were returning by another route. This decided us, we would go first to Malayattur.

The sky turned purple and there was no doubting what lay ahead. That inkiness with its Reckitt's blue suggested bulky vats of rain. Should it be possible we agreed, we would go on to Jessy after the festival. Buses followed one after another, and when we arrived parking-space was completely taken up. I was surprised at such a multitude at Malayattur. Packed buses, packed jeeps and cars filled the immense parking area, and each discharged pilgrims into the dense assemblage. Most would go from the church by transport to the base of Malayattur mountain. There, temporary accommodation was provided, but most would sleep on the bare ground and make the ascent the following day.

The previous time I saw this church I could take in it impressive proportions — there are massive twin towers either side and a many-balconied central spire on the top of which, in conflict with the general proportions, knelt an enormous St Thomas at the feet of an enormous Christ. The style and colour breathed Portugal.

This time the scene was modified, for the large forecourt had been roofed over with plaited coconut matting, supported by myriad poles. The façade of the church had disappeared. Each pole — and there were over a hundred — suspended two vertical fluorescent strips in orderly rows, quite out-shining the weakening daylight. Thunder and lightning had begun. We made our way through the crowd and into the forecourt, for drops were falling. We pushed through to the church entrance and glimpsed a sight of blinding splendour as though the lost sun had shifted indoors.

A passage had been kept clear before the entrance and the sides were defined with filled gunny sacks which I thought held sand. Johnny told me they were full of money brought from the mountain. I prodded one with my foot … it did not budge, full of coins and as heavy as cement. They were a little larger than the cement bags used in our country and were tied to three-quarter capacity.

I was surprised a pilgrimage could generate so much money, but when Johnny told me that was just the day's collection at the chapel on the mount I was astounded. Moreover, he told me these bags contained notes as well. He had counted them and tallied 85.

Eighty-five bags before a fat church. I began an estimate of the value

— say each bag yielded a thousand rupees then the total would be…say there was two or three thousand it would be…a large sum I had no doubt. I had no idea how many coins would be in a bag, surely several thousand and there would be two rupee coins as well, not to mention the more precious notes. I whispered in his ear that I was sure it would be a financial success. My calculating but not malicious mind could see the necessity of maintaining the living tradition.

It was only on this visit that I learned of the existence of the footprints of St Thomas preserved on the mountain. They were chained off and guarded. I presume they must be in rock to have survived nineteen centuries. My earthy mind did not soar at the marvel but wrestled with the problem of impressing stone. Johnny said like St Thomas I was doubting; but disparaging a legend was not important to me. I had seen a list of references to St Thomas in the Apostolic age and very early church and they were few and far between, but the effects of the legend are considerable. I do not want to use such terms as 'incontrovertible' and 'explicit evidence' as I began to realise that what modern minds can propound as they work back, extrapolating from effects, is quite astonishing. At my level of comprehension I concede that if we are to have St Thomas on the mountain, why not his footprint thrown in and … I still want to believe that King Alfred burned the cakes. Why should times which we find empty and undocumented not have their rich repositories of anecdote? I would not deprive them.

This day was the peak day for local visitation, but the national day of St Thomas is July 1st. A multitude of pilgrims has been making its way up the mountain this last week and there will be more in the weeks ahead.

The rain began and we became aware that the roofing was for shade only. Shattering thunder and a lashing wind announced a storm of great magnitude and we were in for a soaking, for no umbrella could withstand such buffeting conditions. Johnny took me to a side door and I was able to stand inside the church. There was no service as the tumult of the elements was already too great. There was a large feature halfway up the church which we could not see before. It was an outline of a map of India in a continuous line of tubed light. I did not think it worthy of the ecclesiastic glory all around. By now the rain had set in. We moved just outside under the protection of the extended eaves. The storm was a sight worth watching as it worked up to a drenching ferocity, with the full orchestration of thunder and wind. The golden sand turned brown as the first drops fell; channels appeared and within minutes all was under water. The largest channel was directly in front of us where the bamboo thatching met the eaves. I saw chappals floating by. The most arresting sight was across the courtyard to large trees 50 yards away where gusts swept up a gully bringing so much rain it obliterated them as they frantically reacted to the elements.

I timed the storm from the first spill from the overfull clouds to when the storm-cocks were turned back, and slow disciplined rain replaced the madness. From the first downpour to the diminuendo it was just under the hour.

I knew we would be soaked to the skin on our return but did not care, it was not cold and thousands of others would similarly be soaked and sopping, who could complain? Only soft rain was falling as we made our way to a teashop. As this shop was half thatched the sodden half was not occupied. The coffee was strong and sweet; it was a most convenient station on our pilgrimage. We looked directly across to a bulky hostelry run by the church. I have not seen anything as ungainly and disproportioned as this building. Even I who cannot draw a straight line could have devised a more harmonious structure — why had the authorities settled on such a botched and bungled design? I think part of the answer would lie with the distorting influence which art deco exerts in South India. In this case it was ruinous. It had not set out to be art deco style but had become distracted and entangled on the way. We set off again. Crowded buses crawled about us. Johnny spotted one which would take us back, and he found a seat for me. I gazed on the sodden landscape passing by its with mute testimony. I said to Johnny who was leaning over me, 'I believe we'll come out of this bone dry.' It was so, for when we got down the slight precipitation was less than rain. There were drips from the trees. It was hard to believe we had emerged from a furious encounter of the elements. We picked our way past the puddles and arrived at our doorstep dry-shod. I should have uttered a prayer of thanks but my mind was off-duty, letting my gratitude arise and drift off I know not where.

The storm had redeemed the day. Until it came I was moping, so I welcomed the stunning distraction. A visitation of the more assertive forces of nature had filled my mind. It was a catharsis.

*

It is a day later. A nutmeg falls by my chair so you can guess where I am — under my green tent. It is split, only the stalk keeps the two halves together. The fruit is not ripe for the tunic around the nut has yet to turn crimson. I see if I can bite it, gingerly, for nothing can be harder than nutmeg. To my disbelief it is soft so that I can bite right through. It is not ripe, so why did it fall? The taste is agreeable but not quite the familiar nutmeg, it has some other aromatic flavour I know but cannot place. It still suggests nutmeg; it has missing ingredients. Later it will be wood and the outside flesh will be a little softer but never truly soft. It has a sweet-sour taste, not too bad, the flesh, but not to go on and on eating.

It is the big day for commencement of the house. I was surprised to see Johnny help place a bag of cement on his stepmother's head to take to the site, almost two hundred yards through the trees on an uneven track. She has kept a young, fresh appearance, and has the reticence of her son. She is slight of build. Her second daughter Sini is more husky and a little heavy in feature. Sojan tells me that Mini, her first one, has not the same strength, nor has Siju. This surprises me, I would not have thought he had any weakness.

I walk the long way round to the site, by the road. Already most of the outside walls are four feet high, not quite so inside. Johnny's father is mixing the cement with a woman worker. Some of the other women are carrying chatties to the bricklayers. Another brickie is grouting. Men are busy setting the door frames in place. They use transparent tubing filled with water which reaches the extremes of the building and gives the levels. It is a different scene from the one I had been watching next door in Trichur where the bricks were standard type and the house more complex in design. The weather threatened again, it was certain it would rain, and by early afternoon the thunder was muttering, its intentions were bad.

Those who remained in the house were committing conversational mayhem upon the rural peace and that is why I transferred again to the nutmeg tree. A few drops fell but they were inconsequential. Sini arrived bringing my heavy chair. She remained there a while to make sure I was settled, then returned to the house. Ten minutes later when it became evident the rain would start up again she returned to warn me. I chose to stay on, but I had to move, and I gathered my papers and Sini forestalled me by grabbing the chair. I knew the workers would not stop as they had a big mix of sand and cement to deal with.

There was a break and I wandered over through the trees, taking care over not to brush the branches. The workers were wet through but cheerful. They would stop only when the mix was finished. Johnny was working, as well as his father, mother, his wife's parents and his brother Anthony. They were volunteers. The paid workers would get a day's wage whether they worked the full time or not.

Shortly after they all came to the house for the meal prepared by Sini — a great number. It was some time before they were able to return to work. I did not follow — my last inspection was enough. That time I had lingered on the return to the house as I because interested in the number of *caladiums* appearing — the painted leaves growing wild in nature are every bit as colourful as the cherished migrants which make their way to the hot-houses of the west. So the third evening came on with rain and gloom, and the houses settled deeper into their foundations. Everybody retired early after the labours of the day, and the light was of too low a voltage to read by — it meant a longer time upon the rack, for I cannot adjust to the rigid bed. There were two pluses, it was not cold and there were no mosquitoes.

Siju did not arrive that evening as arranged, nor the following morning, so Johnny said he would take me back to Trichur. When we were in the fruit shop at Angamally he had arranged with the owner to allow Siju to have the day off for this purpose. I do not like being beholden to anybody but it was Johnny's duty; I had come at his insistence and now that I had enough I had to assert myself. The workers continued the next day, though I had understood they would not be working. Communication between Johnny and me is far from perfect and I often get things wrong. I felt I must go. It was not my fault Johnny had not planned anything for me and that he had gone off doing the things he needed to do. He had first to go to the bank, quite a journey, and also to arrange for iron reinforcing to be delivered. I would have to wait until the afternoon.

The sky was clear but the weather pattern had not broken. There was a morning to fill in. It is a dispiriting exercise to kill time and I was at a low. Each moment is a unique blossom deserving recognition, it is a felony to crush it. I reflected on my self-created emptiness. I had imprisoned myself in this state of mind. The past few days I had looked on stone — for these bricks were from natural rock — being fashioned into a dwelling, and the barred window-frames were there on the site. They spoke to me of cells and dungeons. I followed the thought, and words written by a prisoner surfaced:

Stone walls do not a prison make,
Nor iron bars a cage.

Over-quoted, I blush to use them. This imprisoned poet was in charge of time; I, free, was not. I do not know how long he was there but his passion for Anthea gave wings to his spirit and also gave the English language one of its finest lyrics. I regret what I have been doing to time.

By the temple accosted

Dismay laps against the richness of this place,
It is deeper than anger
That want and hunger flourish here,
Indifference prevails,
Why is man so cruel?
Only the poor are forced to share,
Can wealth and want breathe the same air
And suffering be so normal?

Look at her, in soiled sari
And desperate! I brace my mind.
Dusk heightens her drama, I am out of depth
Some coins clear my way —
Snakes and bedded stones are better off
And no purse deep enough.

ANOTHER FESTIVAL

The void that had been so painful vanished on my return as life flowed back. I was no longer abandoned, not by my friends, but my inner self. My room, so congenial, had more comfort than a star hotel. Purpose flowed back and I could get on with what I wanted to do. A surge of concern for Johnny arose as I thought of his problems, his struggles and pinched existence. He had given Sojan the impression that I was the prompter behind this visit. He is concerned for his good opinion of him. Never mind, he shall have our understanding.

The big event now is the festival of Vishu, in which the local temple plays a central role. Vishu is a thanksgiving festival denoting the end of one growing season and the start of a new year. Each temple district celebrates it in its own way, but generally the god in the form of an emblem is set above an elephant's head and is taken to each household. This portrait or emblem is called a kolam. It is not a symbol but the god's living presence. In the case of our temple the presiding deity is the goddess Durga. Already the golden flag is set in place on a pole waving high above the banyan. It is important it be set in place at least a week before a festival and it must remain some time after all is over — presumably until it fades. A large stage has been erected for the musicians who are to come from Kochi. The piles, beams and joists are from *areca* poles which are long and dead straight, and the flooring is of thick uneven planks. The piles are set in the slope to one side of the playing ground. In front it is six feet off the ground and, at the rear, ten feet. The proscenium, arch and skirting are panelled with a tight trellis of bamboo strips coloured blue and white with touches of yellow and rose in the pattern. Blue tacks are used. The ceiling is of blue cloth and the side walls of plaited palm leaves. It is attractive.

Another structure is best described as an arch with a ten-foot square open chamber behind it. It has the same trellising as the stage. It faces towards the banyan. Much narrower and taller than the stage, it rises to 20 feet. Inside, on the cloth of the ceiling is a design of concentric circles embellished with stylised palmate leaves: the colours are yellow, white, rose and green, and the effect is light and ethereal. This arch is a primitive version of the many-storeyed towers or pandals which we shall see in the major Trichur Puram festival in a few weeks time. From this arch stretch two rows of poles to the banyan which will support the ropes for the decorations.

Valsan is painting the wall that encloses the temple grounds, while Rajendra and Kunjumon are busy with the façade, skirting, and other features of the temple itself. The colours are features of the temple itself. They are blue, beige and a muted red blending with satisfying originality. Small boys are making hanging strips from palm leaves. These are called areng, and are delta or wing-shaped and they have hundreds to do. Others are fixing lighting or hanging pretty strips of flowers from the roof.

There is third temporary structure in front of the temple, half-obscured by the enormous banyan. It is a lofty canopy like the arch but longer — a great banner hangs from the entrance leading from the gate to the temple.

I see Nandakumar lying on the floor of the temple and chivvy him as the only one idling. He tells me he has put his back out and has been to hospital for pain injections as well as medication. The poor man has had extreme pain and still has pain of a lesser degree. He is told to rest for ten days.

I continue my walk to the main road for it is cool and pleasant. Some young men on the other side call out and ask me where I am going and I answer that I am going to Delhi, is this the right way. They accept my attempt at humour and then ask why I am walking. I tell them I am in training for the Olympics. They laugh and think I won't do very well. Some of them cross over to chat. I move on and go only a few yards before I hear a three-note klaxon of an auto sounding repeatedly. I should know its distinctive sound. Vinod is taking Chandran to his home, Chandran the young man who is part-owner of the auto. They invite me to go to his house. It is not far. Only his mother is in and she made me abundantly welcome, cutting up mangoes and squeezing lemons into chilled water for me. The language barrier is formidable but there was no mistaking the hospitality. Chandran hands Vinod a spill of newspaper containing gold which he is to deliver to the goldsmith Vinod; both families are goldsmiths. It is weighty and I hefted it. The weight is 40 grams and the value 20,000 rupees.

Vinod returns me where he met me. He wanted to deliver me back home but I still wished to complete my walk. The only other encounter is with two small children — the little boy who always comes to me to shake hands, and the dearest little girl not much more than three who comes running up to me to kiss my hand. It was a most satisfactory walk.

Loudspeakers from the temple boomed out a rhythmic melody, presumably of a religious nature. This continued well into the night; firecrackers and small bombs sounded. It was a warm-up for the great day to follow. Sojan told me there would be no escape from noise the whole night, it was to be endured. Kunjumon had told me to come to the ground about 10:30 to see some preliminary action.

The day arrived, I went to the ground and there was nothing doing, so I wandered on to Nandakumar's house to see how his back was. He was not at home so I surmised that unless he had gone to the hospital, he was at least no worse.

Back at the house a group of collectors came for donations for the expenses of the festival. Among them was Kunjumon, who told me there would be some action about two in the afternoon. Meanwhile Nandakumar arrived and I had an update on his condition which was tolerable.

That was how the morning went. About 1 p.m. Vinod appeared. Part of his purpose was to take me to see 'something' and part as far as I could make out to help settle a question on his mind. It took some time to get what it was. First he wrote down the word 'dry' and we spent some time making clear its meaning. Then he wanted to know what the vowels are and he wrote down a-e-i-o-u. I confirmed this, and added that 'y' can have a vowel-function, as well as 'j', but the standard vowels were the five he wrote down. I told him that in the word 'dry' the 'y' is a vowel. It was difficult to get what he was driving at. At one stage I thought he mentioned a bet of 50 rupees. Could it be as to whether 'dry' contained any vowels or not? This was my guess but I could get no confirmation. If there were a bet I would like to know which side he took. We left the matter there.

It was two and he wanted to take me 'somewhere' and in ignorance I went along. We passed the stage where many of my young friends had gathered, sitting or lying on the floor. We waved but did not stop and continued on, turning into one of the side-lanes. There we saw a crowd and in the midst an elephant with gold trappings on its forehead and a mahout astride well up in front holding up the holy kolam. The Malayalam word for mahout is papaan.

Again I was surprised at the great size of elephants. This was not so much a procession as a visit, but there were drummers periodically tapping and a couple of buglers to confer a sense of occasion. We followed. The elephant stopped at some houses and there was a collection. Where the entrance was wide enough the elephant entered and it was awesome seeing it go right up to the verandah which visibly diminished in size. After watching for 20 minutes Vinod delivered me back at the house.

There I remained resting and reading while friends called briefly. There was what I can only describe as a complete re-arrangement of the air, so that sounds rarely heard came distinctly from other quarters — there was air movement but only a lazy stirring. One sound I found hard to place and finally concluded it came from a shunting-yard, with the slow panting of an engine as if each pulsation it gathered just enough energy to expend upon yet another turn of the wheel. I rather liked the sound, even though I gave it no attention, it bore more directly upon the subconscious in a comforting rhythm.

I wrote a letter of thanks to Johnny. It was a public holiday so I could not buy stamps, and the next day was an all-India bandh or strike on account of the GATT treaty, so it would be some days before it reached him. Many advisers have told me when the next event of the festivities would take place, and their advice has confirmed what I have now discovered, that in India events follow prediction in their own way, and a clock has only passing relevance. I understood that the next time to note was from 5.00 p.m to 5.30.

Jose called. Jose the extremist, perfectionist and the sceptic — *Il Penseroso*, who would scorn delights and live laborious days. I was like him when young in some respects scorning frivolity. I try to get him to see festivals and celebrations are necessary expressions of a stage of development. It is wrong to deny the child his toys and blocks, and there is a wholesome thoroughgoing therapy in play. The dangerous thing is to assume that the things we have outgrown can therefore have no use for others. This is an egocentric fallacy.

Again I hear the panting from the shunting yards and remarked on it to Jose. 'That is not engines,' he said, 'it's the drums, drums of the procession.' So there it was. Of course, of course. I had been obtuse — the small gathering Vinod and I had seen two hours ago had continued — street by street — throughout the village. The half-hearted drumming that came intermittently was not from a labouring engine but a token rallying as the procession moved from house to house. I might have guessed.

It was now after five so I said we must go and watch, and Jose said he would come with me. There were not many spectators at the ground and they were parents with children. We could hear the tapping much clearer and the measure was unbroken, signifying they were on the last lap. Jose went straight on to his place and I stood on the outskirts of the scene in the shade leaning against a stone wall. The advance took an age, whereas the drum-taps seemingly came from just around the corner.

Two small boys came running over to me all smiles. They were sweet and I shook hands gravely with each in turn, then gave them a hug. The older of the two fished out some roasted groundnuts from his tiny shirt-pocket. Only a child's fingers could have extracted them, and he then handed them to me. They raced back; I suppose the man they went to was their father. They soon came running back to give me more. I grinned over their heads to the man. I had to tell my name and country, and they in turn told me their names. Then Nandakumar came over to me, all smiles, so I felt less an outsider. He told me that now he wore a surgical belt to protect his back and felt a lot better, the pain was slight.

How much longer can the procession take, the sounds are so near? There was a trill of trumpets and bugles scurrying up over the treetops. We were on the farthest corner of the ground from the bend in the lane. When at last the first figures appeared I realised the slow pace was due to the pause at each step.

Vijayan, Kannan and Valsan came running over with some of the younger boys. They seized me and were in a state of high excitement. They were like puppies mauling me, so pleased I was there. I felt conspicuous and staid. Kannan was most affectionate, putting his arm around me. Kunjumon came, then raced back to the band beating time as if he were the conductor.

We watched the band appear — in all there were 40 members. There were drums, bugles, circular trumpets and cymbals. I tried to make a tally of the drums, there were at least sixteen. They were deep and cylindrical in a network of ropes. The drumsticks were curved sticks, insubstantial I thought, but they must be heavy and of hardwood. At last through the treetops I could see the upper trappings of the elephant, the kolam highest of all. It was so astonishingly lofty, reducing trees to shrubs, so splendid and majestic with its immensely rich gold frontlet and its silent, mesmeric dignity.

The band swung into a frenzy as it moved into the ground. The boys and men were jumping up holding one arm aloft and beating with complete identification. They were enjoying their wild party.

The elephant went and stood in front of the arch while the band moved to the centre of the ground. For quarter of an hour it played, maintaining a rapid beat. They dragged me right up to the centre of the ground, and beat my arms for me. What a dill I was and how foolish to be self-conscious. Having saturated this part of the scene with sound the band slowly moved towards the temple to take up its station in the antechamber, in front of the holy place, where none save a priest may enter. My friends made me go up to the elephant and touch it for good luck. The racket continued and we stood watching about half an hour. The rhythm and volume continually changed — it was not all stops out all the time — and fascination grew at the monotone variations. True, the trumpets and bugles were close in attendance but percussion ruled. Every now and then the buglers and trumpeters bowed to the ground, still playing.

The natural light was fading as the lighted temple and grounds grew in brilliance. Someone was plucking at my shoulder, someone tall. 'Uncle, Uncle, come, you must come.' Vinod drew me out from the crowd and took me to his auto. Chandran, his young and immature friend, was waiting in the auto. They had brought beer for me. We went a little distance along the lane where we would not be observed, for though a great deal of alcohol is drunk in India, it still does not wear the cloak of respectability. Vinod's kindness struck at me, for though I have helped him, I never looked upon him as being thoughtful and, he had chosen this way to thank me. How awkward I felt about it. I asked had he been drinking and he said no — he likes only spirits. He pulled the metal cap off with his teeth, his superb teeth.

Chandran shared with me — I do not think he drinks much. Vinod then had a little. I am not much good where it comes to quantity and was glad of help. We went to Chandran's house where they had another bottle. It was good to leave the lane, for it was the not right place.

I received the same welcome from Chandran's mother. This time she was not the only one in the house, there were Mani, Ganesh and two others whose names I did not master. Mother brought me a plate of mangoes and there were oranges and apples in front of me — I was faced with another bottle. Still Vinod did not join us, he simply does not go for it. Ganesh proved the most interesting character, perhaps because he had some English, but attention was upon me and I had to maintain the conversation. In such situations if I can warm to it I find it best to make wisecracks out of any material offering. By the time translations have been made they get the general drift of fun and goodwill. I left, hoping to meet Ganesh again.

Vinod delivered me back at the house. As we passed the temple we saw the crowd had largely dispersed. It would soon swell again as the time for dancing drew near. I had my supper and as I did not feel tired, I decided to wander back to the temple. No sooner had I announced my intention to Sojan than Nandakumar appeared as if on cue. He had seen the auto returning me. We walked back and I felt grateful for his guidance as it was now pitch-black and I could not see a thing — except the merest sliver of moon which appeared as double without my glasses. I tried my strong eye and saw only one moon. It was the other eye that brought upon the confusion. The band had disappeared and the focus had shifted to the stage and the auditorium upon which many were sitting. My friends appeared again eager for the night ahead, but I knew I would not survive more than half an hour. The crowd was there, most seated on the ground. The curtain arose upon a classical dancer of the Kerala tradition. Her appearance was perfection and her dancing flawless. I had seen Kerala dancing before and enjoyed it, though with no informed appreciation. The audience was familiar with the theme and movements, the tradition was very much alive and dear to them. Nandakumar was critical of the amateur lighting and the rough stage.

I soon gave in, not wanting to push on into exhaustion. The explosions which had accompanied the whole evening continued. As I left we passed a man with scrap newspapers and containers of gunpowder. I was glad to give him a wide berth. It was blissful under the cold shower and equally blissful on the soft bed, for I had not fully recovered from Malayattur. The night was not as noisy as foretold.

The following morning I went back and found the ground littered with paper. It looked like an inept and prototype snowfall. Everyone had sat on newspapers. Later in the morning I wandered down again. The litter was cleared and most of the decorations removed. My merry friends were at work, carrying poles, separating the coir rope from the palm leaf hangings and taking off the mango leaves. The entertainment had continued to 4:30 this morning and here they were on the go again.

There had been another visitation of the kolam carried by the elephant, lane after lane throughout the night. I expect when I go there again later in the day I shall see the temporary buildings dismantled.

What I love about the people around me is their animation, their team work, and above all their spirit of affirmation, enhanced in many instances by the tradition of their arts.

Straight talk

I put it to you
Is it right to build a wall
So eye doesn't accidentally fall
Upon a demented woman,
Requiring medication?
To have a garden
Drive, bar, the wherewithal
To run a launch put in a heated pool
When feeble voices call
Of people marginal?

To choose places
As far as you can from the works,
To go in for terraces and vistas
Cultivate the senses
Entertain guests?

The glory of mankind
Is a treaty of goodwill signed
Is medicare, accepting others
Healing the political
Tending what's global.

I put it to you
It's quite impossible
To isolate your skin or soul
For you are joined to the whole
With tissue not separable.

WHAT IS IT THEN?

I am not actually listening to anything or looking at anything and the other messengers and commentators in the employ of the body are around somewhere, apparently doing little. Nor am I thinking of anything in particular, when, without warning, a wave of generosity — that is the nearest word — rushes in and takes over. It comes from an unknown source, it washes in from an unknown sea. It is something other than me, but so completely adaptable and congenial that I am perfectly at ease with it. It is no use trying to portray it, for it contains all dimensions and gives the feeling that nothing is left out. I just pause quiescent, in an indescribable embrace.

I feel that, as scientists have got inside the atom, those who have experiences like this have got inside time. It is as if time is porous and between one moment and the next are other worlds. What is this experience then? It is far too complex for me to grasp, hence I cannot think of defining it, but instead I can indicate some aspects but when my description assumes too concrete a form I know that it is suspect, for form is hard and delimiting and this experience is quite otherwise.

It is an experience subtle enough to slip between two moments; this does not make it unattainable, for we have mastered many subtleties. It is with us in latency and the number who have experienced it is larger than we think, while others go all their days not knowing it, or pushing it aside. It is not conscience; in face of its hugeness conscience seems too careful and rule-bound, but it has links with conscience. What is it then?

It is the golden moment that dances before us like a firefly. Who can seize it and who can ravish it? We all can, but it chooses the time and it does the ravishing.

It is unfathomably deep but is as accessible as our mother tongue. It is an inalienable opportunity, closer than breathing. Nature will see to it that we never lose the capacity to experience it for it contains life's compass. It is not fantasy. Those who find it have unconsciously prepared themselves for it.

It contains all reconciliation and intuition, and it is a source of energy. It is too knowledgeable to contain conflicts. It is such a marvel and compendium that it can bother us, and we fling over it a net of distraction to protect our illusions. Many, including scientists and artists, have experience of it without realising.

It is the place where authenticity resides and is where students make their discoveries; and when we know it and relocate there, we can survive any bewilderment or adversity without too much dismay, for it is the place of ultimate approval. Those who cleave to it lead a delightful and alluring life. It is the place where we ourselves fill with light, and in that light we can see through the form.

Let it speak for itself. What does it say? It says, 'All must return to me, into my light, for I come to you through time, but am myself the timeless present. All that occurs takes place in me. 'Come,' it says, 'I am expecting you.'

A SELECTION OF LATE POEMS

The passing of Annabel

Dear Daryl friend and fellow poet
You stand where desolation spreads its wings
Where all is alchemised into loss
And delight has no place;
But ancient words catch my antennae:
Though in oracular guise:
I am; therefore all is well!
Beloved now and alway.

In all this not single provenance
For gravid with my own demise
I have stormed oblivion
Ablaze with darkness.
Still shines the oracle:
I am; therefore all is well!
Beloved now and alway.

Earth also is one of many mansions
We occupy, then quit as chrysalis,
If so the best is yet to be
And the grand affirmation stands:
I am; therefore all is well!
Beloved now and alway.

March 2003

Noel's last poem, conceived entirely in his mind without the use of paper as he could neither speak nor write, and dictated letter by letter to Howard (with detail to every aspect of punctuation) with the use of an alphabet board. Annabel McLaren was a friend and notable member of the Otaki community, and Daryl is her husband. Annabel's funeral was the last Noel attended before his own.

The final line of the poem was selected by the family for use on Noel's plaque at his burial site in the Otaki cemetery.

Mr Six O'Clock

One of those I have a soft spot for
Yet hardly think of out of sight
I know so little of him,
He'll turn up out of the blue
Any time to play me chess
And despite lack of each other's lingo
Some sort of meaning comes through.
Now he knows six o'clock means
That's when he'll come next, but I know very well
In India no one comes on the dot.
That's why I call him Mr Six O'Clock.

Today out walking for air,
Unfinished thoughts jostling around —
It was that slippery part by the pump —
When he overtook me with his wife or sister
(Here lady friends are ruled out).
He grabbed my arm before I saw him.
We were more pleased than our words could convey
Walking chatting chortling together —
Time and his lady had gone on ahead.
On parting he said six o'clock.
Suddenly I felt cut off.

I thought I was stayed and stable
But the fillip he brought had fled.
It wasn't I had to know him per se
But this day I was on life's outer,
The fix I had on life flawed;
Then saw what is immediate and personal
Against the totality of time
How only the soul can sail the universal
With the specific the keeled catalyst —
That's how Whitman's words brought a nation dreams,
'When lilacs last in the dooryard bloomed.'

Note in November

Spring away and they're at it again
Scratching and chittering in the chimney of
Our space heater, quite futile for it is
Metal and slippy, bits drop down
On the stove — twigs of kowhai pods,
Flax scraps, pine needles — you up
On the roof to see what's going on —
The sillies won't learn from the fires we light.

Lately, though, a fine spell so no fires,
Until yesterday when it poured and poured,
Cold too it called for a fire which
Wouldn't draw and smoked us out —
Up again, to find two small eggs palest blue,
Undoing time with a nod from heaven.

Rhododendron Fragrantissimum
compared to the sermon on the Mount

With dazzling linen to serve five thousand
Seated to eat on the stony mount
Your sweetness enters mundane minds
Never before such teaching.

Though every spring brings such teaching
I narrow it down to the same source;
The slopes, the crowds, the spicy stir
Lodge in the go-down of your branches.

They are never bare, your branches —
After appointed bees have finished serving,
The linen whipped off by wind and rain,
Infant leaves prick up their ears.

Antennae such as leaves or ears
Are equally avid for subliminal news
As the peak of an outpost range,
Or a giant tree bonsai-d by distance.

Ah! The slow kill of distance,
Time and place never in sync,
Why do we flag when we take them on
And tinker with our memories?

And you stout shrub, what memories
Perch on the shelves of your cells,
Of forests in the Himalayas,
Of wilderness and jagged skies?

What draws you to our soil and skies,
Why have you migrated to our lawns,
And what of your catering sprees,
With dazzling linen to serve five thousand?

The fishermen — Travancore

The rough voice of an old fisherman
Set the beat the chant perched on
As all took the strain
On the kilometre rope.

I counted fifteen
And a hundred metres up the beach
Was the other rope with the other gang.
The rear man coiled the rope
And as they all stepped back
Moved to the front.

I could feel the force flowing
As they fed their strength through the rope,
But it is the chant I tell about,
Not an art form, someday a suite,
It was too rough for that, too crude,
But an untutored vibration
Sprung from uncalendared generations,
Not sorrowful, not rejoicing,
But spirit of the unmeasured bonding
That holds the rocks together,
The shore, the thighed ocean
And the heavy water in their net.

From the throat of that fisherman
And the chorus of that crew
Came sounds that shook my shoulder
And tore me from my moorings;

Long before our way of living
Was another life than ours,
Nearer to the awesome time
When the earth broke out singing.

The risk

If I name you it is not you.
What I learn from Lao Tsu.
Mystics teach and tangle with such words,
My guess he tilts at science and reason
That peck away at infinity.
Counting infinity is not wrong though,
Only when you get a certain way
The beginning slips back into the void.
Trying to tally the attributes
Is, to my way of thinking,
Trying to contain the container.

Having put this down
And thinking it makes sense
I feel better
For I've an aversion to logic and reason,
They are too hard to keep up with,
Too fit and eager,
My line of least resistance
Is to immerse in the sway of things
And realise my calling, if any, by osmosis.

So if I name you it is not you.
This is what I have to work out.
You are not second person
Or third,
You are. Full stop.

My days fall in a pleasant place
Though there are those on my mind
As I go to sit on the garden seat,
There are rambler roses over it,
Silver birches and whitey-wood make a thicket
And the sun tries to zig-zag in —
Late romantic
Where eyes are lidded by leaves
And a grey-warbler, first violin,
Bows its thin little song.

There out for inwardness (a kind
Of topping-up with risk of blow-back)
I leave life's penumbra.
What happens can't be explained,
Indwelling, processing, tentative terms.

Later (an aeon is a tentative term)
Brimmed and primed with what went on,
Stumble-heavy, light-headed, winged,
Voice cut off at the main
I leave this unwalled scene
Of light and blaze in another world.
Silence does its work
And leads me back to normal things
Having done what I set out to do
To get the hang of Lao Tsu.

The flying fox

Makes story but nonetheless true
A nun and I spider the introspective river
She not young, I eighty-seven years gone —
A flying fox over the Whanganui River.
Hardest when the other nuns packed me in,
They bent stiff limbs to cage me in,
Tortuous I thought as heaven-storming penance
But once installed safe as a railway train.
They said (how saw?) her knuckles were white
While my poise to them expressed a presumed faith.
I gazed on the roiling sinister flood
But only later considered the perilous thread.
The current made a draught on this stillest of days,
Saw poroporos* below, then gave praise.

Noel crossing the Whanganui River by flying fox.

---

*poroporo is a native shrub, a *solanum*.

To go boating

Is to step out of your ordinary gear.
We labour down to the sandy landing
Where heavy boats of jack-fruit wood are moored,
The planks are thick, the thwarts almost beams
With wooden plugs and interlocking joins,
Simple tools have served an ancient craft;
Two twenty-foot poles of mula wood are used,
Primitive ferns and slimes surprise inside
And six inches of bilge float our sandals;
Some ropes are new, some frayed,
A four-fluke anchor grips the river sand,
Our boat rests on a water bed.

Boatman Siju calls for an appraising word,
Toughened at twenty-four he stands six foot
He is a river god
(he will run to bulk as his frame matures)
His movements are powered, smooth as a tug,
He stands at the stern like a finial,
Spire to some riverine construction,
In furled lungi leans on the stout pole
Showing no sign of his fight with the flood,
His slow smile captivates, reassures,
Embarking or mooring he is at hand,
Focal figure of this particular reach.

The broad Periyar has a three-knot flow,
Upholstered banks attest its opulence,
Look! Upstream mountains have pitched their tents,
From there you can see the Arabian Sea …
The massive welling and weight of river
Is masked by a mirror of changing light;
Our boat slowly parts the sliding water,
No sound is heard yet all is murmurous,
Melodious, addressing an inner ear.
Clarity comes in a burst of splendour —
No wonder there starts up out of itself
If not singing the idea of a hidden choir.

Return to Neeleswaram

Back again and glad to be back
The landscape more lucent than remembered
Away from city filth, dirty streets,
The stink of urine, crush of market place,
Other things are important here
Non-existent to those passing through.

The same side-road down to the fields
With leafage crowding to see nothing,
Twenty houses is not isolation
No bothering with frontages, possessions,
But tucked under the freckling vegetation,
As chickens a hen, image to hand.

Here a goat rips the only unfurled leaf
Of a newly-planted banana palm,
Hens peck rice-straw spread to dry,
It's coarse and sharp but evidently nutritious,
A cow moans, double bass in its belly
And voices sound a hundred yards off.

Sounds carry undistorted,
Whirr of bike tyres on the gravel,
Birds go over their notes *ad infinitum*,
Clang of well bucket, a child's cry,
The cry of fishmonger silver ware packed
In a box on his bike with leaves and ice.

It is noon, sultry after last night's rain
Thunder rolls around, bowls on a bowling green,
Who knows if it means business
Or just flexing, testing boundaries?
Clouds gather, thicken, grow sullen,
Surely it's not going to rain again.

Just now they say, rain means problems
Even though it brings relief to the skin,
It knocks down half-ripe mangos
Flattens hay, brings moulds and diseases,
So I don't cry to Huey to send it down,
Irrigation can serve the crops that need it.

Most are elsewhere working,
Those lucky enough to have a job,
Kids have been carted off to school,
Students bus or bike to their colleges,
The old and the land-workers stay on
And Juli suckles four tan puppies.

Women return, grass stacks on their head,
They have cows but no paddocks
Others file by with coconut branches,
Fodder for kitchen fires.
The main difference from us is the way they walk
Their glide makes our slouch a bit of a laugh.

And the fluid clothing of men and women
Wound, draped and flowing like grass,
The style of this green and floating countryside.
The village scene has no edges,
They are far from processed things that sell in shops
And go by clocks slower than ours.

Action in Te Horo

Crisis and just up,
Liz in white dressing gown,
Cows in the gully garden large as elephants!
We flew out the door, Liz barefoot,
I'm in slippers and Jack-Russell Ellie loud for a fight,
That is from afar.
The mild munchers looked up.
Liz up the other bank scolding, I waving yelling
And Ellie in staccato mode.

The bigger beast tore at a camellia,
Threw up its legs and tried to run past.
We turned up the volume and a breeze
Puffed the dressing-gown to spinnaker size,
That turned the tide.

Meanwhile the lesser beast had gone to the gate,
Ellie barked it through.
The larger downed the bank, passed the gate
And came at me the other side.
It crashed into a whitey-wood
Branches breaking, tongue slurping leaves.
So steep there
I had no foothold, stood on rotten rolling driftwood
Which Ollie now grown-up had collected for rustic seats,
Dear Ollie, I couldn't say bloody Ollie as I slipped.
I grabbed a pole and poked it beyond my balance
To head it back. It looked at me
Calm as if studying Plato
Oceans of innocence in its eyes.
Had it gone further I couldn't have turned it.
It came back, Ellie was waiting,
Liz closed in and victory was clinched.

The old house-gate covered in lichen,
Has spent years awaiting a painter like Constable.
I loved the scene, fences, foxgloves;
Arums and beyond the Tararuas looming.

No it isn't a Mickey Mouse construct,
It does its job when the bolt is shot
And still has work to do.

Deed in the night

In the night in the night
A sound is heard,
Not by me sleeping deep
But by Ellie our hi-tech guard,
She sets up a racket that drags Howard (dreaming
Of Tunui and Mt Hector scaled)
Back to our stamping ground.
He grabs gun and follows out
Where she is pointing.

In a tree in a tree in our kauri tree
Where she is pointing.
Two round lights beam down
Opossum crouched in the crutch of a limb
Stripped by torch of privacy rights,
One shot brings it down
A thing of beauty ends its reign.

Ellie possessed by the high drama
Shakes the fur by the neck
(how rich how exquisite soft)
Chases the final spark into the dark —
How dare it breathe in our domain
How dare it climb where she can't climb
The provocation is extreme!

I the muser who slept through
Am regaled by the deed next day.
Ellie outside drags it about
Parading the spoils of victory.
I the muser think up a new equation,
Life is death, death life —
Is that all that needs to be said?

I go to the kauri,
Now surely a hundred years on,
Planted when the farmhouse was new
Together with pohutukawa and liquidamber.
This tree my joy my astonishment
Will outsee another millennium,
Even now arms cannot encircle it
Pressing its sharp pimpled bark,
There's gum at its base.
So great a tree I cannot bear it
So bold, hefting time itself,
Hefting the weight of what has gone
And braced for what to come.

The rose

A single stem from the rose by the spa
Brought me in a Schweppes bottle
And set, nice thought, upon my table
Is the same colour as the haematoma
I see when my leg is dressed
(Lurid on leg, on petal regal-superb).
It holds its head among its leaves
As would once some toff in furs
To confront me with form and fragrance —
How welcome such unwonted attention!
I wonder where it actually comes from
Along that stony belt straddling Asia —
Iraq Iran Afghanistan —
Time-warping me its proud turbaned head